SDGS,
MAIN CONTRIBUTIONS AND CHALLENGES

Editors

NIKHIL SETH

United Nations Institute for Training and Research

CÁSTOR MIGUEL DÍAZ BARRADO

University of Rey Juan Carlos

PALOMA DURÁN Y LALAGUNA

Sustainable Development Goals Fund

Coordination

MARCO A. SUAZO

United Nations Institute for Training and Research,
New York Office

MARÍA SAGRARIO MORÁN BLANCO

University of Rey Juan Carlos

DIANA M. VERDIALES LÓPEZ

University of Rey Juan Carlos

Chair on Development
and Poverty Eradication
SDG Fund and URJC

unitar

Sustainable Development Goals (SDGs): Main Contributions and Challenges

By Nikhil Seth, Castor Miguel Diaz Barrado, Paloma Duran y Lalaguna, Editors

Published by the United Nations Institute for Training and Research (UNITAR) and Center of Ibero-American Studies, University of Rey Juan Carlos.

Website: http://www.unitar.org/

https://www.urjc.es/ceib

Edited by: United Nations Institute for Training and Research (UNITAR) and Center of Ibero-American Studies, University of Rey Juan Carlos.

Designed by: United Nations Institute for Training and Research

Printed in: New York, United States.

Dep. legal: I.S.

ISBN: 9789211542240

Sales no: 19.xvi.1

SUMMARY

CHAPTER 5

CHAPTER 6

CHAPTER 7

CHAPTER 8

1) **Nikhil SETH.** On 8 June 2015, Mr. Nikhil Seth was appointed by the United Nations Secretary-General Ban Ki-moon as UN Assistant Secretary-General, Executive Director of the United Nations Institute for Training and Research. Before assuming the post of the UNITAR Executive Director, Nikhil Seth was the Director of the Division for Sustainable Development, Department of Economic and Social Affairs (DESA) at the United Nations Secretariat in New York. Mr. Seth's Division was also responsible for supporting the intergovernmental negotiations for the post-2015 development agenda, which was adopted at the United Nations Sustainable Development Summit 2015 in September 2015. During his career with the United Nations since 1993, Mr. Seth has served as Special Assistant and Chief of Office to the Under-Secretary-General for Economic and Social Affairs (Sept 1993 – Jun 2001), Chief of the Policy Coordination Branch in the Division for ECOSOC Support and Coordination (Jun 2001 – Jan 2003), as Secretary of the Economic and Social Council (ECOSOC) and the Second Committee of the General Assembly (Feb 2003 – Aug 2006), and as Director of the DESA Office for ECOSOC Support and Coordination (Aug 2006 – Aug 2011), where he guided the ECOSOC's work in implementing several new key mandates, including its Annual Ministerial Review and Development Cooperation Forum. Mr. Nikhil Seth holds a Masters degree in Economics from Delhi University.

2) Paloma DURÁN Y LALAGUNA is the Director of the Sustainable Development Goals Fund, a United Nations (UN) mechanism that brings together UN agencies, national governments, academia, civil society and business to achieve SDGs. She acted as the United Nations Vice-Chair of the UN Commission for Social Development during her time as Counsellor of Human Rights in the Permanent Mission of Spain to the UN. Prior to that she has served on the EU's Equality Committee and the Council of Europe's Expert Group on Affirmative Action, and worked with civil society in Nigeria, Guatemala, Peru, the Philippines and elsewhere. She holds PhDs in Law, Canon Law and Political Science.

3) Cástor Miguel DÍAZ BARRADO. Head Professor of Public International Law and International Relations at the Rey Juan Carlos University of Madrid. Director of the Centre for Iberoamerican Studies at the Rey Juan Carlos University. Author of several scientific papers internationally recognized in their discipline, which analyzes the issues relating to international protection of human rights and integration processes in Latin America and Iberoamerica. He has been dean of the Faculty of Law at the University of Extremadura. He has been director of the Department of Social Sciences and Humanities, and Vice Chancellor for Academic and Management Studies at the Rey Juan Carlos University. Also, he has developed research and teaching at the Oxford University, Paris University and Lisbon University.

4) Carlos R. FERNÁNDEZ LIESA. Head Professor of Public International Law and International Relations. Carlos III University of Madrid (since 2005). Director of the Expert Title in Prevention and Management of International Crisis of the Carlos III University of Madrid, in collaboration with the Army War College Member of the Ethics

Committee of the Spanish Olympic Committee (between 2007 and 2013). Director of the Time of Peace Magazine since 2015 (edited by the Movement for Peace, Disarmament, and Freedom) (He has published 123 issues since 1983). He is a member of the Advisory Board of the Carlos III University of Madrid Cooperation Office. Member of the Court of Access to the Diplomatic Career in 1999 and 2006. Member of the court of more than 100 doctoral theses.

5) **Juan Daniel OLIVA MARTÍNEZ.** Anthropologist and Jurist. Doctor in International Law and Human Rights. Co-Director of the Expert Title on Indigenous Peoples, Human Rights, and International Cooperation, Director of the Chair on Indigenous Peoples and Vice Principal of the Master Degree in International Solidarity Action and Social Inclusion of the Carlos III University of Madrid. Researcher of the Center of Anthropological Studies, of the Spanish Seminar on Indigenous Studies and member of the Association for Teaching and Research on the Rights of Indigenous Peoples. Former Chief Technical Officer of the Fund for the Development of the Indigenous Peoples of Latin America and the Caribbean, an international organization devoted to the promotion of self-development and collective rights of Indigenous Peoples. Author of numerous books, articles, and chapters of collective works on issues related to International Law, International Cooperation and Indigenous Peoples.

Adriana SÁNCHEZ LIZAMA. Academic Coordinator of the Expert Title on Indigenous Peoples, Human Rights and International Cooperation, member of the Chair on Indigenous Peoples and the University Group of Cooperation with Indigenous Peoples of the Carlos III University of Madrid. Her research fields are Indigenous Peoples Rights, International Relations, International Cooperation for Development, Interculturality, Sexual Diversity, and Gender Identity. She is currently a student of the Doctorate Program of Advanced Studies in Human Rights at the Carlos III University of Madrid, where she has led the Workshop on Sexual Diversity, Gender Identity and Human Rights since 2017.

6) **Marco A. SUAZO.** Senior Adviser to The Executive Director of Unitar and Head of New York Office since October 2015, A carrier Diplomat was previously Ambassador, Deputy Permanent Representative of Honduras to the United Nations, graduated with a Degree in Social Science and Jurisprudence at the Universidad Nacional Autonoma de Honduras, completing is postgraduate studies at The University of Florence (Italy), "Cessare Alfieri Faculty" in International Relations and Law, follow others academic education with courses and seminars in Public International Law, International Negotiations, Economic Integration, Human Rights and Peacekeeping. Ambassador Suazo during he's tour served as Chair two of the Main Comities of the General Assembly, The First on Disarmament and International Security 2008, during the 63 session and the Second Committee on Economic and Social matters during the 57 Session in 2002, in this session the Office of Finance for Development was created in the United Nations Secretariat, Depto. Of Economics and Social Affaires. He has published two Book related to the Honduras History and participation in the United Nations as a funder member, Title: "Our History Honduras in the United Nations 1945- 2005" on the 60 anniversary of the Organization and "We the "People" in 2013, actually is working in a third publication written diplomacy.

7) **Babatomiwa ADESIDA** is the Private Sector and Philanthropy Engagement Consultant for the Sustainable Development Goals Fund (SDG Fund), where his primary role is to engage the Private Sector to establish sustainable partnerships with the UN

through the SDG Fund in numerous countries around the world. With over 15 years of Private Sector experience in the development, implementation and monitoring of projects and policies through the private sector in partnership with numerous governments, Babatomiwa is extremely passionate about Social Reconstruction particularly in developing nations. After receiving a B.Sc with honours in Sociology from the University of Ibadan in Nigeria and MSc. in Public Policy from the University of Bristol, U.K, he has actively participated in the development of some research work in relation to the role of the private sector in ensuring sustainable development.

8) Raúl DE MORA is communications specialist for the Sustainable Development Goals Fund, a United Nations interagency mechanism that promoted the collaboration between UN Agencies, governments, civil society and academia to achieve SDGs. In this capacity, he has overseen the implementation of the SDG Fund's communications and advocacy strategy. His contribution in this book builds on the results of the SDG Fund's Public Diplomacy Initiative. Raul is a communication, advocacy and partnerships professional, with a strong experience in coordinating UN interagency communication initiatives and forging advocacy public-private partnerships to promote sustainable development, both at headquarters and the country level, including crisis and emergency contexts, with an strong interest in the humanitarian-development-peace nexus. He has a Ph.D. in Communications by the University Complutense of Madrid and a M.A. in Communication Management at the Annenberg School for Communications, University of Southern California.

FOREWORD

Cástor Miguel Díaz Barrado

Marco A. Suazo

As we have mentioned in previous editions, the Academic Chair on Development and Poverty Eradication (SDG Chair) is a joint initiative between the United Nations Sustainable Development Goals Fund (SDGF) and the Rey Juan Carlos University. Its objective is to promote the engagement of Universities around the world in achieving the 2030 Agenda for Sustainable Development through training, advocacy and research activities. The research of academics about how to achieve the 2030 Agenda is certainly a useful tool to promote international debate and raise awareness among national governments, international organizations, academia, civil society and the private sector that joint actions are needed to not leave anyone behind. Poverty eradication is the basic and primary objective of the international community to achieve the three dimensions of sustainable development: social, environmental and economic.

Research activities, carried out by academics, enrich the work of development actors, both public and private, and support the understanding of the Sustainable Development Goals and the 2030 Agenda. The main task of the Academic Chair on Development and Poverty Eradication is not only to provide theoretical support, but also to illustrate practical examples that can contribute to the achievement of Sustainable Development Goals, adopted on 25 September 2015 by the United Nations General Assembly resolution 70/1, "Transforming our world: the 2030 Agenda for Sustainable Development". World leaders adopted this Agenda, which is a "plan of action for people, planet and prosperity. It also seeks to strengthen universal peace in larger freedom. We recognize that eradicating poverty in all its forms and dimensions, including extreme poverty is the greatest global challenge and an indispensable requirement for sustainable development".

The present publication is the fruit of an inter-institutional collaboration between the Sustainable Development Fund (SDGF), UNITAR and Universidad Rey Juan Carlos of Spain, in order to benefit future generations' educational curricula and promote the wider implementation and understanding of the 2030 Agenda.

It constitutes an effort to review some of the best examples and progress made by the international community in achieving the SDGs. Since the 2015 Summit, the United Nations System has been supporting efforts to implement them, particularly enabling Member States to deliver on their own commitments; including through the High-Level Political Forum (HLPF) and its National Voluntary Reviews (NVR) mechanism, which constitute the platform where national policies and efforts are disclosed at regional, national and local levels. For the first time since the adoption of the 2030 Agenda, Member States are sharing their experience and difficulties globally, as the capacity-building and training arm of the United Nations, UNITAR, under the pillars of Peace,

People, Planet and Prosperity, has established a Learning Center that also allows civil society, public sector, United Nations agencies and educational institutions like Universidad Rey Juan Carlos to come together and share their contributions toward improving the lives of millions of people around the world. It is our hope that this publication will contribute to that endeavor.

Gender, SDGs and Women's Empowerment have been covered and analyzed in recent publications and open discussions in the University curricula. We are pleased to share an electronic link on gender-related topics which also includes other publications and articles produced by the SDGF and Universidad Rey Juan Carlos: https://www.thomsonreuters.es/es/tienda/search.html?q=Sustainable+development+goals.

This publication collects the contributions and proposals, from different authors, to improve the sustainable development goals from different perspectives.

The analysis and recommendations of this book do not necessarily reflect the official views of the SDG Fund Secretariat, the United Nations or its Member States.

Chapter 1

THE NEGOTIATION PROCESS OF THE 2030 AGENDA [1]

NIKHIL SETH

Executive Director, UNITAR

SUMMARY: I. INTRODUCTION. II. BACKGROUND. III. PHASE I – THE OPEN WORKING GROUP (OWG). III.1 The second innovation. IV. PHASE II: DELIVERING THE GOALS AND TARGETS (JAN 2015-JULY 2015)

* * *

I.   INTRODUCTION

1. The transformational potential of the 2030 Agenda and its resonance, in all parts of our troubled world, could not have been achieved without a transformational negotiating process. I had a ringside seat both as the head of the UN Secretariat for the Rio+20 process, where the seeds of the 2030 Agenda and the SDGs were sown, and head of the DESA support team to the intergovernmental process for the negotiation of the 2030 Agenda. This is the story of how we got there and the complex, inclusive and exhilarating process which gave the world the 2030 Agenda and the SDGs.

2. The political process for negotiating the 2030 Agenda had two distinct phases. The first was the work of the Open Working Group (OWG) mandated by the outcome of the Rio+20 Conference (the OWG met from March 2013 – July 2014). The second phase was the Intergovernmental Negotiations in the General Assembly (January – August 2015).

II.   BACKGROUND

3. On the eve of the Open Working Group's work, multilateral diplomacy, especially multilateral sustainable development diplomacy was at its nadir. The Copenhagen

---

[1] I am indebted to Macharia Kamau, Pamela Chasek and David O'Connor and their book « Transforming Multilateral Diplomacy: The inside story of the Sustainable Development Goals". I have drawn extensively from this accurate record.

climate conference (2009) had been crippled and some of the blame was on the complete lack of transparency, exclusion of many committed to a meaningful outcome, shuffling leadership and a trust deficit among the bigger players. The Rio+20 conference (2012) saw the pendulum moving to the other extreme with line by line, on screen, negotiations with marginal progress leading to a situation where only 30 -35% of the text was agreed to a few days before the Presidents and Prime Ministers were to arrive in Rio de Janeiro. Multilateralism and its processes looked irredeemably broken. While the Rio+20 outcome document, "The Future We Want", was saved by some deft handling by Brazilian diplomacy, the future of multilateral diplomacy and its tried and tested tools from an earlier century were clearly not working. Negotiations, through large interest groups, such as G77 and China, European Union (EU), and Japan, United States, Canada, New Zealand (JUSCANZ), where interests varied as much as they merged, antiquated methods of work, distrust of political leadership and substantive secretariat support, lack of meaningful engagement of non-state actors, fragmented approaches from different UN System entities, were creating processes and structures fossilized in time and outcomes which were far from the needs of our contemporary times.

4. Something had to be done and soon if the 2030 Agenda process was to be freed from the shadow of Copenhagen and the stodgy negotiating process of the General Assembly. What unfolded in the SDG process was a remarkable turnaround which validated multilateralism like never before and placed the UN back at the heart of efforts for peace and prosperity, for a planet which is safe for the future and defining actions with people at the center.

5. What were the ingredients of this innovative process which bolstered the credibility of multilateralism and led to a meaningful and highly ambitious outcome? Was it just a lucky configuration of political leadership and secretariat support or was it the product of a strategic thought through approach, based on an understanding of previous not so successful attempts at forging consensus? The innovations in negotiations as well as the stupendous leadership of the process provided the formula that worked.

III. PHASE I – THE OPEN WORKING GROUP (OWG) (MARCH 2013 – JULY 2014)

6. The Open Working Group started with some birthing pangs. Originally mandated to be a group of 30 representatives nominated by member states, the mandate was interpreted generously providing space for 30 "Troikas" or groups of member states (usually but not always three per group) to accommodate all 70 member states who had expressed an interest in belonging to the OWG. Any other selection / election process would have left 40 member states disgruntled and

excluded. While the" Troikas" were self-defining within different regional groupings, they often cut across the more traditional understanding of interest groups. The most commented on group was "Iran – Nepal – Japan", a rather unusual bonding. EU countries formed small groupings with non-EU countries (e.g. Australia, Netherlands, UK) and with all 70 member states accommodated we were ready to go. This was a significant innovation and became a transparent and "open" method of articulating interest. The more traditional system of one representative speaking for G77 and China (the developing countries), one representative for the EU, is both laborious and time consuming. It also tends to polarize discussions, with positions hardening early on in negotiations, often with the most extreme positions within the group dominating. With the Open Working Group formula all had a place at the discussion table and a voice which was distinct, propelled by national interests tempered by common positions forged within Troikas.

7. **The second innovation** was the openness to all stakeholders, shorthand for governments, civil society, academia, the private sector, and of course the UN System. Bringing non-governmental stakeholders into the negotiating room has had a long history in the United Nations. The door was cracked open in Rio at the Earth Summit in 1992 but by 2012 it was not a question of civil society "observing" negotiations but participating in a meaningful way. However, there is always pushback to this openness and the OWG was no exception. The chairs of the OWG, guided by the secretariat, provided suitable windows for the participation of the non-governmental entities. The secretariat took the extra step of briefing the NGOs every morning, explaining the day's activities and negotiations, urging different interests to align with the day's discussion rather than focusing only on their specific interest. This organized participation helped a more meaningful engagement and provided greater space and ultimately greater ownership of the final outcome.

8. **The third innovation** was the process of confidence building within the room especially between the co-chairs and member states. No texts for negotiation appeared suddenly. Each building block was carefully placed starting with a process of stocktaking which presented issue briefs prepared by the UN System Technical Support Team (TST), high-level and balanced panels, inputs from social media (8 million respondents to MYWorld Survey) and rooting the process in the outcome of Rio+20. Each draft which was put before the OWG carefully reflected the views expressed in the room. The secretariat's strong support to the chairs especially in accurately summarizing comments from the floor, helped in raising their credibility and the credibility of the process. Keeping issues at the technical level, avoiding political loading of debates and the neutral role of the political leadership of the process was crucial to its success.

9. **The fourth effective innovation** was grouping the UN System entities through the Technical Support Team (TST) co-chaired by DESA and UNDP. This helped

a one window entry to the UN System and helped channel their technical expertise through the TST. The inclusive process also helped in controlling the urge of individual UN agencies to lobby the political process prompted, often, by their specific funding and thematic concerns.

10. To summarize the four different and innovative approaches which worked and served the process well were the break-up of traditional negotiating modalities, openness to all views governmental and non-governmental, confidence building, and a single-window entry of the UN System. But these innovations would not have been possible without the leadership required and the secretariat backstopping to overcome the overall political mood, reeling from the impasse at Copenhagen and the mixed results at Rio+20.

11. This brings me to the exemplary political leadership provided by the Ambassadors of Kenya (Macharia Kamau), Hungary (Csaba Korosi) and later Ireland (David Donoghue), backed by support from the UN SG (Ban Ki Moon), now DSG Amina Mohammed, and a strong DESA (Department of Economic and Social Affairs) secretariat. All the right support was in place. The leaders were perceived as neutral, were patient and good listeners, above the dictates of narrow interests, driven by the common goal, set the highest standards, eschewed any surprises, reflected the different positions accurately, guided the discussions, had time to engage with all points of view, occasionally contradicted positions of the groups to which their countries belonged, generally shared a good interpersonal chemistry, rarely demonstrated a sense of despondency and were engaging communicators and negotiators. Quite a lucky configuration of great diplomatic talents. The DESA team I had the fortune to lead were also a group of knowledgeable, hardworking, meticulous, fair, and balanced individuals who won the confidence of the co-chairs, the UN System entities, the NGOs and member states.

12. During the entire process, the Open Working Group and the intergovernmental negotiations, controversies and contentious issues came in waves. Some were large, threatening to engulf everything, while others came as smaller ripples which were minor irritants, at best. Let me give you a flavor of some "contentious issues" during the first phase of negotiation.

13. I have chosen these issues which arose at different stages of the 2030 Agenda process, to provide a glimpse of the substantive difficulties. Obviously, all these were resolved primarily by deft handling by the co-chairs, and their resolution was reflected in the adoption, by acclamation, of the 2030 Agenda. But at various stages of the 30 months of discussions / negotiations, they gave a collective migraine to all who had vested time and effort in the process.

14. At the early stages of the process an inordinate amount of time, especially outside the conference rooms, was spent on debating the issue of whether the world really needed a new SDG agenda or would an MDG+ agenda (MDG plus) be sufficient.

Developing countries, especially from Africa, were arguing that the MDGs were still "unfinished business". Moreover, the ODA and concessional financing systems had put structures into place using the MDG blueprint. Did the Rio+20 issue areas provide a sensible basis for looking at the development needs of the poorest countries? Would bringing in many more "environmental" issues lead to greater conditionalities in aid and trade? Would it lead to a different country direction of aid? What would this do to our traditional understanding of North – South relations? Would the MDGs be lost forever? Many of the field-oriented agencies, like UNDP, were arguing that their country programming was around the MDGs and with the shift would come major disruption. But the inadequacies of the MDG framework were apparent. They were qualitatively inadequate, not comprehensive and derived from UN outcomes of the early 90s. The environmental additions to the MDGs appeared to be an afterthought. Over time, in the OWG this controversy dissipated as it became clear that at the heart of the SDGs would be the follow-up to the MDGs (captured in SDG1 – 6). Calming the fears and apprehensions around the MDGs vs. SDGs debate was necessary for the political acceptance of a broader, and richer, interlinked framework (2030 Agenda).

15. **The second controversy**, more a storm in a tea cup, was around the number of goals which should be part of the SDG framework. In part this debate was fueled by the report of the SG's High Level Panel on the post 2015 Development Agenda (which came up with 12 goals) and the Sustainable Development Solutions Network (championing 10 goals). Members from these two processes argued that 17 goals was taking the SDGs into an incomprehensible zone. The only sensible solution, in their view, would be a severe culling of the total number of Goals. The then UK Prime Minister, the then Administrator of UNDP, and the Head of The Earth Institute of Colombia University were among the many champions of this viewpoint. But in the negotiating process, any attempt to remove or merge SDGs was met by stiff resistance, e.g. merging the stand-alone goal on Oceans was strongly opposed by the Small Island Developing States, merging the goal on inequalities was strongly opposed by the developing countries. In retrospect, this area of contention seems trivial but at that time it loomed as a major disruptor of the process.

16. Until the end of the process, getting agreement on the cluster of issues around "sexual and reproductive health and rights" was problematic. This is the **third** issue I highlight. At Rio+20 too, these issues had created a great deal of dissonance and a sense of frustration. Religion, culture, values, moral beliefs, the Holy See, LGBT rights, the pro-choice / pro-life debates were all part of the heated and toxic discussions on how to reflect, especially on the health related SDG, "sexual and reproductive health and rights". The final text dropped the word "rights" on the judgement of the co-chairs and the term "Sexual and reproductive health-care services" was included instead in target 3.7.

17. SDG 16 on promoting peaceful and inclusive societies was another difficult insertion (my fourth example) into the SDG framework. The report of the UN System Task Team convened by the Secretary-General to advise him on the post-2015 development agenda had strongly argued for the inclusion of peace, justice and good institutions as part of the new Agenda. Developing countries had mixed views. While the principle of "no peace without sustainable development" and no "sustainable development without peace" was self-evident, some larger developing countries argued that the architecture of the peace apparatus in the UN, including the Security Council and Peacebuilding Support Office was separated from the development architecture by an iron wall. The post 2015 discussions were not looking at the reform of the UN in a holistic way and inserting peace and related issues would distract from a development agenda. Some countries emerging from conflict on the other hand argued that peace was essential to sustainable and inclusive development. Developed countries, especially UK, Austria and others, were arguing for two stand-alone goals, one on peace and stability and the other on good governance, rule of law and effective institutions. However, with some give and take, tradeoffs and linkages with other goals of interest for the developing countries, a goal was finally agreed combining both peace and governance, which is SDG 16.

18. The fifth contentious area was SDG 13 on Climate Change. Climate Change has its impacts on the entire SDG framework but parallel discussions were taking place in the run up to the Paris COP (Conference of Parties) of the UN Framework Convention on Climate Change (UNFCCC). Everyone accepted COP21 as the primary negotiating forum on all matters related to Climate Change but a SDG without Climate Change was Hamlet without the Prince of Denmark. The goal survived although the goal had a footnote acknowledging the UNFCCC process as the primary place for all matters related to Climate Change.

19. The issue of a stand-alone goal on inequalities created a minor storm. Countries from Latin America, led by Brazil, argued very eloquently and strongly for a goal on reducing inequalities within and between countries. Developed countries, especially the United States, argued against a stand-alone goal and said that by eradicating poverty and addressing access issues in the other goals, inequality was being, in any case, addressed meaningfully. Apart from ideological differences, defining targets for this goal was problematic as they needed to address fiscal policy, including tax policy, as well as the older debates on North-South issues. Ultimately though, the goal survived with a clear set of accompanying targets.

20. The discussions on sustainable consumption and production, were riven by the legacy of the UN's negotiating history. As far back as 1992 President Bush had publicly stated that American lifestyles were not under negotiation. Developed countries have always been wary of this issue. But this goal was central to the universality of the SDG Agenda and the urgent need for creating the environmental space for the developing countries to grow and for shared

prosperity. It was finally accepted with some tradeoffs with other goals, especially SDG 16.

21. The final difficulty to which I make a reference is to goal 17, on the Means of Implementation. Discussions around aid, trade, technology and finance are always difficult in the UN. Concessionality in non-market transactions between states has always evoked high emotions. The 0.7% of GNI target for developed assistance to developing countries has often been the last issue to be resolved in UN negotiations. Fortunately, the SDG on Means of Implementation and the associated targets were put in the initial drafts and the holding of the Financing for Development Conference in Addis Ababa helped dissipate the storm. By also focusing on policy coherence, strengthened partnerships and data, disaggregated by gender, age, race, ethnicity, migratory status, disability and location, this goal has added great value to the implementation of the agenda.

IV. PHASE II: DELIVERING THE GOALS AND TARGETS (JAN 2015-JULY 2015)

22. The completion of the work of the Open Working Group in July 2014 marked the end of Phase I which was exhausting and exhilarating. Sixteen months had culminated in an agreement on goals and most targets. But many questions remained – an inspirational vision statement was needed for urgent political action; the means of implementation had still to be fleshed out; a follow-up and review process needed elaboration; and concerns had been expressed on the technical precision and level of ambition of some of the targets. The 2030 Agenda had still to be negotiated, into which the goals/targets negotiated by the OWG would be appropriately merged. Here we entered the next phase which defined the post 2015 development agenda.

23. As we entered the 69th General Assembly under the Presidency of Sam Kutesa, the Minister of Foreign Affairs of Uganda, there was change in the air. Ambassador Korosi, co-chair of the OWG, had returned to Budapest, some member states were viewing the next stage as an opportunity to fix the "gaps and deficiencies" in the goals and targets as politically perceived by them, the Troika system was no longer operational, more traditional negotiations were threatening to replace all the innovation of the OWG, the preparation for the Addis Ababa Conference on Finance for Development was taking place in parallel, and the work of the intergovernmental negotiations had to be completed in limited time, in eight sessions, of four days each between January and July 2015. There were, at the start of the intergovernmental negotiations, three features which injected greater optimism – first was the decision to continue with Ambassador Kamau as one of the co-chairs, second was the appointment of Ambassador Donoghue, Ireland, as the second co-chair, and third was the positive momentum generated

by the OWG. The excitement around the imminent 2030 Agenda was growing and those who were following the progress of the OWG, felt the urgency of being part of this momentous end game.

24. The SG's synthesis report on the post 2015 Development Agenda was issued in December 2014. One of the most important and contentious observations in the report was the call for a technical review of the targets which emerged from the OWG, to achieve, at a minimum, consistency with existing UN targets in various agreements. This provided a segway for many countries, especially those part of the West European and Other states Group (WEOG) to argue for an opening of the OWG "consensus". These sentiments caused great disturbance within the G77 / China group (developing countries). There was danger of extreme politicization of the debate. But, once again deft political leadership, openness to stakeholders, and the momentum of the OWG kept the process on track.

25. During the Intergovernmental Negotiations several loose threads had to be brought together – three parallel processes were ongoing which had an impact on the 2030 Agenda process (Financing for Development, Statistical Commission working on the SDG indicators and the Climate Change discussions leading up to COP 21 in Paris); secondly a declaration had to be negotiated to serve as a chapeau to the SDGs; thirdly the targets had to be approved "technically"; fourthly the chapter on financing and means of implementation needed to be aligned with the Addis outcome; fifthly the follow up process had to be clearly formulated. Let me summarize how each one of these issues was handled.

26. The means of implementation chapter of the 2030 Agenda, as expected, was one of the major disruptors. Traditionally this has always been the case in development cooperation discussions in the UN. Compounding the difficulties was the parallel discussions on finance and technology in the FFD conference in Addis Ababa led by two different co-chairs, the Ambassadors of Norway and Guyana. The outcome at Addis was viewed negatively by the group of developing countries (G77) who felt that certain of their priority asks had not been accommodated. On the technology side an agreement to create a technology facilitation mechanism(TFM) was favorably viewed by all and the language of Addis on the TFM was imported verbatim into the 2030 Agenda.

27. The technical "tweaking" of the targets posed another problem. Some had been highlighted in the SG's report. First, these were targets which had not clearly specified numerical percentages and were merely referred to as "x" percentage. There were nine such targets. In addition, some of the agreed targets were less ambitious than similar targets agreed to in different UN contexts. A total of 19 such targets were put before the Inter-Governmental Negotiations (IGN) with detailed justification for their revision. But politics as usual intruded. G77 felt that the opening up of any aspect of the outcome of the OWG would risk opening everything. The to and fro on "tweaking" carried on till the final weeks of the

negotiations. Finally, the logic of "tweaking" won over the politics of no change to an OWG outcome and we had a set of 169 agreed targets.

28. The chapter in the 2030 Agenda relating to its follow up and review created further obstacles. Universality of the agenda meant that all countries, including the developed ones, needed to subject their progress to review. Developed countries were not comfortable with the thought of reporting to the UN and developing countries did not like the idea of a mandatory asymmetric review.

29. It was quite clear that the Universal Peer Review (UPR) model of the Human Rights Council was not going to fly and voluntary reviews would be more likely to find acceptance. Finally, what was agreed was a matrix of review processes at the national, regional and global levels with the High Level Political Forum (HLPF) at the apex and largely based on the target and indicator structure which had been agreed to.

30. What I have tried to do is give the reader a peek at the rollercoaster ride which brought us to a conclusion of the 2030 Agenda process. There were several other boulders on the path including migrants and migration, human rights, people under occupation, LDCs and middle-income countries. There were several other difficulties including language around the issues of sanctions, energy, rule of law, CBDR (Common But Differentiated Responsibilities) but once the process was on a roll then differences melted away in the face of tactics and strategies, diplomatic and technical, that were brought to the process.

31. On Sunday, 2 August 2015, to general applause in the negotiation room, the entire package was adopted. It was a triumph for inclusion, innovation, openness and leadership. The world was now ready to adopt this potentially transformative Agenda in the persons of 160 Heads of State and Government in New York in September 2015.

32. This is the story of the backdrop, the innovations, the leadership and the controversies which were solved during this wonderful if at times nail-biting process. The sense of elation that was experienced when the Agenda was adopted reminded me of June 1992 when Agenda 21 was adopted. It was a feeling of hope, good will and solidarity. A mood which has been difficult to capture in the three years since its adoption.

33. What is so special over all about the Agenda 2030? The UN has adopted so many declarations, agendas and platforms for action in its almost 75 years of existence. Why should we expect the SDGs to endure? To answer this, I turn for inspiration to the UN Charter which enshrines the hopes of humanity for peace and prosperity. It is both inspirational and after so many years is the bible of multilateralism. In the same vein I often feel that the 2030 Agenda actually transforms the Charter into an indicative plan with goals, targets and indicators. Moreover, it was created through a most awe inspiring journey with unprecedented participation and hence ownership. When it was adopted there was applause from every part of the

General Assembly (GA) Hall – from governments of all different political hues and on different rungs of the development ladder, by the UN System, by Academia, business and civil society. It has transcended the North-South way of looking at issues and embraced the future of our common humanity through the principle of universality. It has made sustainable development the business of all and given a fresh flavor to the meaning of global citizenship. Like the UN Charter it will stand the test of time and hopefully shift the trajectory of our world towards an end to poverty, reduced inequality, and environmental sustainability for a just and peaceful world.

Chapter 2

THE TRANSITION FROM MDGS TO SDGS

PALOMA DURAN Y LALAGUNA, PhD
Director of the Sustainable Development Goals Fund

&

TERESA BURELLI
Private Sector and Programmes Analyst at the
Sustainable Development Goals Fund

SUMMARY: I. THE MILLENNIUM DEVELOPMENT GOALS. II. THE GLOBAL CONSULTATION OF SUSTAINABLE DEVELOPMENT GOALS. III. TRANSITION FROM THE MDG ACHIEVEMENT FUND TO THE SDG FUND. III.1 The SDG Fund model. IV. CONCLUSION: LOOKING TO THE LESSONS LEARNED OF THE MDG FUND AND THE SDG FUND FOR THE ACHIEVEMENT OF THE 2030 AGENDA

* * *

I.   THE MILLENNIUM DEVELOPMENT GOALS

Since the creation of the United Nations, many attempts have been made to improve development in a number of countries. Initially the achievement of a lasting peace, after the world wars, was the primary objective of an organization created amidst the shadows and uncertainties brought about by the failure of the League of Nations.

With the signing of the Charter of San Francisco, on June 25th, 1945, the aims of the United Nations organization were established in article 1:

1. To maintain international peace and security, and to that end: to take effective collective measures for the prevention and removal of threats to the peace, and for the suppression of acts of aggression or other breaches of the peace, and to bring about by peaceful means, and in conformity with the principles of justice and international law, adjustment or settlement of international disputes or situations which might lead to a breach of the peace;

2. To develop friendly relations among nations based on respect for the principle of equal rights and self-determination of peoples, and to take other appropriate measures to strengthen universal peace;

3. To achieve international co-operation in solving international problems of an economic, social, cultural, or humanitarian character, and in promoting and encouraging respect for human rights and for fundamental freedoms for all without distinction as to race, sex, language, or religion; and

4. To be a centre for harmonizing the actions of nations in the attainment of these common ends.

The decade of the 50s and 60s saw peace become firmly established, yet also witnessed independence movements in many parts of the world, which did not end until the end of the 20th century after the restructuring of the former Soviet Union, and following the changes in Europe and the independence of various countries in Africa and Asia.

This process of decolonization ushered in an important debate on approaches to development, especially in countries with fewer economic resources.

The conception of development in the 1960s faced two major challenges:

- On the one hand, development was envisioned in almost exclusively economic terms, in such a way that it was measured on the basis of per capita income and the number of inhabitants in a given country. This outlook, typical of the economist's mindset, has since evolved, largely as a result of the work of Amartya Sen. These efforts have paved the way for a more comprehensive approach to the subject, which in the 1970s and 1980s broadened HDI indicators to encompass not just economic development, but also social dimensions.

- At the same time, development came to be rather casually regarded as a by-product of colonialism, in which donor countries maintain their priorities in the territories previously colonized, reflecting political considerations that have an impact on all aspects of development assistance.

This state of affairs was to some extent mitigated by the holding of the great world Conferences, organized by the United Nations. The treatment of the environment; equality between women and men; the protection of children; the summits on aging; the delineation of social rights; the international protection of human rights and the preparation of new international treaties, not to mention a considerable number of other topics, were the focus of international negotiations and agreements.

The decades of the 70s, 80s and 90s witnessed a remarkable increase in global meetings, whose enduring legacy included government commitments strongly focused on the main issues of development.

The turn of the millennium was the perfect framework for then UN Secretary General Kofi Annan to propose the preparation of a short and detailed list of goals to improve the situation of the developing world.

The Millennium Declaration was approved on September 8, 2000, at the end of the "Millennium Summit," which brought together Heads of State and Government. UN General Assembly Resolution 55/2 was unanimously approved at the plenary of the Assembly[1]. The fundamental values for international relations recognized in Section I(6) of the Declaration are as follows:

• **Freedom.** *Men and women have the right to live their lives and raise their children in dignity, free from hunger and from the fear of violence, oppression or injustice. Democratic and participatory governance based on the will of the people best assures these rights.*

• **Equality.** *No individual and no nation must be denied the opportunity to benefit from development. The equal rights and opportunities of women and men must be assured.*

• **Solidarity.** *Global challenges must be managed in a way that distributes the costs and burdens fairly in accordance with basic principles of equity and social justice. Those who suffer or who benefit least deserve help from those who benefit most.*

• **Tolerance.** *Human beings must respect one other, in all their diversity of belief, culture and language. Differences within and between societies should be neither feared nor repressed, but cherished as a precious asset of humanity. A culture of peace and dialogue among all civilizations should be actively promoted.*

• **Respect for nature.** *Prudence must be shown in the management of all living species and natural resources, in accordance with the precepts of sustainable development. Only in this way can the immeasurable riches provided to us by nature be preserved and passed on to our descendants. The current unsustainable patterns of production and consumption must be changed in the interest of our future welfare and that of our descendants.*

• **Shared responsibility.** *Responsibility for managing worldwide economic and social development, as well as threats to international peace and security, must be shared among the nations of the world and should be exercised multilaterally. As the most universal and most representative organization in the world, the United Nations must play the central role.*

A few months before, in March 2000, the UN Secretary General had published the report on which the Assembly resolution [2] was based, in which a review of the international situation, current challenges and projections for the future had been prepared.

Without minimizing the founding principles of the Rule of Law and the protection and defense of human rights, the Secretary General was putting forward a vision of an international community free from poverty, free from fear, and with a sustainable future. To this end, UN reforms and the consolidation of the fundamental values mentioned

---

[1] Cfr. Document A/RES/55/2 *, published on September 13, 2000.
[2] Document 54/2000, Report of the Secretary General, *We the peoples: the role of the United Nations in the twenty-first century [The Millennium Report].*

above and included in the General Assembly Declaration, would continue to have a vital role to play.

In the same vein, the Declaration includes the "Millennium Development Goals" (MDGs), which consist of eight specific objectives encapsulating many of the commitments undertaken at previous UN Summits and Conferences.

The MDGs and their corresponding indicators charted a course for the period 2000-2015:

Goal 1: eradicate extreme poverty and hunger;

Goal 2: achieve universal primary education;

Goal 3: promote gender equality and empower women;

Goal 4: reduce child mortality;

Goal 5: improve maternal health;

Goal 6: combat HIV/AIDS, malaria, and other diseases;

Goal 7: ensure environmental sustainability; and

Goal 8: develop a global partnership for development.

In 2015, at the end of the lifespan of the MDGs, the Inter-Agency and Expert Group on MDG Indicators, under the coordination of the Department of Economic and Social Affairs of the United Nations Secretariat prepared the progress report on MDG implementation ("The Millennium Development Goals Report 2015") (in response to the General Assembly's request for periodic evaluations of the progress made in achieving the Millennium Development Goals)[3]. Although the UN Secretary-General, Ban Ki-Moon began the prologue by welcoming the progress made thanks to the MDGs, the truth is that many challenges remained palpable.

In the same text, the SG noted the fact that poverty was concentrated in certain parts of the world and confirmed that in 2011, nearly 60% of the world's one billion extremely poor people in the world lived in just five countries[4]. The report includes some of the advances achieved, such as the fact that *globally, the number of people living in extreme poverty has declined by more than half, falling from 1.9 billion in 1990 to 836 million in 2015* [5]*;* or that in 2015, *91% of the world's population was using an improved drinking water source, compared to 76% in 1990* [6]*;* However, the data also confirm the existence of important gender gaps, the challenges generated by climate change, the number of people living in extreme poverty and the consequences of conflicts in development [7].

---

[3] The report may be found on the UN website: www.un.org.
[4] Op. Cit., p. 3 [in source].
[5] Ibidem, p. 4 [in source]
[6] Ibidem, p. 7 [in source]
[7] Ibidem, pp. 8-ss

Nonetheless, the fact is that the millennium agenda was government-led. It was the Member States of the United Nations that negotiated the goals and indicators and who approved the final decisions, reflecting an approach to development in which the gap between donor countries and recipient countries could still be clearly perceived. In 2000, the debate on the need for national ownership was still in its infancy, as evidenced by the 2005 Paris Declaration, showing the need for a more proactive role on the part of countries and their stakeholders.

It could be said that the MDGs were a "top-down" road map; a list of objectives directed primarily at developing countries; and an agenda that failed to include some of the needs that were to become obvious by 2015 but which had not yet been recognized as such in 2000.

Nor should we overlook the role of the international community, in which a territorial distribution of power in step with the traditional organization dating back to 1945 was still much in evidence, reflecting only some of the changes unfolding In Eastern Europe or the conflicts experienced in Africa.

For between 2000 and 2015, quite apart from the constraints mentioned above, substantial changes had occurred on the international scene. The areas of concern now included climate change, but also the state of the oceans and the distribution of sustainable energy. Social and economic inequalities affected not only developing countries but also developed countries and (most especially) middle-income countries. South-South cooperation was beginning to take hold in some geographic areas and in other cases, triangular cooperation was being used. Government stakeholders were no longer solely responsible for the implementation of development objectives.

All this meant a clear need to refocus the development roadmap, and the changed international environment ushered in a change of direction in the drafting and negotiation of the Sustainable Development Goals (SDGs).

II.   THE GLOBAL CONSULTATION OF SUSTAINABLE DEVELOPMENT GOALS

The Rio+20 conference[8] (the United Nations Conference on Sustainable Development) in Rio de Janeiro, June 2012, galvanized a process to develop a new set of Sustainable Development Goals (SDGs) which will carry on the momentum generated by the MDGs and fit into a global development framework beyond 2015.

In the interest of creating a new, people-centered, development agenda, a global consultation was conducted online and offline. Civil society organizations, citizens, scientists, academics, and the private sector from around the world were all actively engaged in the process. Activities included thematic and national consultations, and the My World survey led by the United Nations Development Group. Specialized panels

---

[8] https://sustainabledevelopment.un.org/rio20.html

were also held and provided ground to facilitate intergovernmental discussions. The UN Secretary General presented a synthesis of the results of these consultation processes.

In July 2014, the UN General Assembly Open Working Group (OWG) proposed a document[9] containing 17 goals to be put forward for the General Assembly's approval in September 2015. This document set the ground for the new SDGs and the global development agenda spanning from 2015-2030.

The SDGs and their corresponding indicators charted a course for the period 2015-2030:

Goal 1: No Poverty

Goal 2: Zero Hunger

Goal 3: Good Health and Well-being

Goal 4: Quality Education

Goal 5: Gender Equality

Goal 6: Clean Water and Sanitation

Goal 7: Affordable and Clean Energy

Goal 8: Decent Work and Economic Growth

Goal 9: Industry, Innovation and Infrastructure

Goal 10: Reduced Inequality

Goal 11: Sustainable Cities and Communities

Goal 12: Responsible Consumption and Production

Goal 13: Climate Action

Goal 14: Life Below Water

Goal 15: Life on Land

Goal 16: Peace and Justice Strong Institutions

Goal 17: Partnerships to achieve the Goal

The Agenda 2030 and the SDGs build on the MDGs, but the world has substantially changed in these last 15 years and with that the new development agenda is, in many regards very different.

First, the actors have changed themselves. Businesses have incorporated the sustainability, environmental and social dimensions of their work as a part of their operations. NGOs have acquired a more prominent role in societies. As the Edelman Trust Barometer[10] shows, as of 2015, NGOs are the most trusted institutions well ahead of

---

[9] Report of the OWG on SDGs, A/68/L.61, September 2014
[10] 2017 Edelman Trust Barometer

media, business and government. Additionally, more business actors have realized that that investing in low-income communities and in the environment can be profitable and good for the bottom line.

As mentioned above, the process of building this agenda relied on the support of all these new actors. The 2030 Agenda has been the result of one of the most inclusive and widest consultation processes in the UN history. Hundreds of thousands of representatives of governments, civil society, academia, businesses and communities have been engaged in thematic global and national consultations. Now these actors are familiar with the agenda and feel entitled to implement it. For example, some local and national governments have developed their own SDGs plans, as some companies have already started their own. NGOs have been mobilizing the world around the Action 2015 campaign. These new actors are now engaged and feel part of it. They all have ownership and a greater interest in making it happen.

Most importantly, this is a universal agenda. Universal in two manners. Because it applies to all countries, but also universal because it aims at reaching everyone at, as in the words of the high-level panel for the post 2015 agenda affirmed, *"leaving no one behind"*. We have moved from the halves to the universals. (Compare the target 1.1 of the MDGs with the SDG target 1.1. In 2000 it read[11] *"halve, between 1990 and 2015, the proportion of people whose income is less than one dollar a day"* and today it reads *"by 2030, eradicate extreme poverty for all people everywhere, currently measured as people living on less than $1.25 a day"*. In addition, new and important themes have been introduced, like oceans, responsible consumption and issues such as creating decent jobs are now at the core of the agenda. To leave no one behind and to put in a place a universal agenda can't depend only on one party like government or donors who were the more traditional actors of the development landscape. New actors need to be fully engaged and committed.

III.   TRANSITION FROM THE MDG ACHIEVEMENT FUND TO THE SDG FUND[12]

The MDG Achievement Fund[13] (2007-2013) was one of the largest and most comprehensive development cooperation mechanisms created to support the achievement of the Millennium Development Goals. The MDG Achievement Fund was committed to eradicating poverty and inequality and changing people's lives around the world. Set up in 2007 with a total contribution of approximately USD $900 million from the Government of Spain, it implemented the joint programmes that helped to advance the MDGs worldwide. The MDG Achievement Fund financed 130 joint programmes in 50

---

[11] Report: Annan, Kofi A., "We the Peoples": The Role of the United Nations in the 21st Century (2000), United Nations.
[12] This section was prepared by Ekaterina Dorodnykh, former Knowledge Management and UN relations Analyst during her time at the SDG Fund (2016-2018).
[13] www.mdgfund.org

countries around the world, working in 8 areas: Children, Food Security and Nutrition; Gender Equality and Women's Empowerment; Environment and Climate Change; Youth, Employment and Migration; Democratic Economic Governance; Development and the Private Sector; Conflict Prevention and Peace-Building; and Culture and Development.

The MDG Achievement Fund contributed directly and indirectly to the achievement of the MDGs by adopting an inclusive and comprehensive approach to the MDGs:

- The MDG Achievement Fund worked with almost 2000 partners from community organizations, national and local governments, NGOs, UN Agencies and the private sector, taking into account a gender perspective in all its work.

- All programmes were joint programmes, meaning they brought together on average six United Nations agencies in a collective effort, thereby strengthening the UN system's ability to deliver as one entity.

- The MDG Achievement Fund also led a social justice initiative to put the issue of social exclusion and inequality at the center of the fight against poverty to achieve the MDGs.

Building upon the experience and lessons learned from the MDG Achievement Fund, the SDG Fund was created in 2014 to act as a bridge in the transition from MDGs to SDGs, by providing concrete experiences on how to achieve a sustainable and inclusive world post-2015 through its integrated and multidimensional joint programmes. The SDG Fund was the first cooperation mechanism specifically designed to achieve the SDGs. The SDG Fund adapted to the new context of development aid by placing a greater focus on sustainable development and public-private partnerships.

Comparing to the MDG Achievement Fund, the SDG Fund incorporated several relevant changes:

- Greater participation of the private sector and emphasis on public-private partnerships.

- A better selection of UN Agencies involved, limiting to three/four the number of participating UN Agencies in every joint programme.

- Better mainstreaming of gender equality and women's empowerment and integrating environment sensitivity in joint programmes.

- Engagement of local stakeholders. This is a key component in designing and implementing programmes which target the most disadvantaged groups.

- Co-financing through national and international partners. Matching funds of national governments, international donors and the private sector to increase programme sustainability.

- Multi-donor approach. The SDG Fund is open to donors and partners that want to deploy joint programmes for the achievement of the SDGs.

For the design of its joint programmes, the SDG Fund built on the experience, knowledge, lessons learned and best practices of the Millennium Development Goals

Achievement Fund. The SDG Fund worked to turn development effectiveness principles into joint programmes that advance the achievement of the SDGs. SDG Fund joint programmes in 22 countries are directly improving the lives of more than 5 million people. The SDG Fund worked with 14 different UN agencies and hundreds of national counterparts who are involved in making the SDG Fund joint activities a reality. Moreover, the participatory process to formulate joint programmes engaged around 2,000 participants from civil service and government, communities, international development agencies, and the private sector.

The SDG Fund management and organizational structure fulfilled 3 organizational goals:

- Full transparency and accountability with a wide variety of partners: national and local governments, donors, taxpayers, UN agencies and others.

- Operational effectiveness, reducing the organizational size at the global level and keeping small joint programme coordination teams. Embedding work in national institutions and UN country offices.

- National ownership, respecting country leadership and supporting capacity building for such leadership.

Ensuring adequate involvement of local counterparts in decision-making processes from programme design through implementation and evaluation is a key in the work of the SDG Fund. Strong Government leadership, a united UN Country Team led by the Resident Coordinator, and the national Governments' participation were crucial to making strategic.

III.1 The SDG Fund model[14]

Working with the SDG Fund[15] meant working with the UN System as a whole. For each joint programme, the Resident Coordinator, in collaboration with the UN country team, determined which UN agencies should work together to address the challenge more efficiently. By putting together specialized UN agencies in collaboration with national counterparts, the SDG Fund's joint programmes brought integrated and holistic approaches to national and local development issues. Joint programmes helped tackle limitations of a single sector and avoid a silo approach to development.

Governments at municipal, regional and national levels assumed ownership more readily when initiatives are built using their vision, strategy, and framework. Development cooperation need to be people-centric and respond to national priorities. The SDG Fund governance mechanisms ensured the full participation of national government and partners. All the SDG Fund programmes were aligned with national priorities, as agreed by the UN and each national government in the UN Development

---

[14] This section is based in a document of lessons learnt prepared by the SDG fund Secretariat that will be published by 2019.
[15] www.sdgfund.org

Assistance Framework[16] (UNDAF). Moreover, most country programmes contributed their own financial resources. Programme countries provided 25% of the resources. Joint programmes were executed nationally thus increased the participation of national partners in strategic and financial decision-making. Even in the few cases when direct execution by UN agencies could be more appropriate and effective, SDG Fund programmes ensured that important decisions include all relevant national stakeholders.

The 2030 Agenda is a multidimensional roadmap. It takes into account connecting factors, such as that lack of income negatively affects one's health, education and livelihood. Poverty is multidimensional: lack of income overlaps with deprivations in health, education, and living standards. That's why poverty eradication requires multi-faceted, integrated, and holistic approaches and breaking organizational silos is particularly important. Joint programmes contribute to achieving several SDGs simultaneously. Some of the advantages of intersectoral approaches are: reduce overlap and duplication among development programmes; increase cross-sectoral government interventions; and enhance coordination among donors and line ministries; prevent competition for funds; and make positive use of the comparative advantage of each specialized development agency and partner. Most importantly, national counterparts acknowledge that joint programmes improve dialogue at the national level. When partners identify the dimensions that define a complex development issue, institutions and stakeholders work toward common solutions.

---

[16] Report: United Nations Development Group, (2017) "United Nations Development Assistance Framework Guidance"

Graph 1. The SDG Fund model. Key elements for platform analysis

The SDG Fund established a Private Sector Advisory Group, formed by business leaders of several major businesses from various industries worldwide. These leaders have helped the SDG Fund building a roadmap for how public-private alliances can provide large-scale solutions for achieving the SDGs. The Advisory Group's collaborated and discussed practical solutions to the common challenges of contemporary sustainability. It was committed to identifying areas of common interest and deciphering the best methods for an efficient and impactful UN-private sector engagement, as well as offering suggestions for how to work more effectively at the country level. Most importantly, this conversation moved into practice and concrete action: by building on the conclusions of three groundbreaking reports[17] on business engagement in SDGs with Harvard University, Business Fights Poverty and Global Compact, the SDG Fund in 2017

---

[17] SDG Fund Private Sector Advisory Group, Harvard's Kennedy School and Business Fights Poverty (2015). "Business and the United Nations: Working Together Towards the Sustainable Development Goals: A Framework for Action."
SDG Fund Private Sector Advisory Group and Global Compact (2016). "Universality and the SDGs: A Business Perspective."
SDG Fund Private Sector Advisory Group, Pennsylvania University Law School and McDermott Will & Emery (2017). "Business and SDG 16: Contributing to Peaceful, Just and Inclusive Societies."

engaged leading private sector partners in co-designing innovative projects under a new thematic window of public-private sector collaboration. For these partnerships, the SDG Fund brought on board key figures in the creative industries, such as artists, architects or chefs, with their added value in conforming platforms.

A key element of the SDG Fund was the matching funds system, which requires that every financial contribution made by the SDG Fund was matched at least one to one by the joint programme partners. These are national and subnational governments, UN agencies, the private sector and civil society. Matching funds ensured greater national ownership and improve sustainability, since many of these initiatives were scaled up or inform new national policies. As a result, the SDG Fund leveraged in-country resources, with 25% of the resources coming from non-DAC OECD countries.

IV.   CONCLUSION: LOOKING TO THE LESSONS LEARNED OF THE MDG FUND AND THE SDG FUND FOR THE ACHIEVEMENT OF THE 2030 AGENDA

The lessons learned from the SDG Fund's experience highlights that this type of facility, based on matching funds and multi-sectorial approach, supports strategic joint efforts of UN agencies, development partners, governments and private sector to advance sustainable development. Several features from the MDG Achievement Fund and the SDG Fund should be adopted in the design of a new development mechanism to support the 2030 Agenda. These include joint programming principles, involvement of new non-traditional partners (academia and the private sector), full transparency and accountability and increased national ownership.

Chapter 3

POVERTY ERADICATION: A PRIORITY OF THE INTERNATIONAL COMMUNITY[1]

CÁSTOR M. DÍAZ BARRADO

Head Professor of Public International Law and International Relations,

University of Rey Juan Carlos

SUMMARY: I. INTRODUCTION II. MAIN INTERNATIONAL INSTRUMENTS FOR THE ERADICATION OF POVERTY. III. PRINCIPLES OF INTERNATIONAL LAW AND POVERTY ERADICATION. III.1. International Cooperation and Poverty Eradication. III.2. Sustainable development and poverty eradication. III.3. Human Rights Protection and Poverty Eradication. IV. CONCLUSIONS

* * *

I.   INTRODUCTION

One of the key goals of the international community is to eradicate poverty as soon as possible. Eliminating poverty would be a major step forward for mankind and recent data reveals both a drastic reduction in poverty and a strong commitment to eradicating it completely. Data from the World Bank in 2013 confirming this reduction provided a positive backdrop to the 2015 meeting in which new Sustainable Development Goals (SDGs) were approved.

---

[1] This work was conducted within the framework of the project on Development and Poverty Eradication (SDG-FUND y URJC) V528. It is primarily based on my article: La erradicación de la pobreza y los derechos humanos: un laberinto sin salida, published in the journal "Derechos y Libertades: Revista del Instituto Bartolomé de las Casas", nº 38, 2018, pp. 17-52.

How many poor people are there in the world?

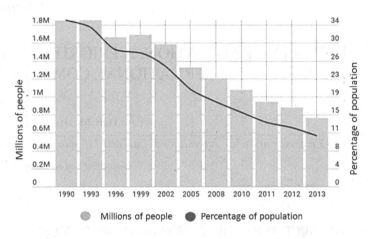

People living with less than 1.90 US dollars per day. Source: World Bank

Source: http://www.europapress.es/internacional/noticia-radiografia-pobreza-mundo-20161018162245.html. Own translation.

The World Bank announced further good news in 2015: "The number of people living in extreme poverty around the world is likely to fall to under 10 percent of the global population in 2015, according to World Bank projections released today, giving fresh evidence that a quarter-century-long sustained reduction in poverty is moving the world closer to the historic goal of ending poverty by 2030"[2]. However, there is still a lot to do.

In political terms, this determination to end poverty has been enshrined in the 2030 Sustainable Development Agenda, contained in Resolution 70/1 of the General United Nations Assembly of September 25, 2015. The inclusion of poverty eradication as Sustainable Development Goal 1 reflects the priority given to this objective. The other SDGs can only be achieved if the international community is able to end poverty in all its forms. Only by ending poverty can we avoid inequalities and enable people to exercise their rights. For this reason, poverty must be considered an essential condition for stability and development in the international community of the 21st century and a necessary condition for the exercise of human rights. International law must also pay a key role in eradicating poverty and is an ideal tool for achieving this goal.

Given that the 2030 agenda is a practical examination of the SDGs, in general and, more specifically, of the central objective of eradicating poverty it does not establish a relationship between poverty elimination and principles of international order, such as human rights. SDGs are designed on the basis of eminently political criteria and employ

[2]http://www.bancomundial.org/es/news/press-release/2015/10/04/world-bank-forecasts-global-poverty-to-fall-below-10-for-first-time-major-hurdles-remain-in-goal-to-end-poverty-by-2030.

purely practical indicators. Therefore, the process of reaching all these Goals and, specifically, the goal of eradicating poverty does not involve the recognition of rights or the imposition of obligations. The aim is to reach these goals via patterns of behaviour, orientations, action criteria, guidelines and, when needed, political commitments[3]. For this reason, the 2030 agenda completely dispenses with juridical precision. The Agenda is an ambitious plan for achieving the SDGs which aims to obtain practical results purely through the actions of States and of other actors in international relations. This is stated in Resolution 70/1: "This Agenda is a plan of action for people, planet and prosperity. It also seeks to strengthen universal peace in larger freedom. We recognize that eradicating poverty in all its forms and dimensions, including extreme poverty, is the greatest global challenge and an indispensable requirement for sustainable development".

However, even if priority is given to political aspects and practical components, poverty eradication must occur inside a specific conceptual and regulatory framework: international law must play a role in conforming these goals; they cannot be achieved purely through political decisions, practical measures and managerial actions. Norms of international law must play a role because the SDGs cannot be fully achieved without adhering to principles and norms of this legal system. International law is a complement to the measures contained in Resolution 70/1, because it, too, is a useful tool for eradicating world poverty. To end poverty, we must use all the instruments that the international community has at its disposal and international law is an ideal mechanism for reaching this goal.

The lack of explicit references to international law should not be taken to mean that the SDGs are not subject to any juridical system. International law is necessary to achieve both the SDGs in general and, more specifically, the goal of eradicating poverty. Some conclusions can be drawn from this. Firstly, poverty eradication is not a purely political goal as it also involves compliance with the obligations established in international regulations. Secondly, juridical measures must also be taken to achieve the SDGs. Finally, we must ensure a convergence between the goal of ending poverty and the international regulations employed to reach this objective. To sum up, International law provides us with a system for understanding international reality and, above all, imposes obligations on States and other actors on the international scene. It is necessary because "it is fundamental that the new era that begins in 2015 is more than a time of grand declarations and paper goals; it must also employ suitable means and mechanisms to achieve the required transformations"[4]. The mechanisms for reaching the SDGs and for eradicating poverty must take into account international law, especially laws and regulations related to human rights.

---

[3] RODRIGO HERNÁNDEZ, A. J., "El concepto de desarrollo sostenible en el Derecho Internacional, Publisher" in Agenda ONU: Anuario de la Asociación para las Naciones Unidas en España, and "El desafío del desarrollo sostenible: los principios de derecho internacional relativos al desarrollo sostenible", Barcelona, 2015.
[4] MARTÍNEZ AGUT, M. P. "Objetivos de Desarrollo Sostenible (ODS, 2015-2030) y Agenda de Desarrollo post 2015 a partir de los Objetivos de Desarrollo del Milenio (2000-2015)", *Quadernsanimacio.net,* n° 21, january, 2015, p. 14.

While the political and practical proclamation of the means to end poverty in Resolution 70/1 does not explicitly express any legal obligations, the SDGs must be conceived in terms that are comprehensible from the perspective of the regulations that recognize and protect rights and establish obligations. Mere programmatic declarations and calls for mobilization, accompanied by itineraries, indicators, and management measures and criteria would be insufficient. It is necessary to adopt regulations that impose precise obligations and ban or allow specific behaviours. At the present time, there is no regulation based on international law that imposes the obligations to eradicate poverty and no legal definition of poverty. There is no consensus regarding which forms of poverty should be banned by international law. We do not know who holds the rights and the obligations in situations of poverty; and any hypothetical obligation to eradicate world poverty would be devoid of any precise legal content. However, there are "structural" principles of international law on which the obligation to end poverty could be based; these principles could be used to give legal content to the obligation to eradicate poverty.

II.   MAIN INTERNATIONAL INSTRUMENTS FOR THE ERADICATION OF POVERTY

The high number of juridical instruments at our disposal for ending poverty prove that this is one of the main aims of the international community. However, there is no regulation inside international law which obliges States to adopt whatever means are necessary to eradicate poverty. Neither is there any regulation inside international law which recognizes the rights of those suffering from poverty, that is, the poor, or imposes obligations, above all on States, to end with all forms of poverty and with the behaviours that generate it. While there are numerous references to poverty eradication in the relevant legal-political instruments, no legally binding precept for achieving this goal has yet crystallized. These instruments contain declarations of intention, endeavours and aspirations of the international community alongside ethical and political proclamations, but none of this has yet been completely translated into juridical terms.

Three conclusions can be drawn from an examination of the instruments that include a commitment to eradicate poverty. Firstly, these instruments cite poverty as one of the main problems facing humanity. The determination to end poverty is absolute. Secondly, the approach of the instruments that mention poverty essentially overlooks principles established by international law, especially those related to the international protection of human rights. The perspectives of these instruments are generalist rather than juridical and are formulated within the framework of development policies. However, instruments which adopt a human rights approach to poverty eradication are slowly being created. Finally, none of the instruments that proclaim the need to eradicate poverty are legally binding and, above all, these tools do not impose precise obligations. However, changes in our approach to eradicating poverty show that this Goal is gradually forming links with some sectors of international law:

i) The general commitment to eradicate poverty is embodied in instruments which have no bearing on the consequences of poverty perpetuation for international law. Resolution 69/234 of the United Nations General Assembly establishing the "Second United Nations Decade for the Eradication of Poverty (2008-2017)" is a case in point. This Resolution states that "poverty eradication is the greatest global challenge facing the world today and an indispensable requirement for sustainable development, and in this regard commits itself to freeing humanity from poverty and hunger as a matter of urgency". This resolution has no bearing on the repercussions of poverty for a particular sector of international law. Declarations of this type do not impose any specific obligations on states with regard to poverty elimination. Its effects are limited to goals, intentions and values and establish no link between poverty elimination and international law. Likewise, resolution 51/178 proclaiming the "First United Nations Decade for the Eradication of Poverty" fails to establish a close relationship between poverty and international law. However, in this case, there are allusions to some sectors of international law. Resolution 51/178 highlights that "special attention should be given to the multidimensional nature of poverty and to the national and international framework, conditions and policies that are conducive to its eradication, which should aim at the social and economic integration of people living in poverty and the promotion and protection of all human rights and fundamental freedoms for all, including the right to development". To sum up, while poverty eradication is a basic commitment of the international community, it has yet to be fully translated into either regulations or juridical concepts in some fields of International law.

ii) Poverty eradication and "development" are regarded as closely related phenomena. This approach enables us to place poverty within a specific, but as yet unformed, sector of international law. Our current lack of a fundamental principle that establishes the "right to sustainable development" affects the legal treatment of the Goal to eradicate poverty. Despite this, the link with sustainable development ensures that poverty is included as a category within the international framework. Let us recall three instruments in which poverty eradication appears both as one of the most serious problems facing humanity in the next few years and one of the development goals.

a) Principle 5 of "the Rio Declaration on environment and development", adopted in 1992, states that "All States and all people shall co-operate in the essential task of eradicating poverty as an indispensable requirement for sustainable development, in order to decrease the disparities in standards of living and better meet the needs of the majority of the people of the world". Fighting inequality and achieving development are inherent parts of poverty eradication. Our sustainable development goals cannot be achieved without ending poverty.

b) In the subsection "the challenges we face", the 2002 Johanessburg Declaration on Sustainable Development places poverty at the top of its list of "overarching objectives of and essential requirements for sustainable development". Poverty eradication is a necessary means of achieving the goals of the international community and of ensuring human development. By exploiting the close link between sustainable development and poverty eradication we may be able to reach both goals.

c) The United Nations Conference on Sustainable Development held in Río de Janeiro in 2012 issued an outcome document titled "The Future we Want", which categorically states that "Poverty eradication is the greatest global challenge facing the world today and an indispensable requirement for sustainable development". It thus expresses a strong determination to fight against poverty and ensure that people enjoy better living conditions in a framework of sustainable development. Poverty eradication is regarded as a priority of the international community.

These declarations are part of the work devoted to expressing the content of the SDGs. Two phases have been determined for reaching these Goals both of which incorporate a set of goals and targets that we must reach if we are to create an international society free from inequality. Poverty eradication is always placed at the top of these Goals and it appears in close association with the "development concept". The formulation of all these Goals, including that of ending with poverty, is essentially based on development criteria and perspectives.

On the one hand, the "United Nations Millennium Declaration", adopted in the year 2000[5], contains a specific section titled "Development and poverty eradication" which sets out criteria, measures, orientations and guidelines that have little bearing on international law. Even the section devoted to "Human rights, democracy and good governance", includes no reference to poverty eradication. It says nothing about the fact that poverty is a violation of international regulations, particularly those related to human rights. For the United Nations Millennium Declaration, poverty eradication is treated purely as a development objective that has no bearing on other sectors of international law.

On the other hand, Resolution 70/1, sets out an ambitious plan that takes into account the Sustainable Development Goals (SDGs).This plan does not once link poverty eradication to international law or human rights. Once more, the SDGs as a whole and poverty eradication in particular are expressed in developmental terms. Resolution 70/1 starts out by stating "This Agenda is a plan of action for people, planet and prosperity. (...) We recognize that eradicating poverty in all its forms and dimensions, including extreme poverty, is the greatest global challenge and an indispensable requirement for sustainable development". The closest they get to providing a legal or human rights perspective is the allusion to human rights in the following statement: "The 17 Sustainable Development Goals and 169 targets which we are announcing today demonstrate the scale and ambition of this new universal Agenda. (...). They seek to

---

[5]A/RES/55/2, 13 September 2000.

realize the human rights of all and to achieve gender equality and the empowerment of all women and girls. They are integrated and indivisible and balance the three dimensions of sustainable development: the economic, social and environmental"[6]. On its own, this allusion to human rights is not enough to ensure that international law and human rights occupy a prominent position in achieving the SDGs.

The declaration does contain other references to human rights some of which go deeper than the statement cited in the previous paragraph. However, none of these references are explicitly linked to poverty eradication. Point 8 of Resolution 70/1 declares: "We envisage a world of universal respect for human rights and human dignity, the rule of law, justice, equality and non-discrimination"; and point 19 states: "We emphasize the responsibilities of all States, in conformity with the Charter of the United Nations, to respect, protect and promote human rights and fundamental freedoms for all"[7]. These are general expressions regarding the need to respect human rights which are applicable to all the SDGs, but are not specifically related to any of them.

We can conclude that there is a general obligation on States to cooperate in the fight against poverty and to ensure sustainable development, by achieving sustainable economic growth and social balance. In any event, these declarations express a political principle that reflects the close link between poverty eradication and sustainable development. Ending poverty is a development goal governed by the largely unregulated indications that inspire the achievement of the SDGs.

iii) However, instruments have also been adopted which establish a relationship between poverty eradication and international law, especially in the area of human rights. These instruments place poverty eradication inside the regulatory framework of recognition and protection of human rights or propose a new approach to poverty eradication. To be more specific, resolutions related to "extreme poverty and human rights" have been adopted: General Assembly, Resolutions entitled "Human rights and extreme poverty" from Resolution 46/121 until the more recent 71/186; Economic and Social Council: "Extreme poverty" and "Human rights and extreme poverty": from Resolution 1988/47; Commission on Human Rights: " Human rights and extreme poverty", from la Resolution 1989/10; and also the Sub-Commission on Prevention of Discrimination and Protection of Minorities: Decision 1990/119, entitled "Human rights and extreme poverty"; and Resolutions entitled "Human rights and extreme poverty", from resolution 1992/27[8]. Nevertheless, it is important to highlight some other instruments that place poverty more firmly inside the human rights sector:

---

[6]A/RES/70/1, 21 of October 2015. Vid., DIAZ BARRADO, C. M., "Sustainable development goals: a principle and several dimensions", DURAN, P.; DIAZ BARRADO C. M.; y FERNANDEZ LIESA, C.R., International Society and Sustainable Development Goals, Madrid, 2016; y DIAZ BARRADO C. M.,"Los objetivos de desarrollo sostenible: un principio de naturaleza incierta y varias dimensiones fragmentadas", Anuario Español de Derecho Internacional 2016, pp. 7-46.
[7]A/RES/70/1, 21 October 2015.
[8]E/CN.4/Sub.2/1996/13, p. 53.

a) In 2001, the Committee on Economic, Social and Cultural Rights (CESCR) stated: "the Committee holds the firm view that poverty constitutes a denial of human rights" and complained that "the human rights dimensions of poverty eradication policies rarely receive the attention they deserve. This neglect is especially regrettable because a human rights approach to poverty can reinforce anti-poverty strategies and make them more effective"[9]. The committee issued a declaration to the Third Conference on the Least Developed Countries, which will be held this year, which contains aspects that have a strong bearing on the need to establish a link between human rights and poverty eradication[10].

It is important to highlight several aspects of the position adopted by the Committee: on the one hand, the Committee offers a definition of poverty: "While acknowledging that there is no universally accepted definition of poverty, the committee endorses [a definition based on] a multidimensional understanding of poverty, which reflects the indivisible and interdependent nature of all human rights"[11]. The committee seeks a broad, pluridimensional definition that describes poverty as "a human condition characterized by sustained or chronic deprivation of the resources, capabilities, choices, security and power necessary for the enjoyment of an adequate standard of living and other civil, cultural, economic, political and social rights"[12]. A link is thus established between poverty and respect for human rights. On the other hand, the committee's decision acknowledges that the application of specific policies that aim to end poverty can- and should- take into account the recognition and protection of rights. The adoption of a human rights perspective guarantees the usefulness of behaviours intended to eliminate poverty. Finally, the Committee's most significant contribution is the decision to place poverty eradication inside the field of rights and obligations, thus ensuring that the treatment of this area goes beyond mere political commitments[13]. The transposition of regulations related to human rights into the field of poverty eradication allows us to contemplate poverty eradication inside a fairly robust legal framework based on International law.

b) Another instrument also establishes a close link between poverty and human rights and places poverty inside a specific legal framework. Putting an end to poverty necessarily involves a comprehensive approach to human rights. The Human Rights Council (HRC) approved "the guiding principles on extreme poverty and human rights", after studying a decade of documents on the subject[14]. These principles are recognized as

---

[9]COMMITTEE ON ECONOMIC, SOCIAL AND CULTURAL RIGHTS, REPORT ON THE TWENTY-FIFTH, TWENTY-SIXTH AND TWENTY-SEVENTH SESSIONS. (23 April-11 May 2001, 13-31 August 2001, 12-30- November 2001), E/2002/22 E/C.12/2001/17, p. 197.
[10]E/C.12/2001/10, 10, May 2001.
[11]E/2002/22 E/C.12/2001/17, p. 199.
[12]*Ibid.*
[13]Cfr., *ibid.*
[14]PÉREZ-BUSTILLO, C., "New developments in International Poverty Law: the UN Guiding Principles on extreme poverty and human rights", *Poverty Brief,* March 2014.

"the first global policy guidelines focused specifically on the human rights of people living in poverty"[15].

These "guiding principles" should guide States in their behaviours intended to end poverty, as this would drastically reduce poverty and even eradicate it completely. From a juridical perspective, these principles show the close link between poverty and human rights, a key sector of international law. The position adopted in the guiding principles is clear. Paragraph 3 of the Preface states: "Poverty is an urgent human rights concern in itself. It is both a cause and a consequence of human rights violations and an enabling condition for other violations. Not only is extreme poverty characterized by multiple reinforcing violations of civil, political, economic, social and cultural rights, but persons living in poverty generally experience regular denials of their dignity and equality"[16].

There is one basic criterion underlying these Guiding Principles: the search for a link between human rights and poverty, the recognition of the rights of the poor and the imposition of obligations upon those whose task it is to end poverty. To sum up, these Guiding Principles reflect issues related to international responsibility. This can be deduced from paragraph 7 of the preface: "A human rights approach respects the dignity and autonomy of persons living in poverty and empowers them to meaningfully and effectively participate in public life, including in the design of public policy, and to hold duty bearers accountable. The norms set out in international human rights law require that States take their international human rights obligations into account when formulating and implementing policies affecting the lives of persons living in poverty"[17]. The key element is the focus on human rights in the eradication of poverty, as it forces us to take into account the regulations that have been introduced in this area.

International law thus has instruments at its disposal that aim to eradicate poverty and, in some cases, establish a link between poverty and human rights. However, we still need to introduce a regulation that imposes the obligation to eradicate poverty, even if this regulation is general in nature. At present, we only have a political declaration stating that eradicating poverty is one of the greatest challenges faced by mankind and that ending poverty is a necessary condition for sustainable development and the respect of human rights.

It is not enough to express the desire to defeat poverty in all its forms. It is also necessary to point to specific measures and indicators that set out the path that needs to be followed in order to eradicate poverty and to introduce regulations that recognize rights and determine obligations. We must go beyond mere political commitments. The eradication of poverty is one of the key aims of the international community and it is urgent to adopt legal measures that require us to end this scourge. In the words of Resolution 69/234, we must acknowledge "(...) the central imperative of poverty eradication in the elaboration of the post-2015 development agenda". This goal must be

---

[15]*United Nations. Guiding Principles on Extreme Poverty and Human Rights. Office of the High Commissioner for Human Rights,* Geneva, 2012.
[16]A/HRC/21/39, 18 July 2012.
[17]*Ibid.*

given legal content and have at its disposal a legal framework from which rights and obligations can be derived. Up until now, the various instruments that have been employed have helped to place this commitment inside the purview of international law but they have in no way established any precise legal obligations.

III. PRINCIPLES OF INTERNATIONAL LAW AND POVERTY ERADICATION

Links can be established between the goal of eradicating poverty and structural principles of international law. Statements on poverty eradication must have some kind of legal embodiment. We should try to create regulations that impose on States behaviours that can lead to the adoption of positive measures for ending poverty, and demand that they abstain from behaviours that could generate more poverty. Three principles of international law form the legal basis for poverty eradication. The International Cooperation Principle; the Development Principle; the Principle of International Human Rights Protection

III.1 International Cooperation and Poverty Eradication

International cooperation plays a fundamental role in the eradication of poverty. International aid and assistance is a cornerstone of global poverty eradication. This is because "The currency of pledges from the international community is by now so severely debased by non-delivery that it is widely perceived as worthless. Restoring that currency is vital (...) to the creation of confidence in multilateralism and international cooperation—the twin foundations for strengthened international peace and security"[18]. The importance of international cooperation in poverty eradication is reflected in the "guiding principles". Resolution 21/11 states that "States have a duty to provide international assistance and cooperation commensurate with their capacities, resources and influence, as established in the Charter of the United Nations (Articles 55 and 56) and in several international human rights treaties" [19]. These obligations to provide international aid and assistance are set out in point VI of this Resolution and they in some way link poverty eradication to human rights. However, since the obligation to cooperate is expressed in excessively generic terms, precise regulations and obligations related to poverty eradication cannot be easily deduced from it. While international cooperation is required to tackle poverty, it is also essential to provide both States and other actors in international relations with a regulatory framework for conducting such cooperation.

---

[18]*Human Development Report, 2005, International cooperation at a crossroads. Aid trade and security in an unequal world*, New York, 2015, p. 40.
[19]*United Nations. Guiding Principles on Extreme Poverty and Human Rights.* Office of the High Commissioner for Human Rights, Geneva, 2012, p. 33.

III. 2. Sustainable development and poverty eradication

The fight against poverty is closely linked to the notion of sustainable development. The main instruments that contain this principle are proof of this. The key defining dimensions of sustainable development show that poverty eradication can only be achieved by taking into account economic, social and environmental aspects of development. Points 11 and 12 of the "United Nations Millennium Declaration", highlight this relationship by stating "We are committed to making the right to development a reality for everyone and to freeing the entire human race from want". In this sense, they talk of the need "to create an environment – at the national and global levels alike – which is conducive to development and to the elimination of poverty."[20]. The link between the development principle and poverty elimination provides a basis for creating legal regulations and obligations. To sum up, "sustainable development" and "poverty eradication" are two closely connected realities and the juridical value of the former will affect the creation of regulations and obligations relating to the latter.

Of course, we can hardly grant a legal character to poverty eradication if we sustain that the "principle of sustainable development" has not yet crystallized into the creation of an essential or structural principle in international law. It is not easy to derive precise and enforceable obligations from this "principle". Sustainable development does not rank as a principle of international law that is fully recognized in international legal practice, firmly accepted in jurisprudence and solidly founded in scientific doctrine. In fact, sustainable development meets none of these criteria; it is simply an embryonic principle that is just starting to crystallize.

However, the fight against poverty is one of the key elements of sustainable development. Progress in the fight against poverty and in the establishment of rights and obligations in relation to poverty will also help to shape the sustainable development principle. In other words, the aim of eradicating poverty as the first and most important of the 17 SDGs is a major component of the "yet-to be formed" principle of sustainable development. Should this principle be consolidated, the obligation to eradicate poverty would become one of the basic regulations that form part of it. The insistence of international instruments on the need to eradicate poverty shows that it is an essential condition for sustainable development. However, there are two different but complementary perspectives:

On the one hand, the SDGs are the last step in the consolidation of sustainable development as a "structural principal" in international law. The States should begin to draw conclusions from the huge number of commitments contained in the 2030 agenda. The SDG are both an action programme and an instrument capable of forcing states to undertake their obligations in areas related to sustainable development. The universal acceptance of these obligations should lead via scientific doctrine and international jurisprudence to the consolidation of a structural principal recognized by all states. "Sustainable development", as a structuring principle of international law, would

---

[20]A/RES/55/2, 13 September 2000.

incorporate the regulation that establishes the obligation on States to adopt as many measures that are required to eradicate poverty along with the regulation that forces States to abstain from behaviours that can generate poverty. At present, the proclaim relating to poverty eradication is merely a political commitment assumed by States. In the current treatment of sustainable development, there is no specific obligation on States to eradicate poverty and no precise indication of the behaviours needed to eradicate it or of the actions or behaviours for which one can be held accountable in international law. The diverse sustainable development instruments outline a general obligation on States to eradicate poverty, but the legal content of this obligation has not yet been determined.

On the other hand, we can make sense of the obligations arising from the commitment to eradicate poverty if we view them from the perspective of the "social dimension", or "human dimension" of development. The human being should be the ultimate point of reference for development. Indeed, the right to development has been proclaimed as a human right[21]. In particular, the 1986 Declaration on the Right to Development makes a real attempt to draw attention to this right. The Preamble to this Declaration is full of references to human rights as is the slide presentation part in which paragraph 1 of article 2 indicates the content of the "human right to development": "The human person is the central subject of development and should be the active participant and beneficiary of the right to development" [22].

Some conclusions can be drawn: Firstly, the right to development is a human right and it is exercised in the context of international protection of human rights. Article 1 of this Declaration states that "the right to development is an inalienable human right by virtue of which every human person and all peoples are entitled to participate in, contribute to, and enjoy economic, social, cultural and political development, in which all human rights and fundamental freedoms can be fully realized". Secondly, the human being is the central holder of these rights, regardless of whether other entities also hold them. Finally, non-compliance with human rights obligations damages the exercise of the right to development. Paragraph 3 of article 6 stipulates that "States should take steps to eliminate obstacles to development resulting from failure to observe civil and political rights, as well as economic, social and cultural rights"[23].

The Second World Conference on Human Rights, held in Vienna in 1993, is a major step forward in this regard. In the opening speech of this Conference, the Secretary General of the United Nations recalled the link that exists between democracy, development and human rights, claiming: "one thing is sure: there can be no long-lasting development without the promotion of democracy and, therefore, the respect for human

---

[21]*Vid.,* CHUECA SANCHO, A. G., "El derecho humano al desarrollo sostenible: de la Cumbre de Río a Johannesburgo", en *Desarrollo humano sostenible: Actas de las III Jornadas de Estudios sobre Cooperación Internacional*: (Universidad de La Rioja, 9-19 de diciembre de 2002), Coord. por Francisco Ernesto Puertas Moya, 2004, pp. 17-30; y GÓMEZ ISA, F., "El derecho al desarrollo como derecho humano", en *Ayuda al desarrollo: piezas para un puzle*, coord. por Irene Rodríguez Manzano, y Carlos Teijo García, 2009, pp. 19-38.
[22]R. 41/128, Declaration on the Right to Development, A/RES/41/128.
[23]R. 41/128, Declaration on the Right to Development, A/RES/41/128.

rights"[24]. Point 8 of the Vienna Declaration established the relationship between democracy, development and the respect for human rights on the following basis:" The international community should support the strengthening and promoting of democracy, development and respect for human rights and fundamental freedoms in the entire world"[25]. Moreover, points 10 and 11 of this Declaration are entirely devoted to setting out the content of the right to development along the lines marked by the Declaration on the Right to development.

Understanding human development as a human right would help us to shape regulations and obligations related to the commitment to eradicate poverty. However, there is still some way to go before development is conceived of as a human right, with precise obligations stemming from it. In any case, the act of affirming sustainable development as a human right will lead to the introduction of specific regulations on poverty eradication, including regulations which focus on this aim from a human rights perspective.

III.3. Human Rights Protection and Poverty Eradication

Ending poverty is a human rights issue. For some time now, we have been declaring the need to link the commitment of States to eradicate poverty and the essential principle of international law that governs the international recognition and protection of human rights. Giving full legal content to this relationship is by no means an easy task, and it is even harder to create mechanisms that enable us to recognize the rights of the poor and impose precise obligations, above all on States with regard to poverty eradication. In any case, the strategies and policies employed in the fight against poverty cannot dispense with the regulatory framework for human rights provided by the international community. Poverty cannot be eradicated without at the same time guaranteeing certain rights that are widely recognized in international law. Current human rights regulations are not oriented towards the recognition of rights and the imposition of obligations in situations of poverty and do not recognize the poor person as a specific holder of rights. The set of regulations related to human rights in International law does not focus directly on poverty.

However, the fight against poverty and human rights are two closely connected phenomena. Poverty could not be eradicated without showing due respect for human rights in general, and particularly for social human rights. This link is reflected in the fact that situations of poverty are an expression of human rights violations. For this reason, the generic obligation to eradicate poverty should be translated into specific obligations in the field of human rights in order to both revert cases of poverty and prevent violations of human rights. Up to now, the approach to poverty eradication that covers human rights has failed to guarantee that poverty forms part of the legal framework for these rights. States are not prepared to draw up and adopt precise and differentiated legal standards

---

[24]*Conferencia Mundial de Derechos Humanos*, Naciones Unidas, 1993, pp. 20-21, *http://www.un.org/es/development/devagenda/humanrights.shtml.*
[25]https://www.ohchr.org/EN/ProfessionalInterest/Pages/Vienna.aspx.

relating to the rights of the poor. One thing is that the view of poverty from the perspective of human rights enables us to contemplate the legal framework for these rights; quite another is ensuring that poverty comes to form an essential part of the set of regulations on human rights. The practical legal content of the link between poverty and human rights is yet to be determined. However, there are two ways of framing the relationship between poverty and human rights that could fulfil the rights of the poor and put an end to poverty.

On the one hand, reinforcing and protecting specific rights could help to eradicate poverty without needing to create specific regulations to this end. Fulfilling social human rights would help to end poverty; or, at the very least, social human rights must be fulfilled in order to try to eradicate it. For example, as the 2030 Agenda for Sustainable development states, we need systems and measures that guarantee social protection and ensure rights to economic resources and access to basic services. Many rights of all types are affected by the reduction or eradication of poverty, although these rights do not make the same contribution to ending this scourge. Consequently, poverty eradication is linked to the recognition and protection of social rights; poverty must be fought by effectively applying regulations that recognize and protect human rights, especially social and economic rights. However, implementing these rights in international law is no easy task. International legal practice reveals that the effective compliance of these rights is still in question and that there are at present no effective mechanisms for ensuring the application of regulations covering economic, social and cultural rights. To sum up, it is hard to ensure poverty eradication, as it is closely linked to rights the exercise of which is not fully guaranteed.

On the other hand, we could introduce specific regulations that adopt a human rights approach to ending poverty. This would involve defining poverty, establishing a catalogue of rights for the poor and implanting control mechanisms to enforce these regulations. This huge and complex task can only be achieved with a strong commitment from member states of the international community. The generic obligation to eradicate poverty should be endowed with legal content and enforcement tools. However, the central question is whether it is necessary and useful to adopt a specific framework for fighting poverty that contains precise regulations related to human rights. The answer is clear. As poverty always involves a violation of fundamental rights, the fight against it requires its own differentiated legal framework.

The international community does not seem to be committed to creating such a framework. The strategies and policies employed in the fight against poverty adopt a human rights perspective, but this is not backed up by specific regulations. In short, the international community has not expressed a specific will to tackle poverty from a legal angle by introducing into international law regulations and obligations which recognize human rights of the poor and impose precise obligations which force States to make these rights effective. Consequently, the International Law on Human Rights lacks a detailed and comprehensive set of regulations related to this question. To sum up, the human rights perspective can lead to the eradication of poverty but for this to occur we require more precise regulations relating to poverty, with specific content and scope.

In any event, International law is beginning to adopt a set of regulations which impose the obligation to eradicate poverty. The political commitment to abolish poverty in all its forms has been incorporated into international legal practice. The most advanced instrument is Resolution 21/11, adopted by the HRC in 2012, which contains "the guiding principles on extreme poverty and human rights". This instrument reveals two things: firstly, that a human rights perspective is necessary in order to abolish poverty once and for all; secondly, that we need to establish the basis for a specific set of norms that enshrines the link between human rights and poverty. The recognition of human and social rights demanded in "the guiding principles" is fundamental in this respect. Resolution 21/11 is a useful instrument for fighting poverty and for creating a conceptual and legal framework that will help us to defeat it.

IV. CONCLUSIONS

Poverty eradication is the first and foremost goal of the SDGs and we must end global poverty and hunger by 2030. While development instruments generally include purely political commitments, they also provide the basis for translating these commitments into legal obligations. Poverty must be attacked on all fronts using every means possible. A human rights perspective must also be adopted. The current international community is a favourable environment for achieving this goal. The recognition of values and the introduction of legal principles will help us to achieve the aim of eradicating poverty across the globe. Development is inconceivable without eliminating poverty. Poverty must be eradicated via the effective application of human rights.

The notion of sustainable development has incorporated poverty eradication as one of its components. Many international instruments for sustainable development provide proof of this. The crystallization of an essential principle of international law relating to sustainable development would give great momentum to the fight against poverty and could spark the adoption of regulations which establish precise obligations in this area. There is legislation which establishes the general obligation of States to abolish poverty, but we can hardly claim that there are any specific obligations related to this goal. Before specific regulations can be imposed in the fight against poverty, a structural principle of sustainable development must crystallize inside customary international law. This principle must have a "social dimension" and a "human dimension" and could give legal content to the link between poverty and human rights.

States have also opted for a comprehensive human rights approach to tackling poverty. The effective application of human rights would bring an end to poverty. Situations of poverty cause or facilitate human rights violations and in themselves constitute a serious violation of such rights. Poverty eradication is essentially a question of human rights. However, there is still a long way to go before the rights of the poor are fully recognized and before specific regulations are adopted with regard to situations of poverty and the poor are legally recognized as a vulnerable group.

Chapter 4

THE GOVERNANCE OF SUSTAINABLE DEVELOPMENT GOALS IN INTERNATIONAL LAW[1]

CARLOS R. FERNANDEZ LIESA

Head Professor of Public International Law and International Relations,

University of Carlos III, Madrid

SUMMARY: I. INTRODUCTION. II. SDG IN INTERNATIONAL LAW OF HUMAN RIGHTS. III.   THE GOVERNANCE OF SUSTAINABLE DEVELOPMENT IN GLOBALIZATION. IV.   AN INTEGRATED CHALLENGE FOR THE INTERNATIONAL   COMMUNITY   V.   PRIVATIZATION   AND SUSTAINABLE   DEVELOPMENT.   VI.   TRANSNATIONAL CORPORATIONS,   HUMAN   RIGHTS   AND   DEVELOPMENT.   VII. INTERNATIONAL LAW BY OBJECTIVES.   VIII. SUSTAINABLE DEVELOPMENT AS A MYTH AND UTOPIA.   IX. SUSTAINABLE DEVELOPMENT: BETWEEN SOFT LAW AND HARD LAW.

* * *

I.   INTRODUCTION

The international community is facing a major economic, social and environmental challenge, which constitutes the central issue of the current international Agenda. The passing by the United Nations General Assembly of the *Sustainable Development Goals in 2015* provided the global route map for the international community. This route map has a number of blank pages, which will have to be filled by the progressive development of international law and by the national and international policies that provide it with content. Sustainable development is in fashion and, according to the accurate opinion of Rodrigo, this has led to an *inflated use of the expression, which runs the risk of it being distorted, if not becoming irrelevant*[2].

If successful, the expression will result in a major development of international law. The challenge faced by sustainable development has a series of *features*. It is a *general, integrated and universal challenge.* As a *general challenge,* its goals are multiple, reaching up to seventeen and deal with a wide range of issues such as poverty, hunger,

---

[1] This work is the result of the research project DER 2014-55484-P, called International Economic Stakeholders and Human Rights. Special relevance for Spain.
[2] -RODRIGO, A.J., *El desafío del desarrollo sostenible*, Tribuna Internacional 17, 2015, p. 18.

health and deprivation, the absence of violence, access to education, physical, mental and social welfare, access to drinking water and sanitation, better hygiene and food, safe human habitats and affordable, reliable and sustainable energy[3].

These SDGs constitute a *universal challenge*, as they require intense cooperation from all the international community (the so-called *Global Alliance for Sustainable Development*) and the adopting of measures by all stakeholders, especially corporations. It is a *new, recent and revolutionary challenge*. New to the extent that awareness only arose very recently, in particular as of the Declaration: *the future we want*, at the 2012 United Nations General Assembly, of the need to "for renewed and strengthened global partnership to implement sustainable development". It also means a novelty that moves from a north south approach to one that affects all countries, as all of them are subject to the SDGs, unlike the MDGs (Millennium Development Goals), which were based on the developed-developing countries logic.

The measures to be taken to achieve the SDGs also mean a qualitative transformation of how the international society functions. It is a challenge that, if reached, will mean that development is compatible with the environment and human rights. It is an *integrated and indivisible challenge* that requires policies that are conceived entirely under this coordinated perspective.

The SDGs can contribute to strengthening the *environment* as well as *human rights*. In this respect, the *2030 Agenda for sustainable development* highlights people, the planet and prosperity[4]. Its target is to *build pacific, just and inclusive societies that protect human rights and create the conditions for economic, sustainable, inclusive and sustained growth*. According to the UN General Assembly, it is a *long journey towards human dignity*, in which no-one should be left behind.

II.   SDG IN INTERNATIONAL LAW OF HUMAN RIGHTS

The expression sustainable development leads to the question if *there exists a human right to sustainable development*. Art.1.1. of UNGA Res. 41/128 (1986) (*Declaration on the right to development*) considers the right to development to be an inherent human right. By virtue of this right, "every human person and all peoples are entitled to participate in, contribute to, and enjoy economic, social, cultural and political development, in which all human rights and fundamental freedoms can be fully realized". Along the same lines, art. 22 of the African Charter on Human and People's Rights, of 27 June 1981 (conceived only as a right of people), Res. 4 (XXXIII) of the United Nation

---

[3] -Vid. in this regard *Transforming our world: the 2030 Agenda for sustainable development*. Resolution passed by the General Assembly on 25 September 2015.
[4] *Transforming our world: the 2030 Agenda for sustainable development*. Resolution passed by the General Assembly on 25 September 2015

Human Rights Commission of 1977, the 1993 Vienna Convention, as well as other international instruments[5].

The 1986 Declaration established the foundations for the concept of the right to development to be considered as a *multidimensional human right of progressive enhancement*. Different international instruments and declarations have stated that the right to development constitutes a human right. Gross Espiell was one of the pioneers in considering the right to development as an individual right, resulting from the recognition of economic, social and cultural rights and the right to life[6].

Along the same lines, Flory[7] claimed that the right to development is to people what human rights are to the individual, as it represents the transposition of human rights to an international community level, with the content of social rights. From this perspective, the right to development constitutes a *right that synthesizes a series of human rights,* as claimed by García-Amador[8].

Some authors believed that the right to development was not a mere addition or juxtaposition of rights, but rather a different right that implied a new approach to the international human rights strategy, whose *conceptual autonomy lies in its nature of a right to means*[9]. In this respect, the rapporteur Sengupta defined the right to development as a *right to a process* – in particular - of development, in which all human rights and fundamental freedoms can be materialized[10]. This approach does not add anything new to the criteria of indivisibility, interdependence and legal nature of all human rights. To not consider the right to development as the sum of a series of rights, but rather as a right to a process adds nothing new, because the materialization of rights is always progressive.

[5] Vid. OLIVA MARTINEZ, D., *El derecho al desarrollo y la cooperación internacional*, Cideal, 2012; MANERO SALVADOR, A., "Cuestiones jurídicas sobre el derecho al desarrollo como derecho humano", *Derechos y libertades*, n° 15, 2006, pages 257-279.

[6] -GROSS ESPIELL, H., *Derecho internacional del desarrollo*, Cuadernos de la Cátedra J.B. Scott, Universidad de Valladolid, 1975, 56 pages; id "El derecho al desarrollo veinte años después: Balance y perspectivas", *Reflexiones tras un año de crisis*, Universidad de Valladolid, 1996, p. 38; PEREZ GONZALEZ, M., "Algunas reflexiones sobre el derecho al desarrollo en su candidatura a derecho humano", *El Derecho internacional en un mundo en transformación. Liber Amicorum en homenaje al Prof. E. Jiménez de Arechaga*, Montevideo, 1995, pages 321 et seq.

[7] -FLORY, M., "Inégalité économique et évolution du Droit International", *Pays en voie de développement et transformation du Droit International*, Colloque d´Aix en Provence, SFDI, 1974, pages 11-40, p. 34.

[8] -GARCIA-AMADOR, F.V., *El derecho internacional del desarrollo. Una nueva dimensión del Derecho internacional económico*, Civitas, 1987; CANÇADO TRINDADE, A., "The contribution of recent World conferences of the United Nations to the relations between sustainable development and economic, social and cultural Rights", *Les hommes et l'environment. En hommage à Alexander Kiss*, Edition Frinon-Roche, París, 1998, pages 119-146.

[9] -ABELLAN HONRUBIA, V., "Algunas consideraciones sobre el nuevo orden económico internacional", *ONU: Año XL*, Revista de la Facultad de derecho de la Universidad Complutense, 13, monográfico, Madrid, abril de 1987, pages 213-221; PEREZ GONZALEZ, M., "El derecho al desarrollo como derecho humano", *El derecho al desarrollo o el desarrollo de los derechos*, Editorial Complutense, p. 96; M´BAYE, K., "Le droit au développement comme un droit de l'homme", *Révue des droits de l'homme*, 1972, pages 503 et seq.; VVAA, Fernández Liesa, C., Mariño Menéndez, F.., *El desarrollo y la cooperación internacional*, Universidad Carlos III de Madrid-BOE, Madrid, 1997.

[10] -SENGUPTA, A., *Tercer Informe del experto independiente sobre el Derecho al desarrollo*, presentado de conformidad con la Res. 2000/5, de la Comisión de derechos humanos (grupo de trabajo sobre Derecho al desarrollo), E/ CN.4/2001/WG.18/2, de 2 de enero de 2001.

To be able to speak of human development with sound judgment does not mean that it can be strictly understood as an individual human right. The construction of development as an individual human right has a purpose and symbolic meaning, due to its ethical dimension[11]. But it does not constitute an individual human right, strictly speaking, as "the consideration of development, the environment or peace as human rights – despite the obvious ideological dimension of including such values into the international legal system -, is difficult to apply to International law, given the problems in identifying the holder, how they are exercised, the mechanisms required to protect and guarantee them and how they can be enforced"[12].

Sustainable development could be defined as a *bridging concept*, according to the General Secretary of the United Nations, aimed not only at joining the three economic, social and environmental development areas, but also developed and developing countries, governments, corporations, the civil society, scientific knowledge and public policy and present and future generations. These new concepts of development are not measured in classical terms of international obligations, but rather by per capita income, GDP, social indicators, human development indicators, nutrition, energy services, loss of species rate and biodiversity, as well as many others. The fundamental aim of sustainable development is for these three foundations to be a single target and to achieve progress in compliance with commitments that enable it. In addition, sustainable development is linked to the three interrelated transitions: demography and stabilization of the global population; development and sharing of profits equally amongst all segments of global society; to ensure that the use of materials and production of waste is compatible with the planet's capacity of regeneration and absorption.

From a human rights perspective, authors such as Juste Ruiz[13] have considered that the *human right to sustainable development* has been formulated and progressively recognized since the declaration of Stockholm on the human environment in 1972, which already retained certain essential elements of sustainable development, as well as by other subsequent international instruments such as the Charter on Economic Rights and Duties of the States of 1974 (art. 30) or the World Charter for Nature; but principally, the *Rio Declaration on Environment and Development* (1992) and other more recent instruments.

[11] -FLORY, M., "A propos des doutes sur le droit au développement", *Les hommes et l'environment. En hommage à Alexander Kiss*, 1998, pp. 165 ss; VASAK, K., "Le droit International des droits de l'homme", *RCADI*, 1974-IV; URIBE VARGAS, "La troisième génération des droits de l'homme", *RCADI*, 1984, t. 359; M'BAYE, "Le droit au développement comme un droit de l'homme", *Révue des droits de l'homme*, 1972, 505 pp; ALSTON, P., ROBINSON, M, *Human Rights and development. Towards mutual reinforcement*, Oxford University Press, 2005.
[12] -ABELLAN HONRUBIA, V., "Sobre el método y los conceptos en Derecho internacional público", *Soberanía del Estado y DI. Homenaje al Prof. J.A. Carrillo Salcedo*, Sevilla, 2005, pages 55-74, p. 73
[13] -JUSTE RUIZ, J., "El desarrollo sostenible y los derechos humanos", *Soberanía del Estado y derecho internacional. Homenaje al Profesor Juan Antonio Carrillo Salcedo*, Universities of Córdoba, Seville and Málaga, Seville, 2005, pages 757-778.

Other authors such as Rodrigo[14] deal with the *nature of sustainable development from a broader perspective, both as a political objective[15] and a legal concept.* In this legal dimension, it would also have a series of manifestations in its increasingly growing legal value. Firstly, sustainable development would be an international legal principle. Legal doctrine is divided with regard to the characteristics of the principle, as either material (giving rise to the obligation of achieving a result) or procedural (a mere process). Rodrigo also reflects on the possible interstitial nature of sustainable development as a legal concept[16], in other words, it would not regulate the conduct of its subjects nor be directed towards them, but rather operate between primary norms with the aim of changing their scope and effects and establishing new relations between them; he also analyzes sustainable development as a primary norm that gives rise to behavioral obligations and as a human right. However, essentially and with sound judgment, the author considers sustainable development to be a methodological framework for the creation and application of public policy and international legal regulations[17]; thus providing a series of tools that helps decisions to be reached with respect to discourse, grounds, analysis, substance, process and interpretation that can help to synthesize, relate, fertilize, harmonize and integrate the different aspects linked to the objective, which can be incorporated into the processes of preparation and application of public policy and international law.

III. THE GOVERNANCE OF SUSTAINABLE DEVELOPMENT IN GLOBALIZATION

Globalization has been linked more to the economy, from a neoliberal perspective, rather than to rights or other values. Globalization is a Western term with different connotations of universalization and internationalization and, as a concept, has not contributed values nor provided a space for politics, by broadening the economic space, without increasing political space and by replacing political reasoning with technical reasoning[18].

Crossing globalization's valley of tears, according to Habermas, appears to delegitimize a system that is subject to market forces and converted into an instrument to achieve its objectives. This situation is not good for sustainable development or human rights. Neither is the phenomenon of the *dual world[19]*, in the sense that together with a

---

[14] -RODRIGO, A.J., *El desafio del desarrollo sostenible*, Tribuna Internacional, op. cit., p. 68 et seq.

[15] As it appears, for example in the Spanish sustainable development strategy passed by the Council of Ministers on 23 November 2007; or in international instruments, such as the preamble to the Convention on Biological Diversity of 1992, the framework Convention of the United Nations on climate change (1992) and the 1997 Kyoto protocol, the United Nations Convention on desertification of 1994 and the Cartagena Protocol on biotechnology safety under the convention of biological diversity of 2000.

[16] -RODRIGO, A.J., *El desafio del desarrollo sostenible*, op. cit., p. 73.

[17] -Vid. RODRIGO, A.J., *El desafio del desarrollo sostenible*, op. cit., pages 76 et seq.

[18] -DE VEGA, P., "Mundialización y derecho constitucional: la crisis del principio democrático en el constitucionalismo actual", *REP*, April/June 1998.

[19] -La expresión es de DUPUY, R.J., "Le dédoublement du monde", *RGDIP*, 1996/2, p. 320.

world of institutions, legality, international organizations and States, there is a world of living forces, in this particular case, transnational corporations and markets. And all this has taken place without a transformation of the international legal and political architecture capable of organizing globalization or the de-territorialization of law or the new digital world in which national and international life takes place. All these phenomena have joined others that are better known, such as the weakening of States and economic globalization. Some predicted the return to the Middle Ages, according to Alan Minc, to a world without authority. Others predicted an irreversible decline in the social welfare state and the European social model. Others referred to the new law of the jungle.

These are not good times for human rights and development, which are not the key issues on the international Agenda. The 2030 Agenda is therefore considered positive, irrespective of its major weaknesses, as it attempts to draw attention and debate to solidarity objectives and the promotion of values. We should avoid preaching catastrophe, as it will only bode for misfortune. The world has always taken steps forward and backward, into light and dark. *Sustainable development* is a strong idea that can avoid the loss of the precious human rights that took the international community so much effort to build in the 20th Century.

To make sustainable development possible under the framework of globalization is not an easy task, as pointed out by the Secretary General of the United Nations in 2005 – *A broader concept than freedom: development, security and human rights for all –* sometimes, the agreements reached by the international community are just hot air[20]. This requires *institutional and regulatory transformation that enables globalization to be humanized and governed*[21].

New *world governance* is necessary. At the time, the proliferation of international organizations changed the structure of the international society, as highlighted by authors such as Reuter, Friedmann and Dupuy. The era of the co-existence of States was overcome and a new international cooperation phase commenced and gave rise to an institutional model of international society that would co-exist with the inter-State model, which was to remain. Globalization has produced a certain weakening of international organizations and the phenomenon of institutional fragmentation, in spite of the proliferation of international organizations. The weakening of the State has not produced the correlative strengthening of international institutions. In present international life, *soft law* and *soft institutions* have proliferated with the so-called *global law*. This term relates to *governance*, a term linked to the neo-liberal process.

---

[20] *Report by the Secretary General of the United Nations,* Kofi Annan, on 21 March 2005, paragraphs 128-131.
[21] - Vid. CARRILLO SALCEDO, J.A., *Globalización y orden internacional,* inaugural lesson of the University of Seville, 2004-2005, p. 25; FARIÑAS DULCE, M.J., *Globalización, ciudadanía y derechos humanos,* Instituto de derechos humanos Bartolomé de las Casas, Dykinson, 2000, 60 pages; FEYTER, K., "Globalization and human Rights", *International human rights law in a global context,* Gómez Isa, F., Fester, K. De (Eds), Universidad de Deusto, Bilbao, 2008, pages 51-96.

The international society of the 21st Century must *manage* the weakening of the State, globalization and the crisis of the nation-State model, the strengthening of a civil society without suitable participation channels, the strengthening of informal groups in international society and the digital society. This *international architecture* comes from the Second World War and is not strong enough to deal with the basic challenges, such as the environment, the economy, ecology, human rights, solidarity, dispute management, peace and sustainable development, amongst others.

The international community now has renewed goals, the SDGs, however they lack renewed architecture. The Secretary General of the United Nations promoted the *Sustainable Development Solutions Network*[22], which advised on the creation of the SDGs that later gave rise to inter-governmental negotiations. At present, the institutional framework for the governance of sustainable development is not capable of meeting the challenge. The 2012 Conference highlighted the need to debate governance and reform the institutions taking part in the implementation of the United Nations sustainable development program, in particular the Commission on Sustainable Development and the United Nations program for the environment; in addition to reforming the sustainable development institutions.

The institutional architecture of sustainable development has to be renewed. It is still entrenched in international conferences, as well in United Nations bodies such as the *Commission on Sustainable Development*, created in 1992 to follow up on the United Nations Conference on Environment and Development and, later, the Johannesburg Plan of Implementation, following the 2002 Sustainable Development Summit. Comprised of 53 members, the UN system promotes sustainable development, encourages policies and supports alliances. Since 2002, more than 360 public-private *sustainable development associations* have been created. Also relevant is the *Executive Committee on Economic and Social Affairs*, as well as initiatives such as UNO-Water, UNO-Energy and UNO-Oceans. At a regional level, commissions have promoted action and development and strategy plans, especially in relation to the fight against poverty. From an environmental perspective, since the sixties, institutions such as UNEP and national institutions and NGOs have been promoted. In the environmental framework, there is greater institutional strength than in the economic framework, which still has post-war institutions and the social foundations. In fact, there still does not exist, for example, an international environmental organization that deals with such a complex issue in an integrated way, but rather a proliferation of bodies and disperse regulations, with thousands of instruments that is extremely difficult to manage in a decentralized society.

In any case, what is required is an *international structure of sustainable development that is equal to the challenge*, which currently does not exist, either under the framework of the United Nations, or that of other international institutions. It is true that a World Alliance has been proposed for revitalized sustainable development, with the support of financial measures for development adopted by the Third International Conference on the Financing for Development (Addis Abeba action agenda) and passed by the General

---

[22] -SACHS, J., *La era del desarrollo sostenible*, cit., p. 563.

Assembly on July 27, 2015 (Res. 69/313, annex), amongst other measures. However, there is a lack of substantial international structure for sustainable development. Accordingly, making a virtue out of necessity, the United Nations highlights the responsibility of governments to reach the SDGs over the next fifteen years. Indicators are therefore being developed to monitor and control government progress in reaching their goals.

IV. AN INTEGRATED CHALLENGE FOR THE INTERNATIONAL COMMUNITY

The United Nations passed seventeen sustainable development goals[23]. Goal number thirteen states that urgent measures must be taken to combat *climate change* and its effects. Amongst other measures, it includes strengthening resilience and adaptive capacity to climate-related hazards and natural disasters in all countries. Another measure is to include integrating climate change measures into national policies, strategies and planning. We should also improve education, awareness-raising and human and institutional capacity on climate change mitigation and implement the commitment undertaken at the Convention on Climate Change for 2020, mobilizing more than 100,000 million dollars annually to address the needs of developing countries, fully operationalize the Green Climate Fund and promote mechanisms for raising capacity for effective climate change-related planning and management. Each one of the seventeen goals has its own route map, with more than 169 measures and major challenges, but more difficulties, meaning that we are faced with a complex task of enormous importance to the international community.

If we continue with climate change and look at what has been done in recent times, we see that each goal is a world in itself. In June 2016, France was the first industrialized country to ratify the Paris Convention, the entry into force of which required a minimum of at least 55% of the global emissions with a greenhouse effect. The convention had been the main result of the *Paris Conference on Climate Change* between 195 countries, which adopted a text on 12 December 2015. The international community pursues the reduction of greenhouse gas emissions, which requires a consensus and the adopting of measures to mitigate, adapt and make ecosystems more resilient to global warming. The difficulties in reaching an agreement resulted from the interests of countries such as China, the United

---

[23] The goals are: 1. end poverty in all its forms everywhere. 2. End hunger, achieve food security. 3. Healthy life. 4. Inclusive and equitable education. 5. Gender equality. 6. Water and sanitation. 7. Affordable energy. 8. Sustained, inclusive and sustainable growth. 9. Resilient infrastructure, inclusive and sustainable industrialization. 10. Reduce inequality in countries. 11. Inclusive cities and human settlements. 12. Sustainable consumption and production. 13. Climate change. 14. Sustainable use of oceans, seas and marine resources. 15. Sustainable use of terrestrial ecosystems, sustainable management of forests, combat desertification, halt land degradation and halt biodiversity loss. 16. Promote peaceful and inclusive societies for sustainable development. 17. Strengthen the means of implementation and revitalize the global partnership for sustainable development.

States, the European Union, India, Russia and Japan, as the main countries responsible for the emissions.

To deal with climate change is an enormously complex challenge for many reasons[24]. It is very difficult to mobilize the international community, because States have different interests and positions (exporters and importers of fossil fuels; rich and poor countries; large and small consumers of energy; more and less vulnerability; democratic governments or not, etc.). In addition, the climate crisis affects future rather than current generations, which does not mobilize politicians. It is a long-term challenge that requires highly complex and coordinated measures that may have powerful opponents with major interests.

The fight against climate change takes place under the framework of a *world risk society*, amongst others. The global risks are mainly of an ecological, financial and terrorist nature. In the international society, this has led to new paradigms and alliances between States and stakeholders to anticipate response to prevent such risks from becoming catastrophes[25]. The international society has also increased its knowledge (*society of knowledge*).

In such a society, the government or governance should be based on knowledge. However, the complexity of the challenges to the international community is so high that it is probably only possible to *manage doubt, on the basis of the criteria of prudence, knowledge and precaution*. According to Innerarity[26], this is because although science has increased the amount of safe knowledge, when it comes to highly complex systems such as climate, it is increasingly more difficult to obtain cause and effect explanations or accurate forecasts. This results in "non-knowledge", the management of decisions in situations of doubt. Neither is this society of knowledge necessarily transferred to institutional strength, as the ability of the State to impose its decisions becomes weaker[27].

We find ourselves at the beginning of what J. Sachs calls the *age of sustainable development*, which is actually a "project" seeking the interaction between complex systems, such as the economy, global society and the environment. All of this requires a *holistic approach*, in the sense that the international society should, at the same time, seek economic, social and environmental goals and good governance[28].

This governance can no longer be limited to governments, but must also include other stakeholders, such as transnational corporations, which must also respect the rules, the environment and goals such as the eradication of extreme poverty. Sustainable development – according to Sachs[29]- seeks to achieve four basic goals in a *good society*:

---

[24] SACHS, J., *The Age of sustainable development*, Columbia University Press, New York, 2014, prologue by Ban Ki-Moon, Secretary General of the United Nations, Paidós Empresa, 2016, 602 pages.

[25] -Vid. BECK, U., *The World Risk Society*, Paidós, 317 pages (original title Weltrisikogesellschaft, published in 2007 in Frankfurt and translated into Spanish in 2008),

[26] -INNERARITY, D., *The democracy of knowledge. For an intelligient society*, Paidós, 2011, 256 pages, p. 64

[27] -INNERARITY, D., *The democracy of knowledge*, op. cit., pages 88 et seq.

[28] -Vid. SACHS, J., *The age of sustainable development*, Prologue by Ban Ki-Moon, Paidós, 2014, pages 19-21.

[29] -SACHS, J., *The age of sustainable development*, cit., p. 21.

economic prosperity; social inclusion and cohesion; environmental sustainability; and good governance by the main stakeholders, governments and corporations.

V.   PRIVATIZATION AND SUSTAINABLE DEVELOPMENT

Another concerning issue for sustainable development and human rights is the phenomenon of *privatization*. Many of the seventeen sustainable development goals can be achieved if corporations contribute. However, the term privatization in international law means that State responsibilities and public services that directly affect human rights are privatized and provided by non-public stakeholders, which can affect the enjoyment and very concept of human rights. The Committee on the Rights of the Child[30] pointed out that a State's obligation to respect the rights of children includes the obligation to ensure that private providers of services act in accordance with legal provisions, meaning that there are indirect obligations for such entities. The obligations undertaken pursuant to international Treaties on human rights directly bind States and the so-called horizontal effect is not produced, however States will only comply with their international obligations if they act in such a way as to protect people against the acts or failure to act by private entities to order ensure that rights are respected[31].

In this context, the responsibility of corporations is particularly evident. At Nuremberg, the issue was raised of the breach of human rights by the forced labor of prisoners, to the benefit of corporations[32]. In any case, there are still current issues relating to the Second World War and the compensation of people that were victims of the holocaust and exploited by different types of corporations, such as banks, insurance companies, manufacturers, etc., which has given rise to global compensation agreements and compensation through other means, such as international claims commissions (insurance companies) and compensation *ex gratia* by foundations, etc.[33].

Nowadays, many of the threats to human rights do not always come directly from States, but rather from non-State stakeholders and the lack of capacity or willingness on the part of States to control them. This has led to an increasingly greater focus on the issue of the *implementation of international human rights law in private matters* and a

---

[30] *General observation n° 5, of 2003 on the general measure of implementation of the convention relating to the rights of the child*, of 27-XI-2003, par. 42.

[31] In this regard, *General observation n° 31. Nature of the obligations imposed on States under the Convention*, 26-V-2004, par. 4.

[32] -Vid. the comment by MARTIN BURGOS, J.A., "Inmunidades jurisdiccionales de los Estados, normas internacionales de la Unión Europea y Derechos humanos", *Libro homenaje a Dámaso Ruiz-Jarabo Colomer*, CGPJ, 2011, page 78 et seq.; ESPOSITO MASSICI, C., *Inmunidad del Estado y derechos humanos*, Thomson, 2007; REQUEJO, M., "Transnational human rights claims against a State in the European area of freedom, justice and security- A view on ECJ judgement, 15 February 2007-C-292/65, Lechoritou and some recent regulations", *The European Legal forum*, 5-2007, pages 206-211.

[33] -Vid. On this issue SHELTON, D., *Remedies in International human Rights law*, Oxford University Press, 2005-2006, 498 pages, page 432.

conceptual change in the traditional view of human rights in the relationship between the State and private entities.

The change would be from a central State approach to international law itself to another approach more in line with current needs. However, it is not easy, as it involves a rupture of the traditional distinction between public/private, State/non-State and government/non-government. The issue of the obligations of non-State stakeholders has been strengthened by phenomena such as the globalization of the international economy – and the power of transnational corporations-, privatization of public services (education, health, prisons, water, communications and police forces), the fragmentation of States and the power of non-State rebel groups, amongst others[34].

VI. TRANSNATIONAL CORPORATIONS, HUMAN RIGHTS AND DEVELOPMENT

The role of transnational corporations in the international society was reconsidered during de-colonization, according to which there were structural injustices that had to be changed[35]. This led to the pursuit of a new international economic order and the beginning of work that would give rise to codes of conduct by the UNO, ILO (1977 Declaration) and the OECD[36].

It gave rise to new debate, for example, on the convenience of granting transnational corporations international legal personality. Authors such as Charpentier objected, considering that it would open up international relations to groups whose main goal is profitability and that are not subject to any kind of political control[37]. The debate was inappropriate, because it confused the notions of sovereignty and legal personality. To acknowledge the international legal personality of transnational corporations and ensure they comply with international law and the national law of the countries in which they operate is not a bad idea and does not involve granting political or any other kind of legitimacy.

In our opinion, it would be advisable to acknowledge the international legal personality of transnational corporations for the purposes of control and liability. We should recall that in the sixties and seventies, the market economy was dominated by

---

[34] -Vid. an analysis in CLAPHAM, A., *Human Rights obligations of non-State actors*, Oxford, 2006, 605 pages. By the same author *Human Rights in the private sphere*, Clarendon Press, Oxford, 1993, 380 pages.

[35] -Vid. as an example of this approach DRAI, R., THUAN, C., MINH, T., BERNARD, J.P., FONTAINE, J.M., *Multinationales et droits de l'homme*, Puf, 1984.

[36] -Vid. SPRÖTE, W., "Negotiations on a United Code of conduct on transnational Corporation", *GYIL*, 1990, 331; MUCHILINSKI, P., "Attempts to extend the accountability of transnational corporations: The role of UNCTAD", Kammirs, T., Zarifi, S., (eds)., *Liability of Multinational corporations under International law*, Kluwer, 2000, pages 97-117; MARTIN-ORTEGA, O., *Empresas multinacionales y derechos humanos en el Derecho internacional*, Bosch, Barcelona, 2008, p. 345; ALSTON, P., *Non State actors and human Rights*, Oxford University Press.

[37] -CHARPENTIER, M.J., "Tendances de l'élaboration du droit international public coutumier", *L'élaboration du droit international public*, SFDI, París, 1975, pages 105 et seq, p. 129.

States and corporations could not change the machinery of the international economic system, but now things are different and the situation has become "uncontrollable"[38].

Furthermore, there are now *codes of conduct for multinational corporations*[39] - which have not been very effective – and coalitions in favor of change, such as the one proposed by Annan[40] in 1999 on good practice. On 31 January 1999, the Secretary General of the UNO, Kofi Annan, presented the *Global Compact* at the Davos Forum, which has been criticized for its non-binding nature, its loopholes and other reasons. ECOSOC created a Commission of transnational corporations. In 1998, a working group was created to produce a new code of conduct which, on 26 August 2003, presented *UN regulations on the responsibility of transnational corporations and other business enterprises in relation to human rights*, which established the obligations to be met by corporations with regard to human rights. The project was non-binding. The Human Rights Commission passed a Resolution on 20 April 2005 addressed to the Secretary General creating the figure of a special Representative of human rights and transnational corporations. Finally, on 16 July 2011, the Human Rights Council passed *guiding principles on the effects of the acts of transnational corporations on human rights*[41]. The Council adopted the report by the special Representative of the Secretary General on human rights and transnational corporations, John Ruggie (A/HRC/17/31 of 21–III-2011). These guiding principles currently constitute a good guide to human rights for both States and corporations, although they raise many issues that are beyond the scope of this study.

VII. INTERNATIONAL LAW BY OBJECTIVES

The SDGs also raise issues relating to the very conception of international law. Initially, the minimum function of international law, according to Kelsen, is to distribute authority amongst States (the spheres of validity of State legal systems). The introduction

---

[38] -BERMEJO GARCIA, R., "Las empresas transnacionales como actores y sujetos potenciales en la sociedad internacional", *Perspectivas actuales de los sujetos de derecho*, Colección Peces-Barba, nº 2, Barranco, C., Celador, O., Vacas Fernández, F., (Coords), Departamento de Derecho internacional, filosofía y eclesiástico, UC3M, 2012, page 89 et seq.

[39] - Vid. MERCIAI, P., *Les entreprises multinationales en Droit international*, Bruylant, Bruxelles, 1993, 414 pages. LADOR-LEDERER, J.J., *International non governmental organizations and economic entities*, Leyden, 1963; ANGEL, H.G., "Multinational corporate enterprises", *RCADI*, t. 125, 1968-III, pages 447-600; SEIDL-HOHENVELDERN, Y., "International economic law", *RCADI*, . 198, 1986-II, pages 21-264; WALLACE, D., *International regulation of multinational corporations*, New York, 1976.

[40] -ANNAN, K., *Common Destiny. New Resolve. Annual Report on the Work of the Organization, 2000*, New York, par. 23, p. 7.

[41] -Vid. MARQUEZ CARRASCO, C., *España y la implementación de los Principios Rectores de las Naciones Unidas sobre empresas y derechos humanos: oportunidades y desafíos*, VVAA, Huygens editorial, 2014, 791 pages. ESTEVE MOLTO, J., "Los principios rectores sobre las empresas transnacionales y los derechos humanos en el marco de las Naciones Unidas, para proteger, respetar y remediar: ¿Hacia la responsabilidad de las corporaciones o la complacencia institucional?", *Anuario español de Derecho internacional*, vol. 27, 2011, pages 317-35. HEINEMAN, A., "Business enterprises in public International law: the case for an International code of corporate responsibility", *Essays in honour of Judie B. Simma*, Oxford University Press, 2011, page 718 et seq.

of objectives into the legal system as a whole, for international law, is nothing new to the international community. What is new is the way it is being done.

It is nothing new, as it is an old technique that has been linked to international human rights law and, more recently, to international development law. Authors like Dupuy[42], Mahiou[43] and Carrillo Salcedo[44] have conceived international law as a *law of aims, committed to change.* According to Dupuy, the specific nature of international law is its aim, whereas Mahiou refers to the law of commitment (with respect to development). More recently, Carrillo Salcedo pointed out the "insufficiency of traditional international law and the need for new international law that, if it wants to meet the challenge (...), must address a community system that is adapted to the dimensions of the planet and whose principal and immediate goal is the balanced and harmonious development of all mankind, considered as a whole".

In this regard, in the sociology of law, the *intentionalists* and functionalists analyze the *aims* that guide the system. In law, authors like Duguit and Scelle analyzed law from a social needs (objectivists) perspective a century ago, thus overcoming the ius positivism of the 19th Century with social concern. In the 20th Century, the postulates of normativism gave way to the internationalists, such as Visscher[45], Friedmann[46], Thierry[47], R.J. Dupuy, P.M. Dupuy and J.A. Carrillo Salcedo. These authors conceive international law according to its *function of transforming international society*, overcoming axiological relativism and formalism. This does not mean understanding international law only from an ethical and finalist perspective, which was criticized by D. Kennedy[48]. However, it is also true that certain projects and commitments have generated the necessary breeding ground for proposals of reform to solve common problems.

The *Right to Development* has traditionally been classified as finalist and theological order oriented towards a mission (right *for* development). This is how it is addressed by authors such as Bollecker-Stern[49], Gros Espiell, Touscoz, Flory, Pellet, Pelaez Marón,

---

[42] -Vid. DUPUY, R.J., "Droit international et disparités de développement. Cours général de droit international public", *RCADI*, 1979-IV, t. 165, page 120 et seq.

[43] -Vid. also the goals (in the area od sources, review of institutions and of principles and norms) of international development law, MAHIOU, A., "Droit international et développement", *Cursos euromediterráneos Bancaja de Derecho internacional*, vol. III, 1999, Cardona, J., (dir), Aranzadi editorial, 2000, pages 29-140, in particular pages 34-40, p. 35-36.

[44] -Cfr. CARRILLO SALCEDO, J.A., "Permanence et mutations en droit international", *Boutros Boutros Ghali. Amicorum discipulorumque Liber*, Bruylant, Bruxelles, 1998, p. 300.

[45] -VISSCHER, C., *Teorías y realidades en derecho internacional público*, Bosch, Barcelona1962, pages 135 and 141.

[46] -FRIEDMANN, W., "Droit de coexistence et droit de cooperation. Quelques observations sur la structure changeante du droit international", page 1 - et seq., p. 9.

[47]-THIERRY, H., "Internationalisme et normativisme en droit international", *Guy de Lacharrière et la politique juridique extérieure de la France*, Masson, París, 1989, p. 371. "L'évolution du droit international. Cours général de droit international public", *RCADI*, 1990-III, 222 pages, pages 17-19

[48] -KENNEDY, D., *Rompiendo moldes en el Derecho internacional: Cuando la renovación es repetición*, Cuadernos internacional 3, Universidad Autónoma de Madrid, traducción y prólogo de Ignacio Forcada, Dykinson, 2002, in particular pages 27-30.

[49] -BOLLECKER-STERN, B., "Le droit international du développement: un droit de finalité", *La formation des normes en droit international du développement*, Flory, M., Henry, J., CNRES, 1984; GROS ESPIELL, H., "El derecho al desarrollo veinte años después: Balance y perspectivas", *Reflexiones tras un año de crisis*, VVAA, Universidad de Valladolid, 1996, pages 27-59, p. 32; TOUSCOZ, J., "Les Nations Unies et

Bennouna, Slinn, Bouveresse, Mahiou, Mbaye[50], Bermejo[51] and Gutierrez Espada[52], Colliard[53]. Sustainable development must be seen in the same classic approach, which still has a mythical-utopian aspect.

VIII. SUSTAINABLE DEVELOPMENT AS A MYTH AND UTOPIA

The objectives of a legal system are related to the concept of law as a *claim to rights*[54], *in which the notion of myth and utopia, as well as soft law and hard law both play a role*. The *development myth*, according to R.J. Dupuy[55] serves a driving and mobilizing force. Unlike myths – which in legal discourse synthesize a legal reality – utopias are more present as *lege ferenda* and serve the ideological function of international law. We use the term utopia as a *project* to be implemented in international law, a driving force towards the transformation and changing of the law[56]. A utopia defines the horizons of legal change, normally to defend the weak and the values of justice. Utopian thinking builds ideal societies, in other words those that still do not exist, which does not mean they cannot be achieved[57].

In this regard, *sustainable development forms part of the utopia of the modern day international community*. Utopia must place us outside a social-historical or real perspective of the legal system, although excess realism can be negative, as what appears to be utopian today may be possible in the future. We cannot envisage or build a world based on disconnected utopian models. We should not wear Walt Disney rose- colored

le droit international économique. Rapport introductif", *Les Nations Unies et le droit international économique*, SFDI, VVAA, Pedone, París, 1987, p. 16; FLORY, M., *Droit international du développement*, Puf, París, 1977; FEUER, G., CASSAN, H., *Droit international du développement*, Dalloz, 2 edition, 1991; PELLET, A., *Droit international du développement*, Que sais-je?, 1731, Puf, París, 2 edition, 1987; BENNOUNA, M., *Droit international du développement*, Berger-Levrault, 1982; SNYDER, F., SLINN, P., *International law of development*, London, 1987; BOUVERESSE, J., *Droit et politique du développement et de la coopération*, Puf, 1990.
[50] -Vid. MBAYE, K., "Le droit au développement en droit international", *Essays in international law in honour of judge M. Lachs*, Martinus Nijhoff Publishers, 1984, pages 163-177, p. 163.
[51] - BERMEJO. *Vers un nouvel ordre économique international. Etude centrée sur les aspects juridiques*, Editions Universitaires Fribourg Suisse, 1982, pages 15 and 16.
[52] -GUTIERREZ ESPADA, C., "Sobre las funciones, fines y naturaleza del derecho internacional contemporáeo", *Homenaje al Prof. Mariano Hurtado Bautista*, 1992, p. 69.
[53] -COLLIARD, C.A., "Spécificité des Etats. Théorie des status juridiques particuliers et d'inégalité compensatrice", *Mélanges offerts à Paul Reuter. Le droit international: unité et diversité*, Pedone, París, 1981, pages 153-180, p. 180.
[54] -Cfr. PEREZ GONZALEZ, M., "El derecho al desarrollo como derecho humano", *El derecho al desarrollo o el desarrollo de los derechos*, Ed. Universidad Complutense, VVAA, p. 96; FLORY, M., "La politique juridique extérieure et le nouvel ordre économique international", *Guy de Lacharrière et la politique juridique extérieure de la France*, De. Masson, 1989, París, 158-266, p. 265.
[55] -DYPUY, R.J., *La clôture du système international. La cité terrestre*, Puf, París, 1989, p. 31.
[56] In this regard, DUPUY, R.J., "Droit, révolution, utopie", *Révolution et Droit international*, p. 435; FRANCK, T., "Legitimacy in the international system", *AJIL*, 1988/4, pages 705-759.
[57] -RAMIRO AVILES, M.A., *Utopía y derecho. Análisis de la relación entre los modelos de sociedad ideal y los sistemas normativos*, Doctoral thesis, Universidad Carlos III de Madrid-Instituto de Derechos Humanos Bartolomé de las Casas, Getafe, April 2000, 779 pages. P. 18.

glasses[58], however we should not forget that certain past visionaries (or visions) have contributed to making things happen. International law has been enriched by concepts and ideas that have guided political acts, resulted in projects and international institutions and, finally, been incorporated into positive law[59].

In the history of international law, *many utopias from the past are reflected in the principles and rules of present day law*. Dreyfus[60] compared the doctrinal images of international law at the end of the 19th Century with the realities of the 20th Century, reaching the conclusion that many of the utopian aspirations of legal doctrine became a reality or, at least, helped progress, for example, towards the utopia of codification, compulsory international jurisdiction, the existence of international Courts and Organizations, the federalist or European Union utopias. These utopias guide legal progress from driving forces, concepts and visions[61]. Today, the utopia is sustainable development.

The mythification of certain concepts is relevant, given that, on occasion, they end up penetrating the legal system. Certain mythical symbols and ideals have great metaphoric potential that contributes to re-affirming the underlying values of the legal system and ideologically transferring the content of its principles and rules: *universal peace, democracy and even abstract humanity*[62]. Here is where the *power of words* comes into play, as the basic fabric of the system.

Caution is required with respect to the virtues of metaphoric myths under the framework of the creation of law, as they may lead to us losing sight of the legal objective of a negotiation and thus benefit the inaccuracy or vagueness of terminology. In such case, the *legitimité annonciatrice*[63], as the idea of the suitability of law to justice, has been present on numerous occasions at United Nations General Assemblies, contributing to the transformation of legality. For example, the new international economic order failed in its maximalist attempts, however, despite certain disappointments, the utopias helped to transform the solidarity approach to international law.

---

[58] -LACHS, M., *Le monde de la pensée en droit international*, p. 18

[59] Utopia has a more important role in international law than it is normally attributed. It performs functions particularly related to *lex ferenda*, by denying and rejecting rules, supporting others and anticipating the future, a frequent characteristic of utopia, according to Serge Sur, being to refer to a transcendental, absolute law and rather produce circumstantial law. Vid. SUR, S., "Système juridique international et utopie", Archives de philosophie du droit, t. 32, *Le droit international*, Sirey, 1981, pages 35-45.

[60] -DREYFUS, S., "D'un siècle à l'autre: Remarques sur l'image du droit international public", *Boutros Boutros Ghali Amicorum discipulorumque Liber. Paix, Développement, démocratie*, Bruylant, Bruxelles, 1998, pages 359 et seq.

[61] -NAFZIGER, A.R., "The functions of religion in the International system", *The influence of religion on the development of International law*, cit., 1991, pages 149 et seq, p. 151.

[62] -CAHIN, G., "Apport du concept de mythification aux méthodes d'analyse du droit international", *Le droit des peuples à disposer d'eux-mêmes. Méthodes d'analyse du droit international. Mélanges offerts à Charles Chaumont*, Pedone, París, 1984, pages 89-115, p.92.

[63] -Vid. in this regard DUPUY, R.J., *La Communauté internationale entre le mythe et l'histoire*, Economica, París, 1986, pages 119, 120.

International law is therefore developed with references to *universal myths* that, on occasion, become part of the legal system, or at least partly. The *utopia* invokes *legal change*, normally in the interests of the weaker members of the system. This means that utopias provide law with an *ideological dimension that projects intellectual and moral representations and references* that are added to its organizational and registry dimension (S. Sur). In this respect, it could be considered, as indicated by Sur with his *utopian dimension of international law for the weak*, which tends or should tend to compensate or correct inequality, his *organizational dimension for equals* and his *registry dimension for the strong*, which reinforces its position and advantages[64].

Certain areas of international law are affected by utopian approaches, such as *international development law, international human rights law, the prohibition of the use of force and the establishment of the collective security system.* The *Universal Declaration of 1948* established a utopian horizon[65]. At present, the so-called third generation rights symbolize new utopias. The *utopia of peace through law* has been shared and has given rise to multiple peace projects, the creation of the Society of Nations and the United Nations[66]. The United Nations Charter therefore has dual legal and utopian (programmatic, ideological, almost religious) dimensions, as well as being a constitutional legal document on the one hand and an ideological-political instrument, on the other, which seeks the ideal of peace through law[67]. The utopia serves the purpose of showing the way, but the road still has to be travelled[68].

In the past, the myth of peace through law was contrasted by the absolute inefficacy of international law and the myth of the state of nature by that of peace through a super-state power[69]. In the same way, a reactionary myth is the mythical, mystical and hyperbolic conception of sovereignty as an absolute notion, which leads to the rejection of the existence of international law. In recent times, the myth of *developism* has prevailed over the *ideology of development*[70], growth being the justifying principle of asymmetric globalization. This is a *reactionary utopia* that should be counteracted by a humanist and alternative project that enables the construction of a *global political system that does not serve the global market, but rather defines its parameters just as the State-nation historically represented the social framework of the national market*[71]. The utopia of

[64] -SUR, S., "Système juridique international et utopie", *Archives de philosophie du droit*, t. 32, Le droit international, Sirey, 1987, p. 41.
[65] -CARRILLO SALCEDO, J.A., *Dignidad frente a la barbarie. La declaración universal de derechos humanos, cincuenta años después*, Minima Trotta, Madrid, 1999, p. 26.
[66] -GOYARD-FABRE, S., *La construction de la paix ou le travail de sisyphe*, Vrin, 1994, pages 225 et seq.
[67] -DUPUY, P.M., "L'enfer et le paradigme: libres propos sur les relations du droit international avec la persistance des guerres et l'objectif ideal du maintien de la paix", *Mélanges H. Thierry. L'évolution du Droit international*, Pedone, París, 1998, pages 186-199, in particular 188 and 191 to 194.
[68] - PONS RAFOLS, X., "La participación de España en el sistema de acuerdos de fuerzas de reserva de las operaciones de mantenimiento de la paz", *Agenda ONU*, nº 2, 1999, pages 123-164, p. 147.
[69] -Vid. sobre estos mitos y sus contra-mitos DUPUY, R.J., "L'illusion juridique. Réflexions sur le mythe de la paix par le droit", *Guy de Lacharrière et la politique juridique extérieure de la France*, Masson, París, 1989, pages 245-257, p. 252.
[70] -DE VEGA, P., "Mundialización y derecho constitucional. La crisis del principio democrático en el constitucionalismo actual", *Revista de estudios políticos*, abril/junio, 1998, pages 13 et seq, p 16.
[71] - AMIN, S., *El capitalismo en la era de la globalización*, Paidos, Barcelona, 1997, p. 19.

sustainable development should therefore not be seen as something that cannot be achieved, but rather as a gradually achievable project.

IX.   SUSTAINABLE DEVELOPMENT: BETWEEN SOFT LAW AND HARD LAW

Sustainable development is becoming a particularly suitable area for soft law, which does not mean that hard law is irrelevant or does not exist. According to Weil[72], there exists a *dual crisis in international law,* with the weakening of the expansion of international law and the appearance of super-laws (*ius cogens*).

In this respect, the blurring of the legality of regulations that can be generated by utopian discourse is the result of mistaking aspirations and the evolution of law, the imaginary and reality, as what occurred with the NIEO[73], which basically constituted a reference to *desirable law (unripe, soft law),* but not to positive law (*hard law*)[74]. However, as pointed out above, we should not overlook the fact that utopia plays a role in *lex ferenda* when it demands a change in the law, the amendment of *lex lata*, as occurs in the international law of sustainable development.

Soft law plays an important role in the interpretation of positive law, the gradual transformation of its content, the behavior of subjects and the transformation of *opinio iuris*[75]. Soft law is important because it evidences the constant transformation of international law and its growth. In the gradual development of international sustainable law, the transformation of *soft law* into *hard law* is also important. What would have helped was the success of the initiative of the Human Rights Council via Resolution 26/9, of June 2014, which consisted in the preparation of a *legally binding instrument to regulate, in international human rights law, the activities of transnational corporations and other business enterprises* [76].

---

[72] - WEIL, P., "Le droit international en quête de son identité", *RCADI*, cit. pages 227 et seq.

[73] -BENNOUNA, M., "Réalité et imaginaire en droit international du développement", *Le droit des peuples à disposer d'eux-mêmes. Méthodes d'analyse du droit international. Mélanges offerts à Charles Chaumont,* Pedone, París, 1984, pages 59-72, p 67.

[74] -PELLET, A., "Le "bon droit" et l'ivraie- Plaidoyer pour l'ivraie (Rémarques sur quelques problèmes de méthode en droit international du développement), *Le droit des peuples à disposer d'eux-mêmes. Méthodes d'analyse du droit international. Mélanges offerts à Charles Chaumont*, Pedone, París, 1984, pages 465-525, p. 470. REISMAN, M., "The concept and functions of soft law in international politics", *Essays in honour of judge Raslim Olawale Elias*, vol. 1. Contemporary international law and human rights, Bello, E., San, A., Edit, Martinus Nijhoff Publishers, 1992, pages 135-144, p. 144

[75] -BOTHE, M., "Legal and non legal norms: A Meaningful existence of non-binding agreements", *NYIL*, 1977, 1980, pages 65-95; SCHACHTER, O., "The twilight existence of non binding agreements", *AJIL,* 1977, pages 294-304 CHINKIN, C., "The challenge of soft law", *ICLQ*, 1989, pages 850-866; EISEMANN, P.M., "Le gentlement's agreement comme source du Droit international", *JDI*, 1979, pp.326-348; VIRALLY, M., "La distinction entre textes internationales de portée juridique et textes internationaux dépourvues de portée juridique", *Annuaire de l'Institut de DI.,* 1983, pages 166 et seq.

[76] -Vid. in this regard LOPEZ, C., SHEA, B., "Negotiating a treaty on business and human rights: a Review of the first intergovernmental session", *Business and human rights journal*, 1, 2015, pages 111-116.

The initiative behind Res. 26/9 was sponsored by Ecuador, South Africa, Bolivia, Cuba and Venezuela and supported by some six hundred civil organizations. However, it was unsuccessful, given that the Human Rights Council received the support of 20 States and the opposition of 14, which included the United States and Member States of the European Union, with the abstention of a further 13 States[77].

From the very beginning of the working group debates, it was clear that there were certain problems that could prevent a Treaty on the issue. The notion of a corporation, scope of business and the stakeholders subject to the Treaty, as well as the human rights that would be at stake and the nature of the obligations that would be imposed upon corporations were just some of the difficulties that arose.

But to make progress in this regard is not an easy task, for a number of reasons. Transnational corporations operate in a context of a weakening of States, in which the scenario is a scarcity of international regulations. Humanizing globalization requires having control over non-subjects (such as corporations), not only to encourage self-regulation but also reduce de-regulation, subject to market law. There are many issues that need clarification, such as the existence of a fragmented legal system in different institutions (the United Nations, European Union, OECD, International Labor Organization, treaties, States, self-regulation) and conventions such as international instruments of *soft law*. This dispersion of law hinders the identification of a legal system based on *soft law*.

On the other hand, progress is being achieved with *new instruments*, such as national and international strategies and national plans. These instruments are different to classic international Treaties and more in line with soft law, however they generate international practice that gradually changes the legal system. Along these lines, although the draft bill of law called the National Plan for Human Rights and Corporations *("Plan nacional de derechos humanos y empresas")*[78] is at a standstill in Spain, this is not the case in other countries where it does exist, such as the United Kingdom, Holland, Denmark, Finland and Lithuania, amongst others. The United Nations working group on human rights and transnational corporations has for several years been recommending that States develop national plans and, in 2015, the United Nations Global Compact published guidelines, as did the Council of the European Union one year before. The aim of the guidelines is for States to develop the relevant international standards in their internal legal systems. The idea has its pros and contras, as although it encourages States to develop their commitments on the issue, there are certain problems. These problems include, amongst others, the fact that the scope, content and practices covered are highly restrictive and the basis of evaluation of corporations is not comprehensive and objective. Finally, the monitoring of the progress in reaching the SDGs may not coincide with the philosophy of international law. As stated in the 2030 Agenda for sustainable development, the

---

[77] -SCHUTTER, O. De., "Towards a New Treaty on business and human rights", *Business and human rights journal*, 1, 2015, pages 41-67.
[78] -Vid. in this regard O'BRIEN, M., MEHRA, A., BLACKWELL, S., POULSEN-HANSEN, C.B., "National action plans: Current Status and future prospects for a New business and human rights governance Tool", *Business and human rights Journal*, 1, 2015, pages 117-126.

processes of follow up and examination are guided by the principle of voluntary performance[79].

Similarly and to conclude, it should be pointed out that the progress of sustainable development in international law gives rise to the appearance of new principles and rules, many of which will have a long road to travel before being consolidated from soft law into hard law. Evidence of this is in the study by prof. J. Rodrigo on the principles of international law relating to sustainable development. They include the principles of sustainable use of natural resources, inter and intra-generational equity, common but differentiated responsibilities, precaution, public participation and access to information and justice, proper management of public issues (good governance) and the principle of integration of the economic, social and environmental aspects of sustainable development[80].

---

[79] -*Transforming our world: the 2030 Agenda for sustainable development*, cit., par. 74.
[80] -Vid. in this regard RODRIGO, J., *El desafío del desarrollo sostenible*, cit., pages 95-191.

Chapter 5

INDIGENOUS PEOPLES AND INDIGENOUS WOMEN IN THE SUSTAINABLE DEVELOPMENT GOALS

JUAN DANIEL OLIVA MARTINEZ

Lecturer of International Public Law. University of Carlos III, Madrid

&

ADRIANA SANCHEZ LIZAMA

Academic Coordinator of the Expert Title on Indigenous Peoples,

University of Carlos III, Madrid

SUMMARY: I. INTRODUCTION. II. INDIGENOUS PEOPLES IN THE 2030 AGENDA. II.1. Paradoxes of Departure. II.2. Cultural Diversity, Indigenous Peoples and Specific Rights. II.3. Dialogue and Intercultural Participation as Possibility Conditions for the Implementation of SDGs in Contexts of Indigenous Peoples. III. INDIGENOUS WOMEN IN THE 2030 AGENDA. III.1. Considerations about the Term Indigenous Women from a Gender and Intersectional Perspective. III.2. Rights of Indigenous Women at the International Level. III.3. Indigenous Women in the Implementation of the Sustainable Development Goals.

* * *

I.   INTRODUCTION

The contributions of Indigenous Peoples to environmental sustainability are internationally known, especially through the popularization of the concept Buen Vivir, which, although it is part of the Latin American experience, has been echoed in broader approaches to sustainable development, which is a reflection of the capacity of incidence that Indigenous Peoples have achieved in the framework of global processes in recent decades, especially since the Earth Summit in 1992.

However, the recognition of the contributions of Indigenous Peoples, and in particular of indigenous women, in other spheres beyond environmental protection is still very tenuous. Although those are part of sustainable development, they need analyzes that allow weaving jointly the problems and the answers given by those whose lives are impacted by them, but who do not remain as spectators of the consequences that this entails and make use of their knowledge to articulate solutions.

In this regard, it is necessary to know how the 2030 Agenda for Sustainable Development, aimed at achieving development based on economic, social and environmental sustainability, and which expresses the commitment to realize the human rights of all and to achieve gender equality and the empowerment of all women and girls is articulated through the 17 SDGs with the rights of Indigenous Peoples.

Indigenous Peoples, meanwhile, can contribute significantly to the proper implementation of SDGs by providing positive experiences, especially from their ancestral knowledge and collective practices, for the continuity of life respectful of the environment and the dignity of human beings.

A fundamental issue of this implementation is to keep in mind the inclusion of the gender and intersectional perspective, not only in relation to SDG 5, but to the entire Agenda, since the fulfillment of the slogan "No One Left Behind" necessarily involves awareness of the specific repercussions for differentiated social groups of the measures taken to comply with the 17 SDG. The absence of intersectional approaches simply perpetuates the notions of unsustainable development that is attempted to be tackled.

The movement of indigenous women at the global level constitutes a series of networks and spaces for dialogue aimed to the construction of strategies that place the diversity they represent at the center of the 2030 Agenda, as well as the contributions they make to improve the conditions for a sustainable life at a global level.

The purpose of this text is to give a brief overview of the implications of the SDGs for Indigenous Peoples and for indigenous women, from a gender and intersectional perspective. To this end, the article is divided into two parts, a general one on Indigenous Peoples in the 2030 Agenda, and a specific one on indigenous women in the 2030 Agenda.

II.   INDIGENOUS PEOPLES IN THE 2030 AGENDA

II.1 Paradoxes of Departure

The Indigenous Peoples around the world are interested in the compliance with the SDGs in both development cooperation policies and the public policies of the states in which they live, but the fact is that the 2030 Agenda does not directly address their concerns. Despite the insistent demands of the indigenous organizations that participated in the process that led to the approval of this framework, which inspires the International Community and serves as a horizon for governments, international organizations, civil society, and companies in their work in favor of sustainable development; the interests, priorities and views of the Indigenous Peoples on the development and the preservation of the environment were incorporated in a limited way.

This fact draws great attention, being that it seems undeniable that these differenciated ethnocultural communities could make important contributions from their particular traditions to a global agenda focused precisely on sustainability, an aspect on which Indigenous Peoples have been particularly active since the Summit of Rio de

Janeiro in 1992, and which they reinforced with their positioning (which we know as the "five messages") at the United Nations Conference on Sustainable Development (Rio + 20)[1].

Only in two of the targets, out of the 169 that make up the document, reference is made to Indigenous Peoples. Specifically, SDG 2.3 on small-scale agricultural production and SDG 4.5, which deals with the elimination of inequalities in access to education[2]. These limitations of origin have already been criticized by the members of the so-called Indigenous Peoples Major Group[3] - which brings together internationally recognized indigenous intellectuals, leaders, and representatives -, during their participation in the previous meetings towards the final adoption of the Agenda.

In all those previous meetings, indigenous leaders insisted that indigenous claims and demands should be given greater importance; that disaggregations of data on sustainable development should be established by ethnicity and differential approach; and that specific indicators should be generated[4] as to know, for example, the number of indigenous people without access to drinking water, minimum income, decent housing or electricity. These demands were not incorporated, which has forced the Indigenous Peoples to develop their own indicators and their own monitoring methodologies in the implementation of the SDGs.

In turn, basic issues for Indigenous Peoples as their expectations regarding self-determination; the preservation of their territories, beyond the patrimonial sense of the possession of the land; the maintenance of their cultural and linguistic identity; or the need to generate new decolonizing public policies that reverse the entrenched discriminatory, racist and oppressive structures that have done so much damage in the states in which they live; were not addressed in the formulation of the SDGs.

This paradox of origin, which is the great interest of Indigenous Peoples in the use of the SDGs as tools to promote the implementation of their rights, but which contrasts with the invisibility of the issues that concern them in the 2030 Agenda, should be taken into account by any scholar who wants to approach the question. In that sense, the Indigenous Peoples do not separate the SDGs from their differentiated rights. For them, it is impossible to work for sustainable development without guaranteeing the practical and real protection of their rights, both individual and, above all, collective.

Therefore, when representatives of Indigenous Peoples meet with governments, companies, universities, NGOs or international organizations to discuss the issue of SDGs, or when they participate in international, regional or national forums on the

---

[1] Vid. *Cambio climático y biodiversidad: Los seis mensajes centrales de los Pueblos Indígenas en Río+20*, 2012, and *Aportes de los Pueblos Indígenas al borrador cero de Río+20*, 2012.

[2] Resolution adopted by the General Assembly on 25 September 2015. Transforming our world: the 2030 Agenda for Sustainable Development, A/RES/70/1.

[3] The statements of the Indigenous Peoples Major Group red in: Indigenous Peoples Major Group, Policy brief on sustaintable development goals and post 2015, development agenda: a working draft, 2015 and Indigenous Peoples Major Group, Los Objetivos de Desarrollo Sostenible y los Pueblos Indígenas, High Level Political Forum, 2017.

[4] Vid. Paragraph 10, World Conference on Indigenous Peoples, 2014.

subject, allusions to their collective rights are constant and serve as the foundational elements of their approach and participation to this international agenda. But as it will be analyzed below, the formulation, language, and nature of the SDGs and the rights of Indigenous Peoples are very different, which adds another paradox that also has to be borne in mind.

II.2 Cultural Diversity, Indigenous Peoples and Specific Rights

To speak of the Indigenous Peoples is to speak of cultural diversity, since they represent 90% of the plurality of cultures that survive in our time (5000 according to some sources), adding almost 400 million people who, in turn, speak thousands of differentiated languages. They are spread all over the world, inhabiting the five continents, from Patagonia to Alaska, from New Zealand to Japan, from South Africa to Norway, using or inhabiting 22% of the planet's territories, many of them distinguished by their great biological diversity both on the surface and in the subsoil. They are, as is well known, guardians of nature, preservers of particularly sustainable subsistence practices, and are very critical of the effects of the globalized economic model that currently prevails.

They are also characterized by their special attachment to the land and their historical territories, of which they usually consider themselves the original inhabitants although among the Indigenous Peoples have also been frequent population movements; and show a strong identity pride for having resisted throughout history to the onslaught of colonization, the assimilationist policies, the ethnocidal attempts that sought to make them disappear as distinctive peoples, the militarization of their territories, or even the macro-programs that, in the name of development, both affected ecosystems in those who inhabit, and consequently their ways of life[5].

Despite the fact that Indigenous Peoples continue to be persecuted in some contexts or their human rights are violated by the actions of companies or governments, today, in many regions and countries, they show a process of undoubted political, social and cultural revitalization. In addition, despite the difficulties, they have managed to open up new opportunities for participation in the main international areas of deliberation, such as the mechanisms for Indigenous Peoples in the United Nations: the Permanent Forum on Indigenous Issues, the Expert Mechanism on the Rights of Indigenous Peoples, and the

---

[5] In the outcome document of the Global Indigenous Preparatory Conference held in the Norwegian town of Alta from June 8 to 13, 2013 during the preparatory work that led to the holding of the World Conference on Indigenous Peoples (A / 67/994), that finally took place in September 2014, the indigenous representatives exposed the historical persecution that their people have suffered throughout the times, which has consisted of 'the continuous usurpation of territories, lands, resources, air, ice, oceans and waters, and mountains and forests of the Indigenous Peoples; in the extensive destruction of the political and legal institutions of the Indigenous Peoples; in discriminatory practices of the colonizing forces with the objective of destroying the cultures of the Indigenous Peoples; in non-compliance with treaties, agreements and other constructive arrangements made with indigenous peoples and nations; in genocide, ecocide and the loss of food sovereignty, in crimes against humanity and war crimes, and in the militarization of indigenous peoples and our lands; in the corporatization and commodification of indigenous peoples and our natural resources; and in the imposition of "development" models that are destroying the capacity to give life and the integrity of Mother Earth and that are producing a series of negative impacts, of which climate change could become the most destructive'.

Special Rapporteur on the rights of indigenous peoples; to which are added others of a regional scope such as the Fund for the Development of the Indigenous Peoples of Latin America and the Caribbean (FILAC), the Working Group on Indigenous Populations / Communities in Africa, or the Advisory Council of the Andean Community of Nations.

Through such spaces, Indigenous Peoples are significantly influencing the public policies of many of the states in which they live, even assuming high representation positions in some governments, serving as ministers, deputy ministers, ambassadors, senior administration officials and general, gaining visibility and capacity to influence, through its most representative organizations, which only a few years ago was unthinkable.

The Indigenous Peoples base their political action and global strategy, as collective subjects of change, on a series of rights recognized in International Law instruments such as the Convention 169 of the International Labor Organization (1989), the United Nations Declaration on the Rights of Indigenous Peoples (2007), the American Declaration on the Rights of Indigenous Peoples (2016), and in some aspects also in the Convention on Biological Diversity (1992); as well as in numerous judgments of the Inter-American Court of Human Rights since 2001 and different pronouncements of the control committees of the main human rights treaties: Committee of the International Covenant on Civil and Political Rights; Committee of the International Covenant on Economic, Social and Cultural Rights; Committee for the Elimination of Racial Discrimination; Committee on the Rights of the Child, among others.

All this serves as legal support to the set of claims of the Indigenous Peoples related to self-government, lands and territories, natural resources, the preservation of their cultural identity, free, prior and informed consultation or consent, their own law and indigenous justice systems, bilingual and intercultural education or their visions of self-development, called Buen Vivir in its own terminology. On the other hand, this international legal framework specialized on the rights of Indigenous Peoples has had an internal projection in many countries, at the constitutional, legislative and also jurisprudential levels with important judgments of the high courts, which are beginning to take on a multicultural approach and are inspired by the principle of valuation and preservation of cultural diversity. All this despite the fact that in a large part of the states with indigenous population, international standards on their rights are not fully incorporated.

In this way, it can also be understood that when Indigenous Peoples work from the dynamics of the SDGs in their discourse and in their organizational or institutional practice, the question of their differentiated collective rights appears, since they understand, as mentioned above, that the 2030 Agenda can be a practical tool to convey many of those rights that have already been formally enshrined in the international order or in the internal legal systems, but on which the real lack of implementation persists.

Since the 2030 Agenda is a document that must necessarily be applied based on internationally recognized human rights, as established in the body of the document, the SDGs and the rights of Indigenous Peoples are articulated. In this sense, the Goals inspire the action of the International Community, serving as references to actors committed to solidarity and inclusive and sustainable public policies. They are an inspiring horizon that is related to the achievement of specific targets through the measurement of specific indicators, but which undoubtedly do not imply a legal link for states or International Organizations, having limitations to be identified as "Soft Law", which refers to a set of mechanisms, such as declarations, resolutions and action programs that demonstrate compliance with the norms established by International Law, but are not binding[6].

The rights of the Indigenous Peoples form an indisputable part of the international norms as they are included in international treaties such as the ILO Convention 169, and therefore constitute conventional norms directly related to some of the fundamental principles of International Law based on the obligation of the states protect human rights. To these rights are added others, also of a conventional nature, relevant to Indigenous Peoples despite not being specific to them, such as those relating to the Convention on the Protection and Promotion of the Diversity of Cultural Expressions of 2005.

The above, together with the Universal and American Declarations on the rights of Indigenous Peoples, and the provisions adopted in the internal legal systems, constitutes an emerging field of consistent, uniform and constant practices, which are gradually becoming generalized among the states that express their conviction that they are obliged to respect them, in some regions more than in others, leading to an international custom of respecting the ways of life and guaranteeing the preservation of the diversity represented by the Indigenous Peoples, ensuring their differentiated rights.

Articulating the rights of Indigenous Peoples and SDGs in order to generate synergy in the implementation of both is a great challenge and a current political commitment of the international indigenous movement, made up of a wide universe of organizations. But, of course, it is also a challenge for all that panoply of allies who identify with their demands, either for empathy and commitment to ethnocultural justice, or because they have been aware that supporting Indigenous Peoples in their demands implies to preserve their cultures and thereby ensure life models, existential principles and positive worldviews that can support a global human development, sustainable and widespread, with respect of particular identities. Allies such as universities, specialized centers, NGOs, associations for the defense of human rights or International Organizations are active international actors in favor of the achievement of SDGs.

II.3 Dialogue and Intercultural Participation as Possibility Conditions for the Implementation of SDGs in Contexts of Indigenous Peoples

Taking into account the foregoing, it seems essential for an adequate implementation of the SDGs in favor of the Indigenous Peoples, which covers the expectations of

---

[6]Although its use and enforcement is of a persuasive nature, the "soft law" causes legal effects, understanding that the adoption of such mechanisms is the first step for them to become "hard law". Although the states are not fully legally bound by the "solf law", they can not fully ignore it and even less act against it.

realization of their differentiated rights, the existence of a process of dialogue and intercultural participation. Only through this process of meeting and adapting to indigenous demands, the SDGs will consummate what Indigenous Peoples expect from them and will fulfill the ethical imperative of the 2030 Agenda "No one left behind".

To this end, international, regional and national channels must be established to consolidate permanent mechanisms of dialogue between states, international organizations, civil society and Indigenous Peoples, and that serve to develop concrete initiatives based on the priorities of Indigenous Peoples and to promote self-development or Buen Vivir, as well as policies and programs consistent with the basic standards of the internationally recognized collective rights. It is through those means that it is possible to facilitate the development of indicators that reflect the real situation of Indigenous Peoples and help close the gap between the international recognition of their differentiated rights and their real enjoyment within the countries and regions in which they live.

This process must take into account the multidimensionality and multidirectionality with which Indigenous Peoples identify their own models of development, something that they try to project in their community life plans[7], and that goes far beyond the economic and materialistic dimension of development, in addition of the understanding that sustainability has cultural, identity, social, environmental, territorial, political, organizational and spiritual components. A much richer conception of development, based on cosmovisions that offer an alternative perspective to global and immersive dynamics, and which is based on a renewed vision that seeks to ensure human beings an integral, sustainable way of life, respectful of the people and the environment, as well as community cultural traditions.

Therefore, the implementation of the SDGs should have an intercutural approach[8] and be based at least on the following parameters of action to be taken into account in public agendas, state policies and cooperation actions, both governmental and non-governmental, aimed at ensuring sustainable economic, social and environmental development for Indigenous Peoples:

1.- The main beneficiary should be the community. Understanding that Indigenous Peoples are collective subjects, they must be the recipients of public policies and programs linked to SDGs, without forgetting due respect for the individual rights of their members. In the indigenous sphere, the community is the center of development, since its activity is centered on the collective, based on a dense organizational network rooted in mechanisms of reciprocity and complementarity, in criteria of community valuation of

---

[7] Vid. J. D. Oliva, *La cooperación con Pueblos Indígenas: desarrollo y derechos humanos*, CIDEAL, Madrid, 2005.

[8] In this regard, it is relevant the adoption in 2014 of the Montevideo Consensus on Population and Development, promoted by ECLAC of the United Nations, which includes specific chapters with the objective of having statistics and disaggregated data that provide real and verifiable information on the situation of the Indigenous Peoples. LC/L.3697

goods, of social control of the accumulation, of ritualization of the surplus, and logics of harmonization of activities with the environment.

2.- The special conception of the Indigenous Peoples on the land, their ancestral territories and the environment must be respected, since those play a structuring role in the life of the community, their identity and differentiated culture. While the development of human beings must be pursued, the natural environments in which they inhabit must be preserved, including all the animal and plant species, that is, the set of biodiversity with which the Indigenous Peoples relate holistically in their traditional ways of life. It is precisely the territorial component that is the most sensitive element in any intervention based on the SDGs that is to be carried out in favor of Indigenous Peoples, especially since in many geographical contexts they face the lack of effective protection of their rights over their lands, territories and natural resources before the imposition of projects promoted by their governments or by extractive companies, often without timely and due free, prior and informed consultation, nor counting with the consent of the affected communities, in addition to the omission of agreements for Indigenous Peoples to participate of the obtained benefits in a fair and equitable manner. Likewise, many of the projects involve forced displacements of the indigenous population.

3.- The active participation of Indigenous Peoples[9] through their legitimate representatives, as well as their assemblies and grassroots communities, should be a priority, in full compliance with the rights to political participation and self-determination of Indigenous Peoples that should guide all public policy, development project or initiative that aims to intervene in their territories and life contexts within the framework of the 2030 Agenda. Although efforts were made in the International Organizations to integrate indigenous representatives in the debates, negotiations and previous work that led to the adoption of the Agenda, as was the case of the Indigenous Peoples Major Group, it is necessary to ensure that such participation is sustained in time. Likewise, it should be the communities and the representative organizations that set their own indicators, participate directly in each of the phases of the interventions and monitor the results, both in the framework of public policies and in the development programs or projects of international cooperation, taking center stage throughout the process. In the same way, Indigenous Peoples must be consulted in a free, prior and informed manner, regarding actions to monitor and evaluate compliance with the 2030 Agenda, as well as actively

[9] Initial premise that was already pointed out by the Permanent Forum on Indigenous Issues of the United Nations, stating that the implementation of the SDGs should "guarantee the participation of indigenous peoples in the implementation, follow-up and review of the 2030 Agenda: indigenous peoples can contribute to the development of national action plans, follow-ups and reviews at all levels, including voluntary national reviews in the high-level political fórum". The Forum also added that "the 2030 Agenda should be implemented by fully respecting the rights of indigenous peoples: By protecting and promoting the rights of indigenous peoples, as reflected in the United Nations Declaration on the Rights of Indigenous Peoples, states will be able to address the challenges faced by indigenous peoples and ensure that they are not relegated", and "promote the visibility of indigenous peoples in the data and the review of the 2030 Agenda: At the national level, there should be identified relevant indicators for indigenous peoples, which will be included in the lists of national indicators. The disaggregation of data and the recognition of indigenous identity in national statistics, as well as the integration of community data from indigenous communities, will allow the evaluation of progress for indigenous peoples". Vid. Permanent Forum on Indigenous Issues, *Los Pueblos Indígenas y los ODS*, ONU, Nueva York, 2016.

participate in the design, execution, monitoring and evaluation of national plans of sustainable development adopted in coherence with the Agenda, especially in those areas that affect them or that involve interventions in their lands and territories. These national plans must also take as reference the life plans generated by the communities themselves, fulfilling the internationally recognized rights of Indigenous Peoples in a real and effective way. To account for such compliance, national plans must have specific indicators on indigenous issues and disaggregate data by ethnicity[10]. Indigenous Peoples must also have well-established mechanisms that allow them to provide data to the National Voluntary Reports presented by the countries to the United Nations on the implementation of the Agenda[11]. Although the participation of Indigenous Peoples in the implementation and monitoring of the SDGs is part of the due observance of their rights by the states, it remains very limited in the main international specialized frameworks such as the Forum of the Countries of Latin America and the Caribbean on Sustainable Development of ECLAC, or at the High Level Political Forum on Sustainable Development[12]. In contrast, the incorporation of the indigenous perspective on the SDGs in the Ibero-American Plan of Action on the rights of Indigenous Peoples and the Declaration of Iximuleu "For a prosperous, inclusive, sustainable and intercultural Ibero-America" should be highly valued, both of which are instruments impulsed by FILAC in the framework of the First Meeting of High Authorities of Ibero-America on Indigenous Peoples, held in April 2018[13].

4.- The training on the SDGs of the technical personnel of the representative indigenous organizations, as well as of the specialized technical personnel of the public administrations and the International Organizations, and the diffusion of information among the base communities on the potentiality of the same, is fundamental to motivate their participation in the intercultural and collective processes of implementation that

---

[10] In this regard, it is important to acknowledge the efforts made by several countries in the Latin American region (Colombia, Ecuador, Mexico, Paraguay, Panama and Uruguay, among others) as set out in the *II Informe sobre la situación de la implementación de los ODS en América Latina y el Caribe desde la Visión de los Pueblos Indígenas*, FILAC, Bolivia, 2017. The report focuses on SDGs 6, 7, 11 and 15.

[11] The paragraph 79 of the 2030 Agenda states that as part of the monitoring and review mechanisms, states can conduct periodic and inclusive reviews, led by countries, of national and subnational progress. These reviews should take into account the contributions of Indigenous Peoples, civil society and the private sector and other interested parties, regarding the political circumstances and priorities of each country.

[12] *Ibídem.* p. 25.

[13] It was a preparatory activity for the XXVI Ibero-American Summit of Heads of State and Government, scheduled for November 2018. The meeting was attended by government delegates, representatives of Indigenous Peoples, officials of International Cooperation and International Organizations. In the Declaration adopted (Declaration of Iximuleu) the signatories committed themselves to establish mechanisms for the participation of the Indigenous Peoples, in harmony with their own worldview and culture, for the implementation and follow-up of the national plans to reach the SDGs. On the other hand, the Ibero-American Action Plan for the Implementation of the Rights of Indigenous Peoples assumes some specific objectives related to the topics of this article. The first one, adjust the national legal frameworks to the full incorporation of the international standards of the rights of Indigenous Peoples, and the second (there are two others), include the indigenous perspective in each of the national plans for the implementation of the SDGs , ensuring that they are in line with the provisions of the Declaration on the Rights of Indigenous Peoples, while promoting the participation of Indigenous Peoples in programs, projects and other activities related to the implementation and review of the 2030 Agenda , including indigenous women, persons with disabilities, the elderly and indigenous children.

reinforce their incidence at the national, regional and global levels. There can be no participation of Indigenous Peoples in the implementation of SDGs if those are not able to intervene successfully, remembering that many indigenous people do not know the real scope of the Agenda[14] and therefore it is important, in joint work with the most representative organizations, to establish mappings by regions and countries on the real capacity they have to participate in the implementation, follow-up, and review of the achievements related to the SDGs in indigenous territories. At the same time, the technical capacities for the elaboration of their own reports and indicators on SDGs should be improved from the perspective of the Indigenous Peoples and their particular visions regarding self-development, their differentiated rights and social, economic and environmental sustainability, applying their knowledge, innovations and traditional practices, especially in regard to the conservation and use of biological diversity[15].

5.- Consistent with what has been pointed out so far, any action related to the implementation of SDGs should be linked to the specific rights of Indigenous Peoples, understanding that SDGs and the rights of Indigenous Peoples cannot be seen as separate bodies but as interrelated and complementary areas. Likewise, the principle of non-discrimination, the preservation of the diversity they represent and the principle of self-determination[16] must be respected. Rights can be classified into those of a political nature (self-government, autonomies, own systems of decision-making, own political organizations); of territorial-environmental nature (rights to the collective property of the land, to the preservation of their reference ecosystems, to natural resources, to the delimitation and titling of their territories, to a healthy environment); of a legal nature (right to own law, to their own justice systems, to their internal mechanisms of conflict resolution, to their traditional judicial authorities, to the collective legal personality, to access to justice); of an economic and sociocultural nature (right to the preservation of their cultural heritage, both material and immaterial, to the preservation of their identity and protection of their traditional knowledge, to their collective intellectual property rights, to bilingual and intercultural education, to intercultural health, to self and autonomous development, to their traditional systems and livelihoods, to their own entrepreneurial models, to technology and the satisfaction of basic material and human needs); and of participatory nature (right to consultation and free, prior and informed consent)[17].

6.- In the same way, in the planning and implementation of SDGs, specific targets and indicators should be incorporated in relation to women, youth, children, LGTBI[18] people, migrants, seniors and indigenous people with disabilities, as well as affirmative measures, recognizing that these groups tend to see their rights violated and be recipients

---

[14] *Op. Cit.* FILAC, 2017. The knowledge of the Indigenous Peoples of the Latin American and Caribbean region on the 2030 Agenda and the SDGs remain very limited and inaccesible.

[15] A good practice in this regard is the Latin American Diploma "The Indigenous Peoples Route to reduce inequality in the 2030 Agenda", recently held in La Paz, Bolivia (October 2018).

[16] With the logical limits that the borders of the states in which they live can not be modified.

[17] Vid. J.D Oliva, *Los Pueblos Indígenas a la conquista de sus derechos,* BOE, Madrid, 2012; J. Anaya, *Pueblos Indígenas y Derecho Internacional,* Trotta, Madrid, 2005.

[18] Accronym for Lesbian, Gay, Trans, Bisexual and Intersexual.

of discriminatory treatment both outside and within their communities. Therefore, addressing their rights from a gender and intersectional perspective, respecting their collective identity, is an essential task in the process of implementing, monitoring and evaluating compliance with the 2030 Agenda in favor of Indigenous Peoples[19]. This should permeate public policies, programs or cooperation projects to boost their empowerment, based on the awareness that through their participation they can contribute to the welfare and sustainable development of their own communities.

III. INDIGENOUS WOMEN IN THE 2030 AGENDA

III.1 Considerations About the Term Indigenous Women from a Gender and Intersectional Perspective

The women subject is today understood as an inhomogeneous political subject, an analysis that has been the result of the advances of the women's movement at a global level and its reflection in feminist theories, as well as the expansion and deepening of women's rights in a long historical journey, in which indigenous women have played a prominent role, especially in the resistance against the onslaught of colonization processes that largely silenced them for a long time, both because of their belonging to Indigenous Peoples, and because of their condition of women.

The presence of indigenous women as political subjects in the arena of debate of rights is increasingly visible, especially because of the role they play in the construction of the discourse on sustainable development, and in which they, through their knowledge and ancestral practices, have their own voice, so it is necessary to know their specific demands as women belonging to Indigenous Peoples, and therefore, as individual and collective subjects.

The term indigenous women is here understood from the criterion of self-identification, referring to those women who are part of Indigenous Peoples, taking as a reference definition the common Article 1 of both ILO Convention 169, and the United Nations Declaration on Rights of Indigenous Peoples of 2007. This criterion does not depend on the State Parties officially recognizing Indigenous Peoples.

As part of the analysis with a gender approach[20], it is also necessary to recognize the self-identification of the individuals as women, in full respect of the right to identity

---

[19] Vid. *Memoria del Taller de Estrategia Global para Mujeres Indígenas sobre la Participación Efectiva en la Implementación de la Agenda 2030,* (26-28 de octubre de 2017, Mandaluyong, Filipinas).

[20] The definition of gender analysis adopted in this article is the one referred in OHCHR, *Integrating a Gender Perspective into Human Rights Investigations. Guidance and Practice,* 2018, at 7: "Gender analysis is a key tool to help recognize, understand and make visible the gendered nature of human rights violations, including their specific and differential impact on women, men and others, as well as human rights violations based on gender that specifically target LGBTI. It can help to identify differences in the enjoyment of all human rights and fundamental freedoms in all spheres of life. It also seeks to analyse power relations within the larger socio-cultural, economic, political and environmental contexts to understand the root causes of discrimination and inequality. Gender analysis is an integral part of a human rights-based approach1, allowing one to see the many ways that gender affects human rights. As a starting

contained in Article 33 of the Declaration on the Rights of Indigenous Peoples, expanding the notion of gender beyond biological criteria, and recognizing gender as a social construction.

In this regard, it is important to clarify that the gender women will be dealt with from a broad point of view, including all trans and non-binary identities[21], especially referring to those that are included in what, in the different cultures in which they have a presence, is understood as a spectrum of the feminine, although from the full respect and understanding of the uniqueness of each of these diverse gender identities.

This approach responds mainly to the lack of information regarding the diversity of gender identities, which is why, for the purpose of this article, has been chosen to use the term women from an extended perspective. Of course, this diversity is also present among the Indigenous Peoples, existing numerous examples around the world such as the Two Spirit people in the Indigenous Peoples of North America, the Muxe in Mexico, the Hijra in the Indian Subcontinent, the Fa'afafine in Samoa, among other non-binary indigenous identities[22].

Although these notions are not necessarily contemplated in the reference documents for this article, they are required to be able to carry out more in-depth analyzes of the implementation of the 2030 Agenda, as well as to ensure the due respect for the human rights of all people.

According to the OHCHR[23], analyzes with a gender perspective can reinforce investigations and reports by contributing to the task of accounting for differentiated forms of impact on human rights that certain situations or crises may have on individuals or populations, including women, men, girls, and boys, as well as LGTBI people and people with non-binary gender identities; and in a related way, also contribute to the construction of more adequate responses to human rights violations on certain groups of individuals.

In the UN Women 2018 Report on the 2030 Agenda, it is highlighted that, in order to carry out a comprehensive and effective monitoring of the SDGs, it is necessary to have data on gender identity, and that these should be generated using definitions, norms well-designed statistics and concepts, which provide the basis for exchanging statistical

---

point for gender integration, it can propose measures that will close the gender gap between international human rights standards and the everyday human rights situation on the ground".

[21] *Ibidem* at 8: "Gender identity refers to a person's deeply felt and experienced sense of their own gender, which may or may not correspond with the sex they were assigned at birth. It includes the personal sense of the body and other expressions of gender, such as clothing, speech and mannerisms. Everyone has a gender identity. Transgender or trans are umbrella terms for people with a wide range of gender identities and expressions who do not identify with the sex they were assigned at birth. A transgender person may identify with different gender identities including man, woman, transman, transwoman, and with specific terms, including non-binary identities such as hijra, fa'afafine, two-spirit, among other terms. Cisgender is a term for people who identify with the sex that they were assigned at birth."

[22] More information on this topic can be consulted in: UN. *Living Free& Equal. What States are doing to tackle violence and discrimination against lesbian, gay, bisexual, transgender and intersex people*, 2016. HR/PUB/16/3

[23] *Op. Cit.*

data between countries and to improve their accessibility, comparability and interpretation possibilities.

One of the main problems facing the implementation of the 2030 Agenda is the lack of gender-disaggregated data, with a radical lack of data on people whose identities do not fall within the male / female gender binomial, which is to a large extent consequence of the lack of international standards to collect and measure data on gender identity. In this sense, it is important to generate relevant information from a gender perspective, which considers the rights of both women, trans and non-binary persons, and intersex people.

This analysis also takes into account the rights of indigenous girls, considered as those under 18 years of age, in accordance with the provisions of the Convention on the Rights of the Child, approved in 1989 by the General Assembly, and in force since 1990, and which also ensures the protection by states of the right of indigenous girls in common with the other members of their group, to have their own cultural life, to profess and practice their own religion, or to use their own language. This without forgetting that the Committee on the Rights of the Child, in its General Comment No. 11[24], indicates that the foregoing excludes pernicious practices, such as early marriages and female genital mutilation. Attention is also drawn to the need to take into account the content of General Comment No. 13[25], which refers to the potential vulnerability of indigenous girls to be exposed to violence.

Added to this, it is necessary to address the social reality that we want to analyze from an intersectional perspective[26], in order to be able to account for the different discriminatory practices to which women and LGTBI people are subjected, being particularly relevant the recognition that poverty is the result of discrimination, which generates contexts of vulnerability for people who suffer from it, that is in turn, an aggravating factor of discriminatory practices. It is therefore significant that women who are racialized and/or who live with multiple intersections are among the poorest.

Discrimination against women as a fact linked to other factors that affect their lives, resulting in complex and differentiated experiences of gender-based violence that need adequate legal and regulatory responses, is recognized by the Committee for the

---

[24] General comment no 11: Indigenous Children and their Rights under the Convention (January 2009). CRC/C/GC/11

[25] General comment no 13: Freedom from all forms of violence. CRC/C/GC/12

[26] A. Stephens, E.D. Lewis, and S.M. Reddy, 2018. *Inclusive Systemic Evaluation (ISE4GEMs): A New Approach for the SDG Era*. New York: UN Women. ISBN: 978-1-63214-125-5, at 15: "Another way to view complexity is through the notion of intersectionality. Coined by Crenshaw in 1989, intersectionality suggests that different social divisions (e.g., gender, race) interrelate to produce social relations and personal life experience. Originally a triad of gender, race and class, other social categories such as sexuality, faith and disability, amongst others, have been added to the framework. The importance of understanding intersectionality has extended beyond race and gender to development contexts".

[26] UN Women, *Recomendaciones Generales y Observaciones Finales del Comité para la Eliminación de la Discriminación contra la Mujer sobre mujeres indígenas y/o afrodescendientes realizadas a Estados de América Latina*, 2017. Recomendación General No. 35 (2017) Sobre la violencia por razón de género contra la mujer, por la que se actualiza la Recomendación General No. 19.

Elimination of Discrimination against Women. Women (CEDAW Committee) through General Recommendation No. 35, which considers factors such as:

> [...] the ethnic origin or race of women, minority or indigenous status, color, socio-economic status and / or caste, language, religion or belief, political opinion, national origin, marital status, motherhood, age, urban or rural origin, state of health, disability, property rights, lesbian, bisexual, transgender or intersex status, illiteracy, asylum application, refugee status, internally displaced or stateless, widowhood, migratory status, the condition of head of the family, cohabitation with HIV / AIDS, deprivation of liberty and prostitution, as well as women trafficking, situations of armed conflict, the geographical remoteness and stigmatization of women fighting for their rights, in particular human rights defenders[27].

One of the first advances in the recognition of the race/gender intersection within the framework of the United Nations is reflected in the Durban Declaration and Program of Action of 2001[28], which indicates that indigenous women and girls suffer from exacerbated forms of discrimination when racism and sexual discrimination are combined, leading to a deterioration of their living conditions, to poverty, violence, multiple forms of discrimination and the limitation or denial of their human rights.

Likewise, the document calls for states to incorporate the gender perspective in all programs of action against racism, racial discrimination, xenophobia and related intolerance, addressing in a timely manner the forms of discrimination that fall particularly in indigenous, African and Asian women, those of African or Asian descent, migrants and women from other disadvantaged groups, so as to ensure their access to production resources on equal terms with men, as a means of promote their participation in the economic and productive development of their communities.

Analyzes with a gender and intersectional perspective regarding indigenous women need to account not only for their individual rights but also for their collective rights, as a starting point to ensure respect for their dignity and value as human beings. The materialization of their rights to lands, territories, and resources, to maintain their cultures, to the recognition of their own identities, to self-government and self-

---

[27] UN Women, *Recomendaciones Generales y Observaciones Finales del Comité para la Eliminación de la Discriminación contra la Mujer sobre mujeres indígenas y/o afrodescendientes realizadas a Estados de América Latina*, 2017. Recomendación General No. 35 (2017) Sobre la violencia por razón de género contra la mujer, por la que se actualiza la Recomendación General No. 19.

[28] Durban Declaration and Programme of Action. World Conference against Racism, Racial Discrimination, Xenophobia and Related Intolerance (WCAR), 2001, Durban, South Africa. The inclusion of the gender perspective in these documents followed up the General Recommendation No. 25 on gender-related dimensions of racial discrimination of the Committee on the Elimination of Racial Discrimination, publicated in 2000, which addresses the need of recognition or acknowledgement of the different life experiences of women and men, in areas of both public and private life, in order to detect circumstances in which racial discrimination only or primarily affects women, or affects women in a different way, or to a different degree than men.

determination, and to be asked for their free, prior and informed consent in decisions that may affect them depends on the possibility of their collective affirmation.

Indigenous women, although they share many of the concerns and interests with other women around the world in the areas of human rights and economic and social development, also provide a unique and important perspective on these issues. The fact that indigenous women do not constitute a homogeneous category, since they represent a wide variety of cultures with different needs and problems, should be a central premise in the formulation of norms and programs, taking into account that as members of the Indigenous Peoples share a history linked to colonialism, oppression, and discrimination, whose legacy is still present and is reflected in the shortcomings they suffer in terms of the effective enjoyment of their individual and collective rights[29].

Therefore, the set of international instruments for the recognition and protection of the rights of Indigenous Peoples cannot operate separately from the global principle of participation of indigenous women, one of the spaces being the discussion of proposals to integrate their social rights, political, cultural and economic development strategies in the UN system[30], focused on the 2030 Agenda since its adoption in 2016.

III.2 Rights of Indigenous Women at the International Level

The Convention on the Elimination of All Forms of Discrimination against Women (CEDAW), adopted by the General Assembly of the United Nations in 1979[31] and in force since 1981, states that:

> Article 1.- For the purposes of the present Convention, the term "discrimination against women" shall mean any distinction, exclusion or restriction made on the basis of sex which has the effect or purpose of impairing or nullifying the recognition, enjoyment or exercise by women, irrespective of their marital status, on a basis of equality of men and women, of human rights and fundamental freedoms in the political, economic, social, cultural, civil or any other field.

This definition does not refer to the intersectional dimension of discrimination, in the sense of not including concomitant forms of discrimination against women, such as the dimensions of race, ethnicity, disability, sexual orientation or gender identity. These issues would only appear later thanks to the efforts of the women's movements globally,

---

[29] ECOSOC. Twenty-year review of the Beijing Declaration and Platform for Action and beyond: a framework to advance indigenous women's issues. Permanent Forum on Indigenous Issues, 2015. E/C.19/2015/2

[30] Grupo de Apoyo Interinstitucional sobre Cuestiones Indígenas (IASG). Directrices sobre las cuestiones relativas a los pueblos indígenas del Grupo de Naciones Unidas para el Desarrollo. Nueva York, 2009. ONU.

[31] It took over thirty years of work by the United Nations Commission on the Status of Women, a body established in 1946 to monitor the situation of women and to promote women's rights, to reach this important achievement towards the recognition of the specific rights of women.

being reflected in the General Recommendations and Resolutions of the CEDAW Committee[32].

It is necessary to remember that at the time of its entry into force, the rights of many women around the world were not yet fully contemplated, as is the case of black women who saw their rights denied even at the legislative level, of South African women during Apartheid, of transgender women who are victims even now of laws that deny their identities and their bodies, and of indigenous women, central subjects of the analysis presented here and who began the long journey through the recognition of their differentiated rights several decades before of the official recognition of the Indigenous Peoples in 1989, through ILO Convention 169, and of which they are part.

Despite not containing specific mentions on the differentiated rights of indigenous women, Article 3 establishes the application of Convention 169 to both indigenous men and women, in addition to establishing in Article 20 the principle of equal treatment and opportunities for men and indigenous women in employment, as well as protection against sexual harassment[33].

In the years in which the aforementioned documents were adopted, many of the crimes against humanity that particularly affected women in recent history, and which are now used as a point of reference to deepen the special impact of the violence over their bodies and identities, had not yet been clarified, were about to occur or continued to be perpetrated, this being the case of the genocide of the Mayan women of Guatemala[34], being these issues that would bring to light novel treatments on violence against women, including International Criminal Law.

The preamble of CEDAW refers to the indispensable elimination of apartheid, of all forms of racism, racial discrimination, colonialism, neocolonialism, aggression, foreign occupation and domination and interference in the internal affairs of states as a condition for the enjoyment of rights for both men and women. These issues had already been addressed in the International Convention on the Elimination of All Forms of Racial Discrimination adopted by the General Assembly in 1965, and in force since 1969, making reference both to the Declaration on the Granting of Independence to Colonial Countries and Peoples of 1960, and the United Nations Declaration on the Elimination of All Forms of Racial Discrimination of 1963, although without reference to the ways in

---

[32] With particular emphasis on indigenous women in General Recommendation No. 35 (2017) on gender-based violence against women, updating General Recommendation No. 19; General Recommendation No. 34 (2016) on the rights of rural women; General Recommendation No. 33 (2015) on women's access to justice; General Recommendation No. 30 (2013) on women in the prevention of conflicts and in situations of conflict and post-conflict; General Recommendation No. 27 (2010) on elder women and the protection of their human rights; and the resolutions that are specific to women's issues: the Resolution 49/7 "Indigenous women: beyond the ten-year review of the Beijing Declaration and Platform for Action" (2005); and the Resolution 56/4 "Indigenous women: key actors in poverty and hunger eradication" (2012).
[33] Convention 169 on indigenous and tribal peoples in independent countries. Part III Hiring and Conditions of Employment, Art. 20 (3) (d).
[34] Vid. C-01076-2012-00021 OF.2°. Tribunal Primero de Sentencia Penal, Narcoactividad y Delitos Contra el Ambiente. Guatemala, 25 February 2016.

which such processes impact gender relations, or how the effects of racial discrimination[35] are when there is a presence of other intersections.

In addition, the CEDAW preamble affirms other elements that would subsequently appear central to the construction of the International Law of Indigenous Peoples: the realization of the right of the peoples subject to colonial and foreign domination or foreign occupation to self-determination and self-determination. independence. This, following the precepts on the self-determination of the peoples contained in the Charter of the United Nations of 1945 and reaffirmed in Article 1 of both the International Covenant on Civil and Political Rights, as well as in the International Covenant on Economic, Social and Cultural[36].

The above, without forgetting a conceptual precision on this right, which is the reference to the permanent virtuality that has the right to self-determination of peoples, since it does not end with the initial exercise done to obtain the free political determination, taking into account that many countries that no longer suffer from colonialism in its classic and traditional sense continue to suffer because of neocolonialism and imperialism in its various forms[37].

The recognition of women's rights as human rights was transcendentally reinforced in the Vienna Declaration and Program of Action, adopted after the World Conference on Human Rights held in Vienna in 1993, affirming that they are an inalienable, integral and indivisible part of universal human rights; in addition to having highlighted the intrinsic dignity and incomparable contribution of Indigenous Peoples[38] to the development and pluralism of society[39].

The Fourth World Conference on Women, held in Beijing in 1995[40], in which 189 Member States of the UN participated, having unanimously adopted the Beijing Declaration and Platform for Action, which is the main global policy document on equality of since then, was a watershed for the participation of indigenous women

---

[35] According to the article 1 (1) of the International Convention on the Elimination of All Forms of Racial Discrimination: "In this Convention, the term "racial discrimination" shall mean any distinction, exclusion, restriction or preference based on race, colour, descent, or national or ethnic origin which has the purpose or effect of nullifying or impairing the recognition, enjoyment or exercise, on an equal footing, of human rights and fundamental freedoms in the political, economic, social, cultural or any other field of public life".

[36] Both pacts were adopted by the General Assembly in 1966, and are in force since 1976.

[37] UN, The right to self-determination. Implementation of the resolutions of the United Nations. Study prepared by Héctor Gros Espiell, Special Rapporteur of the Subcommission on Prevention of Discrimination and Protection of Minorities. New York, 1979.

[38] Mentioned as Indigenous People in the document, and not as Indigenous Peoples, which is the agreed concept adopted in the ILO 169 Convention.

[39] Vienna Declaration and Programme of Action, adopted by the World Conference on Human Rights in Vienna, 1993. Paragraphs 18 and 20. 1993 was also the International Year of the World's Indigenous People.

[40] This conference was preceded by three other world conferences on women, which set a precedent for the political agreements agreed upon in the Beijing Platform for Action: the World Conference of the International Women's Year: Mexico City (19 June to 2 July 1975) , with the participation of 133 states; the World Conference of the United Nations Decade for Women: Equality, Development and Peace: Copenhagen (14 to 30 July 1980), with the participation of 145 states; and the World Conference to review and appraise the achievements of the United Nations Decade for Women: Equality, Development and Peace: Nairobi (15 to 26 July 1985), with the participation of 157 states.

globally. On this occasion they presented the Declaration of the Indigenous Women of the World in Beijing[41], where the collective actions proposed by indigenous women for sustainable development are articulated, a term that had previously been coined at the Summit on Sustainable Development in Rio de Janeiro, Brazil, in 1992, when Indigenous Peoples also presented their positions through the Kari-Oca Declaration[42] and the Earth Charter of Indigenous Peoples[43].

One of the main aspects highlighted by indigenous women in the Beijing document is the intersectional discrimination and violence historically suffered by them[44], their active role in defending the right to self-determination and the right to their territories, as well as the need to incorporate the term Indigenous Peoples in all documents, declarations and conventions of the United Nations.

On the other hand, they highlight the prevailing extractivism of natural resources in their territories and the appropriation of their knowledge by transnational corporations, all linked to the emergence of free trade agreements, in a moment of an accelerated global opening towards neoliberalism. These practices are considered as ethnocidal and genocidal policies, intrinsically linked to models of monocultural economic growth and opposed to the territorial rights of Indigenous Peoples, as well as to the non-economic activities of indigenous women that allow the survival of Indigenous Peoples.

---

[41] Beijing Declaration of Indigenous Women, NGO Forum, UN Fourth World Conference on Women Huairou, 1995. Beijing, Peoples Republic of China.

[42] Kari-Oca Declaration, World Conference of Indigenous Peoples on Territory, Environment and Development, 1992, Kari-Oca, Brazil. La noción sobre desarrollo sostenible desde la perspectiva de los pueblos indígenas se evoca en la siguiente frase: "We, the Indigenous Peoples, walk to the future in the footprints of our ancestors".

[43] Indigenous Peoples Earth Charter, Kari-Oca Conference, 1992, Kari-Oca, Brazil. Paragraph 64 of the Charter makes an important reflection that will be present in subsequent documents on sustainable development, including the 2030 Agenda: "Any development strategy should prioritize the elimination of poverty, the climatic guarantee, the sustainable manageability of natural resources, the continuity of democratic societies and the respect of cultural differences ". This approach to a new form of development is used as a criticism of the development models then in force, whose adverse effects for Indigenous Peoples are denounced in paragraph 66 of the letter "The concept of development has meant the destruction of our lands. We reject the current definition of development as being useful to our peoples. Our cultures are not static and we keep our identity through a permanent recreation of our life conditions; but all of this is obstructed in the name of so called developments."

[44] *Op.Cit.* Beijing Declaration of Indigenous Women,1995. Formas de violencia especialmente relevantes para las mujeres indígenas son denunciadas en el documento, como es el caso de las esterilizaciones forzadas, que pueden ser entendidas como crimen de lesa humanidad. Párr. 33: "Demand for an investigation of the forcible mass sterilization and anti-fertility programs done among Indigenous women. Identify which international and national agencies are responsible for these and make them accountable". La violencia hacia las mujeres indígenas como resultado de modelos de desarrollo que no consideran los derechos de los Pueblos Indígenas se resalta en el Párr. 14: "The violence and sexual trafficking of Indigenous women and the increasing numbers of Indigenous women becoming labor exports, has been aggravated by the perpetuation of an economic growth development model which is export- oriented, import-dependent, and mired in foreign debt. Military operations conducted on Indigenous peoples lands use rape, sexualslavery, and sexual trafficking of Indigenous women, to further subjugate Indigenous peoples. The development of tourism to attract foreign capital has also led to the commodification of Indigenous women and the dramatic increase in the incidence of HIV/AIDS. This reality is not addressed by the Platform. Domestic violence and the increasing suicide rates among Indigenous women, especially those who are in highly industrialized countries are caused by psychological alienation and assimilationist policies characteristic of these countries".

One of the current forms of economic colonialism denounced in the Declaration of Kari-Oca II in the framework of the Rio + 20 Earth Summit in 2012 by the Indigenous Peoples is the "Green Economy", which due to its devastating effects on nature , derived from the perpetuation of capitalist extractivism with ideas such as "sustainable mining" or "ethical oil", intensifies the violations of the rights of Indigenous Peoples, especially collective rights such as self-determination, land and territory, traditional knowledge and natural resources, in addition to the right to life and physical integrity of indigenous human rights defenders[45].

In the Beijing Declaration, as well as in the Platform for Action, based on 12 areas of special concern[46], some of the demands of indigenous women, which had been conceived since the beginning of the process of several decades of deliberation on the rights of women within the United Nations, as well as discussions on the rights of Indigenous Peoples, were incorporated.

Such efforts by the indigenous women's movement at the global level were reflected in the United Nations Declaration on the Rights of Indigenous Peoples, adopted in 2007 by the General Assembly after approximately 25 years of deliberation[47], in which mention of the special monitoring of the needs and rights of indigenous women are made in Articles 21, 22 and 44, mainstreaming the gender approach in the implementation of all the provisions contained in the document.

After 37 years of CEDAW's entry into force, whose implementation has been reinforced and accompanied by multiple efforts at the global level, disparities persist in the enjoyment of rights for many women, as is the case of the approximately 185 million indigenous women around the world, a number that represents 50% of the total number

---

[45] Kari-Oca II Declaration "Indigenous Peoples Global Conference on Rio+20 and Mother Earth". Rio de Janeiro, Brazil, 2012.

[46] Beijing Declaration and Platform for Action, 1995, United Nations. In the Declaration, there is only one mention related to indigenous women in the paragraph 32: "Intensify efforts to ensure equal enjoyment of all human rights and fundamental freedoms for all women and girls who face multiple barriers to their empowerment and advancement because of such factors as their race, age, language, ethnicity, culture, religion, or disability, or because they are indigenous people". The Platform of Action, based on 12 critical áreas of concern (1.-Women and Poverty; 2.-Education and Training of Women; 3.-Women and Health; 4.-Violence against Women; 5.-Women and Armed Conflict; 6.-Women and the Economy; 7.-Women in Power and Decision-making; 8.-Institutional Mechanism for the Advancement of Women; 9.-Human Rights of Women; 10.-Women and the Media; 11.-Women and the Environment; 12.-The Girl-child), refers to indigenous women in several Strategic Objectives and Actions, considering them as one of the groups of women that are the most disadvantaged, requiring special attention.

[47] The long journey covers since the Economic and Social Council established in 1982 the Working Group on Indigenous Populations, which had among its functions since 1985 the preparation of the first draft of the Declaration, presented in 1993 to the Subcommission on Prevention of Discrimination and Protection of Minorities, which in 1971 commissioned the preparation of a study on the forms of discrimination against the so-called indigenous populations, which was finally published under the title "Study of the Problem of Discrimination Against Indigenous Populations", known as Martínez Cobo Study, in relation to the name of the Special Rapporteur of the Subcommittee responsible for the study, José Ricardo Martínez Cobo, and which was presented in three chapters between 1982 and 1984, one per year. For its part, the first draft of the Declaration was adopted by the Subcommittee in 1994, and submitted to the Human Rights Commission, which established the Working Group on the draft declaration in 1995, which aimed to review the document, having prolonged the discussions until 2006, when it was approved by the Human Rights Council, an organism that replaced the Human Rights Commission that same year.

of people belonging to Indigenous Peoples, and whose specific needs are invisible, to a large extent, as a result of discriminatory treatment both outside and within their communities, which accompanies their trajectories of life, a situation that has a symbolic reflection in the lack of representation in statistics, which in turn derives in the absence of public policies and programs adapted to the achievement of their specific rights.

Likewise, it is linked to the still insufficient participation of indigenous women in decision-making, which to be valid must be based on key principles of human rights on individual autonomy and self-determination as part of basic human dignity, linked intimately to the rights of freedom of expression and information, the freedom of association and assembly and the right to participate in cultural life[48]. This follows the words of indigenous women at the Global Conference of Indigenous Women 2013, "Nothing about us, without us", and "Everything about us, with us", referring to the right to self-determination, which comprehends direct participation, full and effective of Indigenous Peoples, always bearing in mind the voice of indigenous women in all matters related to their human rights, political condition, and well-being[49].

This was one of the commitments made by the representatives of the states that participated in the high-level plenary meeting of the General Assembly of the United Nations in 2014, known as the World Conference on Indigenous Peoples, as well as having expressed their support to achieve the empowerment of indigenous women and their organizations through the formulation and implementation of policies and programs aimed at promoting capacity-building and strengthening their leadership.

The recognition of alliances for the social fabric of common efforts towards sustainable development in the Agenda 21 of 1992 was crucial to highlight the importance of active participation in the decision-making on the development of both women, through the Women's Major Group, as well as Indigenous Peoples, through the Indigenous Peoples Major Group, providing substantial elements for the implementation of the rights of both groups, affirming also the unique contributions of indigenous women and the importance of reinforcing their role in development sustainable. These groups have continued their work since then, being crucial in the implementation of the 2030 Agenda.

A necessary detail about the participation of women is the reference in the Report of the International Conference on Population and Development of 1994, held in Cairo[50],

---

[48] FAO, *Consentimiento libre, previo e informado. Un derecho de los Pueblos Indígenas y una buena práctica para las comunidades locales. Manual dirigido a los profesionales en el terreno*. Roma: FAO, AECID, IFRC, WVI, AA, ACF, GiZ, 2016.
[49] Declaración de Lima ¡Mujeres Indígenas Hacia la Visibilidad e Inclusión!. Conferencia Global de Mujeres Indígenas, Avances y desafíos frente al futuro que queremos. Lima, Perú, 2013.
[50] UN Report of the International Conference on Population and Development. Cairo, 1994. A / CONF.171 / 13 / Rev.1. New York, 1995. ISBN 92-1-351116-7. The report includes the following definitions on reproductive health and sexual health (Chapter VII, Reproductive Rights and Reproductive Health): "Reproductive health is a general state of physical, mental and social well-being, and not merely the absence of diseases or ailments, all aspects related to the reproductive system and its functions and processes. Consequently, reproductive health implies the ability to enjoy a satisfying and risk-free sexual life and to procreate, and the freedom to decide whether or not to do it, when and how often "; "It includes [reproductive health] also sexual health, whose objective is the development of life and personal

about the need for equal participation with men in productive and reproductive life, taking into account the division of responsibilities in terms of raising children and maintaining the home. In the case of indigenous women, participation in productive activities related to their collective rights to land and territory is of particular relevance; and in reproductive activities, making decisions related to sexual and reproductive health, as well as community and family division of care tasks.

A significant premise in the analysis of social contexts is the fact that, what is not stated, does not exist, so visibility is crucial for indigenous women, and some significant steps have been achieved in the 2030 Agenda in this regard, a result of the tireless work of indigenous women's movements to position their demands at all levels of incidence.

III.3 Indigenous Women in the Implementation of the Sustainable Development Goals

Women, in all the diversity they represent around the world, contribute daily and substantially to the maintenance of society, through the various tasks they perform, and many of which are interpreted as part of the actions to achieve sustainable development, whose bases are contained in the 2030 Agenda on three pillars of sustainability: economic, social and environmental. The Agenda represents an important framework of action for the achievement of the rights of Indigenous Peoples, and significantly for indigenous women since an effort to address the SDGs from an unprecedented gender perspective has been made.

When we talk about sustainability, we are not talking about anything other than the sustainability of life, which must dialogue with the criteria of human rights, in accordance with the spirit of the Rio Declaration on Environment and Development of 1992, which establishes that "The right to development must be fulfilled so as to equitably meet developmental and environmental needs of present and future generations"[51], a document that also recognizes the fundamental role of women and Indigenous Peoples in the

---

relationships and not merely counseling and care in terms of reproduction and sexually transmitted diseases."

[51] Rio Declaration on Environment and Development, 1992. A/CONF.151/26 (Vol. I). Principle 3. This definition of sustainable development follows the one reflected in the Report of the World Commission on Environment and Development: Our Common Future, publicated by the World Commission on Environment and Development (WCED) in 1987, commonly known as Brundtland Report, which indicates that "Sustainable development is development that meets the needs of the present without compromising the ability of future generations to meet their own needs" (Chapter 2: Towards Sustainable Development. I. The Concept of Sustainable Development). The Brundtland Report also addresses to some relevant ideas related to Indigenous Peoples that were further developed through the consolidation of the sustainable development concept and the role of Indigenous Peoples to achieve it: "Sustainability requires views of human needs and well-being that incorporate such non-economic variables as education and health enjoyed for their own sake, clean air and water, and the protection of natural beauty. It must also work to remove disabilities from disadvantaged groups, many of whom live in ecologically vulnerable areas, such as many tribal groups in forests, desert nomads, groups in remote hill areas, and indigenous peoples of the Americas and Australasia"; as well as a statement made in a WCED Public Hearing in 1986 by Louis Bruyere, President od the Native Council of Canada, which approaches to several indigenous peoples concerns such as the need of consultation over the development projects on their lands and territories (Chapter 2: Towards Sustainable Development. III. Strategic Imperatives)

management of the environment and in development, g¡being their full participation a requirement to achieve sustainable development[52]. For its part, the Convention on Biological Diversity, also presented at the Rio Summit in 1992, recognizes the vital role that women play in the conservation and sustainable use of biological diversity, as well as the value in this respect of knowledge, innovations, and practices of Indigenous Peoples[53].

Therefore, it is necessary to value the knowledge of indigenous women in this continuity of life: as women who cultivate the land and safeguard the biocultural heritage, women who heal, women who keep alive the languages of their people and give renewed continuity to ancestral knowledge, women who rebuild the social fabric sometimes devastated by conflicts and who demand justice; among other accomplishments that, being crossed by the own experiences of the women with an indigenous identity and a strong communitarian sense, constitute an invaluable contribution for the world if we recognize the cultural diversity as one of the pillars for this continuity of the life, being this one of the sources of sustainable development, as expressed in the Universal Declaration of UNESCO on Cultural Diversity of 2001.

The SDGs address a much broader treatment of the gender perspective than the MDGs, which had significant shortcomings in this regard despite having two MDGs directly related to women's rights: MDG 3 "Promoting equality among genders and women's empowerment" and MDG 5 "Improve maternal health ". In this regard, the "agreed conclusions"[54] adopted by the CSW at the end of its fifty-eighth session[55], which represent the first assessment of each of the MDG targets from a gender perspective and which established the bases for women's rights to be reflected in the 2030 Agenda, highlight the limited compliance with the MDGs, denoting special difficulties in the case of indigenous women and girls.

It is stated that the meager improvements that the MDGs represent for the implementation of women's rights are largely related to the fact that the gender perspective was not systematically integrated into the design, application, supervision, and evaluation of the Goals, having had important faults in the breakdown, based on pertinent factors, indicators, statistics, and gender data. To address such lags in achieving the MDGs, the CSW evaluation emphasized the need for gender equality, the empowerment of women, and the human rights of women and girls to be considered as one only goal to incorporate by targets and indicators in all the goals of any new development framework that is prepared, a premise that was reflected in the 2030 Agenda

---

[52] *Op. Cit.* Principles 20 and 22.

[53] UN. Convention in Biological Diversity, 1992. According to the article 2 of this document: "Biological diversity" means the variability among living organisms from all sources including, inter alia, terrestrial, marine and other aquatic ecosystems and the ecological complexes of which they are part: this includes diversity within species, between species and of ecosystems.

[54] Emphasis added in the original document.

[55] 58th session (10-21 March 2014). Agreed conclusions: Challenges and achievements in the implementation of the Millennium Development Goals for women and girls. E/2014/27. This document was elaborated previous to the MDG deadline. Nevertheless, the final outcomes of the MDG were not outstanding regarding to women's rights.

through its 17 SDGs and 169 targets, all of which are integrated and are indivisible, and most of which are gender sensitive.

Meanwhile, the global indicator framework was adopted by the General Assembly of the United Nations through the Resolution on "Work of the Statistical Commission pertaining to the 2030 Agenda for Sustainable Development"[56], where the indicators contained therein are susceptible to being refined annually, as is the case of the adjustments made by the Statistical Commission in 2018[57], and which will be reviewed in full in 2020 during the 51st session of the Statistical Commission, as well as in 2025 at its 56th session. It is indicated in the aforementioned Resolution that, when relevant, the indicators should be disaggregated, among other categories, by income, sex, race, ethnicity, immigration status, disability, and geographic location.

In total, there are 232 individual indicators that have been agreed, of which nine are repeated in two or three different targets[58], giving a total list of 244 indicators, which were developed by the Inter-Agency and Expert Group on Sustainable Development Goal Indicators (IAEG-SDGs), and that are complemented with indicators developed by the member states at the national and regional levels, which opens a window of opportunity for the generation of pertinent indicators for the issues that concern indigenous women.

The 2018 UN Women report on the 2030 Agenda[59], shows that there are 54 of 232 indicators for women and girls, 14 of which correspond to the SDG 5. Similarly, it registers that the indicator framework is gender-sensitive in 6 of the 17 SDGs (SDG 1, 3, 4, 5, 8 and 16), but highlighting the lack of clarity regarding gender in other crucial areas (SDG 2, 10, 11, 13 and 17), as well as an absence of gender issues in the rest (SDG 6, 7, 9, 12, 14 and 15). Among the most noteworthy aspects is the approach to domestic work and unpaid care and violence against women and girls, which are problems incorporated in a new way in global monitoring initiatives.

Regarding the approximation to the rights of Indigenous Peoples, it should be stated that they have significant relevance in the 17 SDG, despite having only 6 explicit mentions in the Agenda, which, although are few in comparison with the initial proposals of the Indigenous Peoples, might be observed as a relevant gain taking into account that no mention was made in the Millennium Declaration, and that it ultimately led to the absence of disaggregated data relevant to Indigenous Peoples at the time of the implementation of the MDGs.

According to the "Update on Indigenous People and the 2030 Agenda" of 2017 of the Permanent Forum on Indigenous Issues[60], of the 169 targets, 73 are directly related to

---

[56] Resolution adopted by the General Assembly on 6 July 2017 "Work of the Statistical Commission pertaining to the 2030 Agenda for Sustainable Development". A/RES/71/313
[57] ECOSOC. Report of the Inter-Agency and Expert Group on Sustainable Development Goal Indicators. 2017. Statistical Commission. E/CN.3/2018/2
[58] The repeated indicators are: 8.4.1/12.2.1; 8.4.2/12.2.2; 10.3.1/16.b.1; 10.6.1/16.8.1; 15.7.1/15.c.1; 15.a.1/15.b.1; 1.5.1/11.5.1/13.1.1; 1.5.3/11.b.1/13.1.2; 1.5.4/11.b.2/13.1.3.
[59] *Op. Cit.*
[60] Update on indigenous peoples and the 2030 Agenda. Permanent Forum on Indigenous Issues. Economic and Social Council, 2017. E/C.19/2017/5

the rights contained in the United Nations Declaration on the Rights of Indigenous Peoples although not all of them mention Indigenous Peoples, and 156 are closely related to human rights, denoting that connection can also be made between indicators and the specific rights of Indigenous Peoples. However, it is alarming that, of the 232 indicators for the 17 SDGs, only 4 explicitly mention Indigenous Peoples, in addition to the fact that the Agenda does not reflect fundamental collective rights such as the right to self-determined development, and the right to free, prior and informed consent.

The SDG 2 "Ending hunger" and the SDG 5 "Gender equality and empowerment of women and girls" are the SDGs that have specific indicators for Indigenous Peoples and that are raised from a gender perspective, being relevant the fact that they are particularly aligned with the two specific Resolutions on indigenous women adopted within the CSW[61], highlighting that in the case of Resolution 56/4, the value of the knowledge and roles of indigenous women in the eradication of poverty is highlighted, as well as in sustainable development and the conservation of biodiversity and natural resources, which are very relevant contributions to face the worrying panorama of incremental feminization of poverty.

The follow-up and review of the implementation of the SDGs is carried out by the High Level Political Forum on Sustainable Development (HLPF), under the auspices of the General Assembly and the Economic and Social Council of the United Nations, through Annual meetings in which evaluations of a set of SDGs are carried out, being only SDG 17 of mandatory revision. During the HLPF, the presentation of voluntary reports by the countries is expected. The participation of civil society in the HLPF is carried out through the nine major groups[62] that were created at the Rio de Janeiro Conference in 1992, among which the Women's Major Group and the Indigenous Peoples Major Group stand out as main platforms for the participation of indigenous women.

One of the controversial aspects of the 2030 Agenda, which directly affects the possibility of fulfilling the rights of indigenous women, is that it does not include any independent goal or specific targets on the regulation of the private sector, and that the language of the Agenda reinforces the idea that there are automatic positive synergies between the activities of the private sector and development, noting the special risk represent those that do not have adequate fiscal regulation[63], or whose practices are based on the plundering of land and natural resources of Indigenous Peoples, largely with the acquiescence of the states.

On the other hand, a pressing problem in the implementation, follow-up, and review of SDGs is the lack of disaggregated data by gender as well as pertinent criteria for Indigenous Peoples, which is reflected in the reports that have been produced up to now

---

[61] *Op. Cit.*

[62] The oficial nine Major Groups focus on the following sectors of society: Women, Children and Youth, Indigenous Peoples, Non-Governmental Organizations, Local Authorities, Workers and Trade Unions, Business and Industry, Scientific and Technological Community, and Farmers.

[63] C. Rodríguez, 'Corporate power: a risky threat looming over the fulfilment of women's human rights', in *Spotlight on Sustainable Development 2017. Reclaiming policies for the public. Report by the Civil Society Reflection Group on the 2030 Agenda for Sustainable Development*, at 64 – 68.

in this regard, referring disparities in the collection of relevant data in the countries, with significant global lags. Indigenous Peoples can contribute to this work providing data generated through their organizations, such as, for example, what is already being collected through the Indigenous Navigator, which is an online platform dedicated to providing tools for the evaluation of the realization of the rights of Indigenous Peoples[64].

In this sense, addressing progress towards achieving the SDGs of the 2030 Agenda based on actions aimed at meeting the needs of indigenous women, as well as their participation in these processes, not only fulfills a discursive function but also of appropriation of processes by indigenous women. Since the 2030 Agenda is of voluntary attainment for states, and gives an important role to the private sector, whose actions are most often contrary to human rights, the participation of indigenous women as active subjects of civil society becomes a central axis in the fulfillment of the SDGs, in accordance with the implementation of the rights of Indigenous Peoples in general, and of indigenous women in particular.

---

[64] The Indigenous Navigator is available online (http://nav.indigenousnavigator.com) and is a collaborative initiative realised with the support of the European Union by a consortium of seven partners: Asia Indigenous Peoples Pact (AIPP); Forest Peoples Programme (FPP); International Labour Organization (ILO); International Work Group on Indigenous Affairs (IWGIA); Tebtebba Foundation; The Danish Institute for Human Rights; and Indigenous Peoples Major Group for Sustainable Development.

Chapter 6

SDGs AND PUBLIC POLICIES

H.E.MR. MARCO A. SUAZO
Head of UNITAR New York Office

&

ADITYA KANKIPATI
Researcher

* * *

I.   INTRODUCTION

Public policy is the set of government actions, whether it be legislation or regulation, that aims to address the concerns of government entities or constituents of a nation. The 2030 Agenda for Sustainable Development, more commonly known as the Sustainable Development Goals (SDGs), is a collectively envisioned path towards sustainable development created by the governments of the world, to help move our planet live a more sustainable way of life. It is possibly the biggest, and most ambitious public policy effort for sustainable development ever attempted. However, while it is good to think about the benefits of sustainable development, without implementation it is just a fantasy. National governments must make an effort to implement the goals into national public policy. Even if national governments are able to do this, the subnational levels of government (state, local etc.) must shoulder responsibility to ensure implementation by creating public policy that embodies the aim of the Sustainable Development Goals, whilst fulfilling the needs of their constituents.

For there to be effective implementation of the 2030 Agenda into public policy, a variety of factors must be considered by the governments of nations. Firstly, implementation of the 2030 Agenda must be incorporated into all relevant national frameworks so that future legislations and policies can be created with an SDG-focused lens[1]. Governments also must consider integrating the SDGs into the national budgetary processes, to maximize "all available domestic resources to achieve the best possible results"[2]. National governments have the power, and therefore the responsibility to pursue implement of the goals into public policy. However, implementation may require national governance reform to remove structural challenges, from tackling corruption, to creating or strengthening institutions of government[3]. Additionally, governments need to create measurable outcomes, with clear data-gathering and verification of the implemented policies[4]. All parties must be involved in the creation of this monitoring and feedback system and have open access to it.

Secondly, implementation cannot be centralized to just the national level of government. Effective SDG implementation can only be done through the integration of policy between all levels of government and must decentralize SDG implementation to subnational levels of government (state, local etc.). This will allow the subnational levels of government to lead more locally-specific policies and service quality improvements[5] (Global Centre for Public Service and Excellence, 3). Furthermore, decentralization of power will allow the context of reform to continue to prioritize local interests and prevent possible failure and delay of implementation.

Thirdly, government institutions must leverage collaborative leadership skills to make implementation of the Sustainable Development Goals at a local level "a multi-stakeholder process" that can effectively engage non-governmental partners "including the representatives of civil society, businesses, academia and science, for collective problem-solving"[6]. While governments at all levels may have the power to initiate and enact these policies, advocacy from non-governmental actors can also "influence public policy through education, lobbying, or political pressure"[7] (Dean G. Kilpatrick). Advocacy has the ability to bring attention to pertinent issues and educate policy makers and the public. This can create a more grassroots movement towards awareness and help the public move towards a more sustainable lifestyle, alongside the legislation and policies created by governments.

Despite the 2030 Agenda being internationally agreed, countries still face major challenges in achieving the 2030 Agenda. Countries are prioritizing which goals to address, instead of attempting to tackle the goals simultaneously. While high-income nations are close to completely addressing the social and economic goals, such as eradicating extreme poverty and hunger, these countries are scoring very low on goals

---

[1] United Nations Department of Economic and Social Affairs (DESA), "Handbook For The Preparation Of Voluntary National Reviews: The 2019 Edition", October 2018, 24
[2] Inter-Parliamentary Union and UNDP, *Parliaments and the Sustainable Development Goals*, 2016, 11
[3] Global Centre for Public Service Excellence and UNDP, *SDG Implementation Framework: Effective public service for SDG implementation*, , 3
[4] Global Centre for Public Service Excellence and UNDP, *SDG Implementation Framework: Effective public service for SDG implementation*, , 4
[5] Global Centre for Public Service Excellence and UNDP, *SDG Implementation Framework: Effective public service for SDG implementation*, , 3
[6] Global Centre for Public Service Excellence and UNDP, *SDG Implementation Framework: Effective public service for SDG implementation*, , 2
[7] Dean G. Kilpatrick, *Definitions of Public Policy and the Law*, 2015

concerning the environment, but have the resources to, in theory, achieve all the goals. However, poorer countries don't have the resources nor the infrastructure to tackle certain goals, particularly those that pertain to the environment.

The Sustainable Development Goals can be grouped into broad themes and for the purpose of this chapter, three themes have been selected: 1) education, 2) eradicating poverty, 3) human rights and inclusive societies. Multiple countries will used as case studies to what strategies, initiatives, and programs each are implementing to address the three themes. To see what each country is doing, the Voluntary National Reviews (VNR) is the primary source of information. The aim of the VNRs is to facilitate the sharing of experiences, including successes, challenges and lessons learned, with a view to accelerating the implementation of the 2030 Agenda. The VNRs also seek to strengthen policies and institutions of governments and to mobilize multi-stakeholder support and partnerships for the implementation of the Sustainable Development Goals.

The theme of education only pertains to SDG 4 Quality Education. SDG 4 is comprehensive in its approach to education, trying to guarantee accessibility to quality education to all demographics. SDG 4 intersects with a lot of the other Sustainable Development Goals, particularly those concerning human rights.

II.   AUSTRALIA

The VNR on Australia was produced in 2018. The Australian Government has made education a multi-stakeholder process, working with state and territory governments, as well as the education sector and civil society. Australia provides universal access to preschool, primary and secondary education, with school attendance compulsory until the age of 16. The Government has created a large number of policies aiming to increase quality and access to education for all, which includes building lifelong learning opportunities and supporting workforce participation and prosperity for all, ensuring no one is left behind. All schools in Australia have computer and internet access, and are adapted for students with disabilities. The Government aids eligible students pursue higher education through loan provisions and the subsidisation of eligible higher education places. The system allows graduates to earn a threshold salary before paying off the financial aid, to reduce the financial burden at a crucial time for young adults.

The Australian Government has created initiatives to fund target students and disadvantaged schools, such as students with disabilities. All levels of government work with civil society organisations (CSOs) to provide additional support where needed. For example, the Smith Family's Learning for Life program, funded by the Australian Government, hopes to support around 56,200 disadvantaged students by 2020 to achieve improved educational and post-school outcomes. The Australian government is also trying to guarantee access to quality education to those in rural and remote communities, particularly Aboriginal and Torres Strait Islander populations. The Rural and Regional

Enterprise Scholarships is one national effort to improve education opportunities for students in rural and remote areas. The Government provides support students from regional and remote areas to undertake STEM (Science, Technology, Engineering and Mathematics), agriculture and health courses. Other programs aim to improve the provision of essential infrastructure such as computers, printers and internet access points to improve internet literacy and educational outcomes for both children and adults.

Vocational training is also addressed, with industry taking a central role in designing and delivering training to ensure it meets employer and community needs. All levels of government support inclusive and equitable access through subsidies, programs and a student loan scheme. There is a broad range of community institutions, which provide and promote lifelong learning and adult and community education, delivering foundation skills training. For example, the South Australian Government, through its Office for Women, works with TAFE SA to offer vocational courses for women from diverse backgrounds, to gain knowledge, confidence and skills for employment and further studies. Informal learning programs are available through institutions like community libraries.

Many Australian schools and universities have implemented sustainability programs to teach children and young people about resource sustainability and to improve resource management within their institutions. Sustainability is one of three national cross-curriculum priorities and has been incorporated in programs like ResourceSmart Schools in Victoria. Many Australian universities are actively incorporating the SDGs into their curricula and student activities, including institutions that have signed up to the Principles for Responsible Management Education, which is working to embed the SDGs into management education.

III.   BAHAMAS

The VNR on The Bahamas was produced in July 2018. The Government of the Bahamas believes that a well-educated country can increase research and innovation capacity, leading to greater productivity and attracting new, higher value-added investments. To this end, the Government has committed to investing in human capital through education and training. Education is compulsory for children between the ages of 5 and 16, and the nation's public-school system provides tuition free education. Currently, education expenditure is approximately 13% of the national budget, with the Department of Education expecting a budget increase for the next biennial period ($205.6 million in 2018/2019, to $247.4 million in 2020/2021). In their efforts to ensure quality education for all, the Government established a Student Achievement Unit in August 2014, with the aim of bringing equity and efficacy to the education system. The Unit collects and analyses data to guide educational interventions where deficiencies in subject areas in schools are identified. The Unit also tracks every student to ensure that necessary intervention and support is given to address the challenges each faces.

The Government has also created programmes for At Risk Students, one of these being 'Providing Access to Continued Education' (PACE), coordinated by the Department of Health in collaboration with the Ministry of Education, Science and Technology (MOEST). PACE is designed to help first-time teenage mothers complete high school, thereby giving them a better chance of breaking the cycle of poverty. MOEST has also mandated that technical and vocational education should be prioritized to help meet the nation's development needs. The Government has allocated $2.6 million for scholarships to The Bahamas Technical and Vocational Institute (BTVI), and increasing BTVI's 2018/2019 budget with an extra $600,000. Learning for Adults with Developmental Disabilities has also been addressed by the Government, with the establishment of a Multi-Service Centre for Adults with Developmental Disabilities in Nassau in February 2016. The facility provides a safe and nurturing environment for such adults, in the attempt to provide opportunities for training and development of people in the facility.

The Government have found some challenges in trying to implement programmes on education. There is challenge for continue sustainable funding for education and training at all levels, particularly for early childhood education and vocational training. Another challenge is an equal distribution of the mechanisms to ensure equity in education. They also identified educational outcome gaps between boy and girls between private school and public-school students, and bridging this gap is a challenge.

IV.   MEXICO

The VNR on Mexico was produced in 2018. The Mexican Government have taken steps to ensure that there is access to child development services, improvement in the physical infrastructure of educational facilities, a guaranteed quality education, particularly for vulnerable populations, and integrate the education system with the demands of the labor market. One of the most recent and comprehensive strategies created by the government is the New Educational Model, launched in 2017. The model is structured around five axes: curricular planning, schools at the centre of the educational model, teacher training, inclusion and equity and governance of the education system. To have greater integration of ICT into education, Secretaría de Educación Pública (SEP) (Secretariat of Public Education) has created the Digital Inclusion Program, part of the Learning 2.0 strategy, that aims "to develop digital skills and computational thinking of students and teaching staff". Another strategy from SEP is the Schools at the Centre Strategy, which has the goal of improving the quality of education. The Schools at ONE HUNDRED PERCENT Program, operated by the National Educational Infrastructure Institute (INIFED), has improved the physical infrastructure of more than 33,000 educational facilities across the country. SEP's Full Time Schools Program looks to increase human capital through maximizing academic, athletic and cultural development. To ensure quality teaching, Instituto Nacional para la Evaluación de la Educación (INEE) has a Professional Teaching Service that guarantees teachers have the proper knowledge and skills.

However, there are challenges that have presented themselves in this pursuit for more inclusive and equitable education. One of these challenges is incorporating children and adolescents of marginalized communities into the education system, such as those with special needs, indigenous or Afro-Mexican communities, and those who live in isolated areas. Another is increasing the supply of quality education, particularly in high schools and at the college level, and reducing the dropout rate.

One commonality in the VNRs that have been looked at is that very few of them talk about educating people on the Sustainable Development Goals. As a leading provider of high-quality learning solutions and other knowledge products and services, the United Nations Institute for Training and Research (UNITAR) is deeply committed to helping Member States and other United Nations stakeholders implement the 2030 Agenda. . UNITAR is committed to educating people on the Sustainable Development Goals, as shown with its 'Introduction to the 2030 Agenda for Sustainable Development' e-course. This could be of use to nations as to how to structure potential educational courses on the 2030 Agenda.

The second theme of Eradicating poverty can be applied to any public policy addressing SDG 1 No poverty, SDG 2 Zero Hunger, SDG 6 Clean Water and Sanitation, and SDG 7 Affordable and Clean Energy. The reason for including SDG 6 Clean Water and Sanitation and SDG 7 Affordable and Clean Energy is that studies have found a correlation between poverty and the two respectively. The World Bank has found a lack of access to clean water and sanitation holds people back from moving out of poverty, whilst also compromising health due to water-related diseases[8]. Additionally, UN officials have said having access to affordable and clean energy can not only help mitigate environmental damage, but also aid in eradicating poverty through increased development[9].

V.   NIGERIA

The VNR on Nigeria was produced in June 2017. Eradicating poverty is an area of major focus for the Government of Nigeria, given the country has a poverty profile of 62.6 percent. All levels of government are pursuing strategies to eliminate poverty in Nigeria. The Federal Government created the National Social Investment Programme (NSIP) which provides social safety nets for the poor, welfare for the unemployed, and job creation and skills enhancement with a target of creating about 3 million jobs. NSIP is made up of four components: the first is the N-Power Programme, which is designed

---

[8] The World Bank, *Millions Around the World Held Back by Poor Sanitation and Lack of Access to Clean Water*, 2017

[9] United Nations Departmetnt of Economic and Social Affairs, *Shift to clean, affordable energy critical to attaining Global Goals – UN officials*, 2017

to help young Nigerians gain and develop life-long skills to become solution providers in their communities and players in the domestic and global market. Another is the National Home-Grown School Feeding Programme (NHGSFP) which is increasing the enrolment and completion rate at the primary school level, creating jobs for cooks, and increasing the demand for local agricultural produce, thereby building a community value chain. This particular programme is done in collaboration with state governments, with the Federal Government providing subsidies for the programme and states giving their own investments to increase the pool of beneficiaries. Early findings have found the programme has increased enrolment rates, retention and completion; improved the health of the children; empowered and improved the local economy. The National Cash Transfer Project (NCTP) is another programme within the NSIP, which provides targeted cash transfers to the poor and vulnerable households with the final aim of graduating them out of poverty. The Government Enterprise and Empowerment Programme (GEEP) is another government programme that aims to provide "financial services access to a wide range of actors, from traders, farmers and agricultural workers, to enterprising youth, market women and women cooperatives. Subnational governments are also involved in a variety of ways. One is the 'Unconditional Cash Transfer' programme (UCT), which provides social security allowance for the physically disabled people and the elderly, and empowers people living with disability to earn a living that will eventually get them out of poverty.

Hunger & food insecurity is a constant threat to Nigeria, as in most parts of Sub-Saharan Africa. Severe food insecurity within the population based on the Food Insecurity Experience Scale stood at 26.4% based on data from the National Bureau of Statistics. There are a number of policies to achieve zero hunger: The Green Alternative Agriculture Promotion Policy 2016-2020 was introduced with the objective to achieve self-sufficiency in food production, reduce imports, stimulate exports and create jobs. The Government offers incentives by providing access to land and finance, inputs, storage, processing, marketing and trade. The Rural Finance Institution Building Programme (RUFIN), a US$27.2 million loan agreement between the Nigerian Government and the International Fund of Agricultural Development (IFAD), aims to enhance access of rural populations to basic banking services, thereby developing and strengthening Micro Finance Banks (MFBs), other member-based Micro Finance Institutions (MFIs), leading to the expansion and improvement of agricultural productivity and Micro-Small Rural Enterprises. The Central Bank of Nigeria (CBN) created the Anchor Borrowers' Programme (ABP), designed to lift thousands of small farmers out of poverty and generate millions of jobs for unemployed Nigerians. It is to complement the Growth Enhancement Support (GES) Scheme of the Federal Ministry of Agriculture by graduating GES farmers from subsistence farming to commercial production.

The Nigerian Government has also taken measures to ensure clean water and sanitation. The 2016–2030 Partnership for Expanded Water Supply, Sanitation and Hygiene (PEWASH), launched in November 2016, is a framework for rural water supply that builds upon the National Rural Water Supply and Sanitation Programme which ended in 2015. It is designed to coordinate and complement planned and ongoing projects and programs by all stakeholders in the rural water supply and sanitation sub-sector, including all levels of government; development partners; private sector; and civil society to help Nigeria ensure the availability and sustainable management of water and sanitation for all. The main challenges are lack of services or poor-quality services for the poor in urban and rural areas, mainly in the sanitation and hygiene subsector. Coverage and quality of services vary across the geopolitical zones with water-related deprivations greater in the North, while open defecation is rampant in the Southwest. Furthermore, WASH services insufficiently address the needs of the disabled[10].

VI.   VIETNAM

The VNR on Vietnam was produced in June 2018. The Vietnamese Government have created a system of poverty reduction policies which are relatively comprehensive in terms of content and supported targets. The National Target Program (NTP) on Sustainable Poverty Reduction (NTP-SPR) in 2016-2020 to reduce the number of poor households every year, improve income and living conditions of the poor, has innovative mechanisms to organize its implementation and is more specific on the integration of gender and vulnerable groups than previous programs, and build essential infrastructure to increase the livelihoods of low-income residents[11]. Additionally, the 2011-2020 Development Strategy of the Viet Nam Bank for Social Policies outlines the Government's efforts in defining solutions in order to develop more effective support service products for poor and near-poor households and the beneficiaries of support policies. There is recognition that while the policies are relatively comprehensive, the rate and coverage of support is not high, and the content of support remains fragmented.

The Government has also created policies addressing zero hunger. The National Nutrition Strategy 2011-2020 with a vision to 2030, focuses on improving nutrition for mothers and children. The Government also approved the project "Agricultural restructuring towards improving added value and sustainable development" until 2020. The project aims to develop hi-tech agriculture to enhance the application of science, technology and technical advances to production, develop clean, resilient and climate-smart agriculture. The National Target Program on New Rural Development 2016-2020 is another public policy addressing zero hunger, and aims to build modern socioeconomic infrastructure in new rural areas[12].

---

[10] Federal Republic of Nigeria, Federal Ministry of Water Resources, "Nigeria Overview: Water, Sanitation and Hygiene", 2017, 1

[11] "National Target Programme on Sustainable Poverty Reduction Approved." National Target Programme on Sustainable Poverty Reduction Approved - Nhan Dan Online, 5 Sept. 2016, en.nhandan.org.vn/politics/item/4596002-national-target-programme-on-sustainable-poverty-reduction-approved.html.

[12] "UN Support to the Vietnam's National Target Program on the New Rural Development." The United Nations in Vietnam, The United Nations, 12 Jan. 2016, www.un.org.vn/en/media-releases3/69-un-press-releases/3916-un-support-to-the-vietnam's-national-target-program-on-the-new-rural-development.html

The Prime Minister has issued many important policies pertaining to SDG 6-related issues, such as the National Strategy on Water Resources to 2020, National Strategy for Environmental Protection up to 2020 with a vision to 2030, National Programme on Safe Water Supply 2016-2025, National Plan of Action to improve efficiency of water resource management, protection and utilization during 2014-2020 and NTP on new rural development during 2016-2020. However, national water resources planning and a baseline water resource master plan have yet to be formulated. There are still shortcomings in implementation of activities to achieve goals and other documents relating to conservation and sustainable development of wetlands.

The Vietnamese Government has issued many important policies to ensure access to sustainable energy for all. The Law on Electricity aims to provide sustainable electricity to meet people's and the nation's socio-economic development needs. The Electricity Plan VII is also aimed at "Ensuring that most rural households have access to electricity by 2020". Because of the goal to increase the share of renewable energy in the country's total primary energy consumption, the Renewable Energy Development Strategy to 2030 with a Vision to 2050 has set specific targets on the ratio of renewable energy within the country's energy structure, power production and ratio of power produced from priority renewable energy sources up to 2050. Moreover, Vietnam has also enacted the Law on Economic and Efficient Use of Energy and Viet Nam National Energy Development until 2020 with a Vision to 2050 to promote more efficient use of energy in production and consumption.

VII. HUNGARY

The VNR on Hungary was produced in 2018. Poverty eradication is an area of focus in Hungary. Even though the number of people in poverty is decreasing significantly, in 2016 26.3 percent of the population was affected by the risk of poverty or social exclusion. The Hungarian Government has shown its commitment to eradicating poverty with various efforts being implemented. The Hungarian National Social Inclusion Strategy II (2011-2020) sets the framework for government intervention to increase children's wellbeing, promote inclusive education, broaden employment opportunities for people with low-level educational qualifications, further economic integration, ensure access to proper medical care, decrease geographical disadvantages, and eliminate housing problems.

The Hungarian Government believes that eradicating poverty is closely linked with ensuring sustainable agricultural production and strengthening protection against extreme weather. One government policy to ensure agricultural production is the National Water Strategy, approved in 2017, which fosters the protection of agricultural areas against damages caused by water (flooding, inland inundation). There is also the Irrigation Development Strategy, which began to be developed in 2017 with the aim of increasing irrigated areas in the country. In 2016, the Government created the National Hail

Prevention System to protect agricultural production, and became operational on 1 May 2018.

The Hungarian Government have a wide array of policies on providing clean water and sanitation, and mirrors the expectations of the EU Water Framework Directive. The Government's major clean water and sanitation public policy is the National Water Strategy. It aims to achieve better rates for water retention and distribution, increase the efficiency of water usage, and maintain the high quality of public water utility services and the management of rainfall-runoff. In addition, risk prevention measures against water damage have also been considered, along with the improved quality of water resources in a sustainable manner. Furthermore, the improvement of the relationship between water and society, the renewal of planning and management measures, and the reorganisation of the regulatory structure pertaining to water management have been considered essential. Additionally, a "Water Reuse in Hungary" project, initiated in 2018, aims to conduct a nationwide mapping of possible water reuse. It will serve as a basis for the elaboration and realisation of measures aimed at improving water reuse in Hungary.

In order to enhance the security of supply, ensuring sustainability and competition in the field of energy supply, in October 2011 the National Energy Strategy 2030 was adopted. The objective of the Energy Strategy is to guarantee the safe energy supply in Hungary at all times, by also taking into account the country's economic competitiveness and environmental sustainability needs and the load-bearing capacity of consumers. For the period between 2014 and 2020, the Hungarian Government has allocated over 2.5 billion EUR to Operational Programs supporting energy. These Programs are intended to support areas and sectors of the economy that predominantly focus on developing renewable energy sources, increasing energy efficiency, and reducing GHGs emissions.

The last theme being discussed is Human Rights and Inclusive Societies. This covers a lot of the Sustainable Development Goals because a lot of the goals have to do with securing human rights and creating more sustainable and inclusive societies. Public policies that address to human rights and inclusive societies would also address SDG 3 Good Health and Wellbeing, SDG 5 Gender Equality, SDG 8 Decent Work and Economic Growth, SDG 10 Reducing Inequalities, and SDG 11 Sustainable Cities and Communities.

VIII. KENYA

The VNR on Kenya was produced in June 2017. The Kenyan health sector aims to give Kenyan citizens access to equitable, affordable and quality healthcare. All levels of government have created a wide array of strategies and initiatives to tackle health. The two comprehensive health policies are the Kenya Health Policy 2014-2030, and the Kenyan Health Sector Strategic and Investment Plan (KHSSP) 2014-2018. These policies aim to eliminate communicable diseases, halt and reverse burden of Non-communicable diseases (NCDs), reduce the burden of violence and injuries, provide essential health care, minimize the exposure to health risk factors and strengthen collaboration with sector providers. Another initiative is the Health Insurance Subsidy Programme (HISP), which aims to improve quality of life and human development, as well as alleviate poverty by meeting the health needs of the people. Additionally, it attempts to remove financial barriers to health care and reduce incidences of extremely high health costs. These goals can be achieved by consolidating and expanding social health subsidy mechanisms with view to achieving Universal Health Coverage (UHC). This project targets about 21,530 households of which 17,612 households have been registered to access health services from the hospital of their choice. However, some challenges have presented themselves such as increasing prevalence of NCDs and no significant lifestyle changes in the general population, health financing and purchasing of healthcare services still having implications on access and quality of healthcare, and childbirth related challenges such as the inadequacy of emergency delivery services and the competences of appropriate health workers.

The Kenyan Government has recognized that women empowerment and gender equality is a significant factor in the not only eradicating poverty, but also stimulating sustainable development. Kenya has gender-based Violence (GBV) Helpline 1195 that affords quick access to GBV services including referral after violation. The goal of the hotline is to involve community members and survivors to fight against all forms of violence against women and children. Various affirmative action programmes for empowering women, Youth and PWDs are also being implemented: Women Enterprise Fund, UWEZO Fund, National Government Affirmative Action Fund and the Youth Enterprise Fund. However, there are still challenges when it comes to reducing gender inequalities. Harmful and prohibitive socio-cultural traditional practices and beliefs such as female genital mutilation/cutting (FGM/C) continue to exist in some communities. There is also a high level of tolerance of Gender Based Violence in some communities. Finally, gender inequalities continue to exist regarding access and control of resources, economic opportunities, political as well as power.

There are also initiatives to provide decent work for all. The government through the Ministry of Education initiated a programme to construct Technical Institutes in every constituency to bolster the capacity of the existing ones to increase the number of youths with skills and enhance employability. The government has developed a National Industrial Training and attachment policy to guide industrial training and attachment in the country. Between 2013/14 and February 2017, 64, 899 trainees were placed on industrial attachments. An online industrial attachment portal has been established. This is aimed at equipping the youths with the relevant skills and increase employability and productivity as well as improved linkages between industry and training institutions. The youth enterprise fund has been streamlined to empower youth to start and grow their own businesses. The National Youth Service programme has engaged the unemployed youth and imparted skills thereby opening employment opportunities. The implementation of the preferential procurement policies (affirmative action on government procurement) supports enterprises run by the vulnerable and thereby creating jobs and employment opportunities.

In order to reduce inequalities within the country, the government, along with other stakeholders (Government ministries and agencies, the private sector, communities etc.) has been implementing specific interventions targeting the most vulnerable sectors of the population. The constitutionally created Equalization Fund aims at correcting the disadvantage of the previously marginalized areas. It is allocated one half percent of all revenue collected by the national government each year to provide basic services including water, roads health facilities and electricity to marginalized areas. It has ensured that regions with more development challenges receive more public resources to accelerate equality within regions and communities. Other programmes include Hunger and Safety Net Programme, Women Enterprise Fund, Youth Enterprise Development Fund, Affirmative Action Social Development Fund. These programmes aim at addressing the plight of the less disadvantaged in society, combatting poverty, and promoting equity. However, challenges remain, such as resource constraints in its desire to expand its social protection transfers, as well as being next to countries who have been unstable for a long time leading to illegal immigration as well as trafficking in persons and illegal fire arms which pose perpetual security concern in the country.

The Kenyan Government has also taken steps to create sustainable cities and communities. The policy and legal frameworks are aimed at improving the sustainability of cities and urban settlements in line with the aspirations of Kenya Vision 2030. The Government developed the National Solid Waste Management Strategy in 2015 as part of the efforts to promote environmental sustainability in our cities and other urban settlements. The Government made an investment of Kshs. 7.6 billion in 2016 in street lighting in all major towns in Kenya including all county headquarters, to not only increase the security, but also to create employment opportunities and facilitates the realization of a 24-hr economy in these towns. In addition, CCTVs cameras have been installed in Nairobi and Mombasa to help towards enhancing security and prevent crime. Similar projects are planned for implementation in other cities. To ensure the programme's sustainability, the national government has reduced the tariff charges to sub-national governments. The private sector contributes towards making cities and communities sustainable through the construction of more than 20,000 houses for both government and non-government employees through public private partnership model which, commenced in October 2016.

IX. IRELAND

The VNR on Ireland was produced in 2018. A key priority for Government of Ireland is to constantly improve the health and well-being of people in Ireland: by keeping people healthy; providing the healthcare people need; delivering high-quality services and getting best value from health system resources. They have created a number of initiatives. Healthy Ireland 2013-2025 is the national framework for action to improve the health and well-being of the people of Ireland. The Government has also created initiatives, such as the National Maternity Strategy 2016-2026, Tobacco Free Ireland,

National Suicide Strategy, National Substance Misuse Strategy etc., that tackle a variety of public health issues prevalent in Ireland. The Healthy Ireland Framework is having a positive impact, with daily smoking rates, consumption of alcohol and the number of obese people decreasing.

Ireland has a comprehensive policy and legal framework to promote gender equality and the empowerment of women and girls. The National Strategy for Women and Girls 2017-2020 delineates the set of priorities concerning gender equality for all levels of government, from changing attitudes and practices preventing women's and girls' full participation in education, employment and public life, to improving services for women and girls, with priority given to the needs of those experiencing, or at risk of experiencing, the poorest outcomes. The Strategy has six objectives: to advance socioeconomic equality for women and girls, advance the physical and mental health and wellbeing of women and girls, ensure their visibility in society, advance women in leadership at all levels, combat gender-based violence, and embed gender equality in decision making.

The Government of Ireland also has policies that help people get decent work. One of the early initiatives was the Action Plan for Jobs, launched in 2012, to rebuild the Irish economy and create jobs. The top priorities of the programme are to support the creation of 200,000 additional jobs by 2020, and to stimulate the domestic economy and generate employment in locally traded sectors. Ireland has adopted a national plan to battle youth unemployment called Pathways to Work, which is based on the EU's Youth Guarantee. The Department of Children and Youth Affairs operated a Youth Employability Initiative in 2016, which assisted almost one thousand young people aged 15 to 24 years to build skills to enhance their employability. While youth unemployment in Ireland has fallen, it continues to remain high.

To address the issue of Sustainable Cities and Communities, the Government of Ireland launched its Action Plan on Housing and Homelessness Rebuilding Ireland in 2016. It addresses specific challenges such as addressing homelessness, accelerating social housing, building more affordable housing, improving the rental sector, and utilizing existing housing. Another initiative is the Rural Transport Programme (RTP), which aims to provide a quality nationwide community based public transport system in rural Ireland which responds to local needs. Along with providing rural populations with access to public transportation, the government has created the National Disability Inclusion Strategy 2017-2021 as the latest public policy on public transportation that has accessibility features for disabled populations.

X.   JAMAICA

The VNR on Jamaica was produced in June 2018. 'A Healthy and Stable Population' is one the priorities outlined in 'Vision 2030 Jamaica', the strategic guide created by the Jamaican Government for sustainable development. The Jamaican Government has created a wide range of strategies and initiatives to address a number of issues, ranging from maternal and child mortality (Programme for the Reduction of Maternal and Child Mortality (PROMAC)) and substance abuse prevention, to promoting healthy lifestyle practices and mental health and well-being (Mental Health Action Plan 2013–2020). One of their initiatives to achieve this priority is a 10-year Strategic Plan 2017-2027, which provides direction for the government's commitment to advance universal access to health, universal health coverage and Vision 2030 Jamaica. The plan seeks to establish an integrated service delivery framework as well as development of an operating tool for early detection of non-communicable diseases (NCDs). The strategic priorities for the reduction and control of NCDs are guided by the National Strategic and Action Plan for the Prevention and Control of NCDs in Jamaica 2013–2018. The goal of the Plan is to reduce the burden of preventable morbidity and disability and avoidable premature mortality due to non-communicable diseases and injuries by 25.0 per cent by 2025.

The Government of Jamaica is committed to gender equality and through its gender mainstreaming efforts, which seek to promote the economic, social, cultural and political empowerment of women and men. Within all policies and programmes are gender mainstreaming initiatives in keeping with the goals and core principles of the National Policy for Gender Equality, 2011 (NPGE). The Gender Sector Plan of the Vision 2030 Jamaica and the NPGE provide the framework for gender mainstreaming and non-discrimination within the Jamaican context. These frameworks seek to ensure that all forms of discrimination against women and girls are eliminated.

The Government of Jamaica is also focused on reducing inequality within the nation. In the financial year 2016/2017 the Government focused on the provision of welfare and safety nets for the most vulnerable in the society through four major projects: GOJ/World Bank Social Protection Project, the GOJ/IDB Integrated Social Protection and Labour Programme, the GOJ/IDB Integrated Support to the Social Protection Strategy, and the GOJ/WB Support to the Socio-economic Inclusion of Persons with Disabilities. These four projects complemented each other and provided support in the form of cash transfers, training and other critical resources to vulnerable populations including poor children and persons with disabilities, and were executed through the Ministry of Labour and Social Security.

Over the past decade Jamaica has undergone gradual urbanization. It is estimated that 54 percent of the population live in urban areas. Despite urbanization presenting an opportunity towards development, urban centres in Jamaica continue to face challenges especially as it relates to sustainable growth. In 2017, the National Housing Trust (NHT) introduced lower mortgage rates specifically targeting minimum wage earners/low earning contributors, as well as persons with disabilities (PWDs) under the Home Grants Programme. Another important aspect is that NHT increased housing loan limits for first time home owners, more accessible construction loans, increased scheme affordability and deferred mortgages.

The Voluntary National Reviews give significant insight into country policies to achieve the 2030 Agenda. The fact these are voluntary, and 102 countries have conducted a VNR, with 8 countries doing more than one, is a statement to the commitment of achieving the 2030 Agenda. One policy recommendations that is important concerns education. For the most part, while VNRs have talked about environmental sustainability and stewardship education, very few educational policies focus on discussing the 2030 Agenda, the Sustainable Development Goals, and making sure how the Agenda works for all people. Curricula on the 2030 Agenda should be integrated into all levels of education, so that the leaders of tomorrow understand how to frame issues concerning sustainable development, and the understand the holistic and interconnected nature of sustainable development.

XI. SOURCES:

AUSTRALIAN GOVERNMENT, Department of Foreign Affairs and Trade. "Report on the Implementation of the Sustainable Development Goals.", 2018.

FEDERAL GOVERNMENT OF MEXICO, "Voluntary National Review For The High-Level Political Forum On Sustainable Development: Basis For A Long-Term Sustainable Development Vision In Mexico", 2018

FEDERAL REPUBLIC OF NIGERIA, "Implementation of the SDGs: A National Voluntary Review", June 2017

FEDERAL REPUBLIC OF NIGERIA, Federal Ministry of Water Resources, "Nigeria Overview: Water, Sanitation and Hygiene", 2017

GLOBAL CENTRE FOR PUBLIC SERVICE EXCELLENCE AND UNDP, "SDG Implementation Framework: Effective public service for SDG implementation", 2016

GOVERNMENT OF HUNGARY, Ministry of Foreign Affairs and Trade of Hungary, "Voluntary National Review of Hungary on the Sustainable Development Goals of the 2030 Agenda: Transformation towards sustainable and resilient societies", 2018

GOVERNMENT OF IRELAND, "Ireland: Voluntary National Review 2018 – Report on the Implementation of the 2030 Agenda to the UN High-Level Political Forum on Sustainable Development", 2018

GOVERNMENT OF KENYA, Ministry of Devolution and Planning, "Implementation of the Agenda 2030 for Sustainable Development in Kenya", June 2017

GOVERNMENT OF VIET NAM, "Viet Nam's Voluntary National Review On The Implementation Of The Sustainable Development Goals", June 2018

GOVERNMENT OF THE BAHAMAS, "The Bahamas: Voluntary National Review on the Sustainable

DEVELOPMENT GOALS TO THE HIGH LEVEL POLITICAL FORUM of the United Nations Economic and Social Council", July 2018

"NATIONAL TARGET PROGRAMME ON SUSTAINABLE POVERTY REDUCTION APPROVED." *National Target Programme on Sustainable Poverty Reduction Approved - Nhan Dan Online*, 5 Sept. 2016, en.nhandan.org.vn/politics/item/4596002-national-target-programme-on-sustainable-poverty-reduction-approved.html.

"Millions Around the World Held Back by Poor Sanitation and Lack of Access to Clean Water." The World Bank, 28 Aug. 2017, www.worldbank.org/en/news/press-release/2017/08/28/millions-around-the-world-held-back-by-poor-sanitation-and-lack-of-access-to-clean-water.

"Shift to Clean, Affordable Energy Critical to Attaining Global Goals – UN Officials ." *United Nations Department of Economic and Social Affairs*, United Nations, 2 Nov. 2017, www.un.org/development/desa/en/news/sustainable/clean-energy-for-global-goals.html.

THE GOVERNMENT OF JAMAICA, Planning Institute of Jamaica, "Jamaica: Voluntary National Review Report on the Implementation of the 2030 Agenda for Sustainable Development", June 2018

UNITED NATIONS DEPARTMENT OF ECONOMIC AND SOCIAL AFFAIRS (DESA), "Handbook For The Preparation Of Voluntary National Reviews: The 2019 Edition", October 2018

"UN Support to the Vietnam's National Target Program on the New Rural Development." *The United Nations in Vietnam*, The United Nations, 12 Jan. 2016, www.un.org.vn/en/media-releases3/69-un-press-releases/3916-un-support-to-the-vietnam's-national-target-program-on-the-new-rural-development.html

Chapter 7

SDGs AND PRIVATE SECTOR

PALOMA DURÁN Y LALAGUNA

The Sustainable Development Goals Fund Director

&

BABATOMIWA ADESIDA

Private Sector and Philanthropy Engagement Consultant for the

United Nations SDG Fund

SUMMARY: I. A TIMELINE OF THE UN AND PRIVATE SECTOR ENGAGEMENT. II. THE ESTABLISHMENT OF THE UNITED NATIONS. III. THE CHANGING ROLE OF THE PRIVATE SECTOR- A REDEFINED PARTNERSHIP. IV. A PRACTICAL APPROACH TO PRIVATE SECTOR PARTNERSHIPS- THE SUSTAINABLE DEVELEMENT GOALS FUND. V. THE SDG FUND AND THE PRIVATE SECTOR. VI. STRATEGIES FOR PRIVATE SECTOR ENGAGEMENT. VI.1. Private Sector Advisory Group (PSAG). VI.2. Creating the PSAG in Nigeria- A case of Local Ownership. VI.3. Private Sector Advisory Group Reports. VII. FRAMEWORK OF ENGAGEMENT WITH PRIVATE SECTOR. VIII. CASE STUDIES. VIII.1 Co-Design and Co-Implementation Case Study: Food Africa. VIII.2. Private Sector engagement in Colombia Joint Programme Case Study: Ferrovial IX. MITIGATING REPUTATIONAL RISKS

* * *

I.   A TIMELINE OF THE UN AND PRIVATE SECTOR ENGAGEMENT

Different forms of partnership arrangements have always existed between the UN and the Private Sector. From traditional consultative and procurement arrangements to more advanced types of cooperation in the past couple of decades, the engagements have ranged from the development and promotion of global norms and responsible business standards to the joint design, financing and implementation of projects on the ground. In fact, evidence suggest that certain specialized UN Agencies have had long-standing working relationships with the private sector as far back as decades before the official creation of the UN. These organizations include the following:

1. The International Telecommunications Union (ITU) established in 1865 – the UN specialized agency saddled with the responsibility of protecting and supporting everyone's fundamental right to communicate.

2. The Universal Postal Union (UPU) established in 1874 – established to coordinate postal policies among nations in addition to the world wide postal system.

3. International Labour Organization (ILO) established in 1919 – to promote international labor rights.

These agencies were formed back then in a bid to meet the growing need at the time to for States and International organizations (private sector) to cooperate on specific matters.

II.   THE ESTABLISHMENT OF THE UNITED NATIONS

After the two World Wars and several intergovernmental consultations on the need for global peace, the United Nations was established in 1945. Of course, global peace meant a greater opportunity for businesses to expand into new markets including in regions that were hitherto either impossible to reach due to political reasons or were just completely unsafe for operation. Therefore, even at the creation of the UN itself, business was an ardent supporter of the organization. Numerous business representatives participated in the 1945 San Francisco conference, including the International Chamber of Commerce, whose own creation in 1919 was premised on the belief that commerce and peace were complementary sides of the same coin.

It is recorded that Philip D. Reed, who was President and Chief Executive Officer of General Electric from 1940 to 1942 and from 1945 to 1959, sent a telegram to the Chairman of the US Senate Foreign Relations Committee expressing the "earnest and enthusiastic support of the US Chamber of the Charter" and urging unanimous ratification.

In the following decades, the UN-Private Sector relations would face some setbacks resulting from the need for neutrality on the part of the UN and mistrust among States. This preempted the UN's publishing of a seminal study on Multinational Corporations in World Development in 1973.

Following the publication was the appointment by the Economic and Social Council (ECOSOC) of a Group of Eminent Persons to advise the Council on the role and influence of transnational corporations (TNCs) in development. The Group called for the "continuing involvement in the issue of multinational corporations of the Economic and Social Council assisted by a commission specifically designed for that purpose ". It also recommended the establishment of an information and research Centre "to provide services for the commission."

Other important timelines in the UN and Private Sector engagement are highlighted below:

- 1974- The UN Commission on Transnational Corporations (UNCTC) commenced work in 1974 and dealt with a wide range of developmental finance issues. The main concern throughout its existence was negotiation of a code of conduct on transnational corporations consistent with the UN General Assembly call for the establishment of a New International Economic Order. Negotiations eventually stalled over the legal nature of the code, with Northern countries insisting that it should be purely voluntary while the Southern argued that it should be binding.

- 1989-The toppling of the Berlin Wall in 1989 became the principal catalyst for rapid regime change across Eastern Europe and elsewhere. This was concurrently fueled by liberalization and technology resulting in many developing countries embracing export-led growth and trade and investment liberalization.

- 1991/1992-The 46th Session of the UN General Assembly held where there was a Rejection of the Code of Conduct on Transnational Corporations following the concerns raised over the work of the UN Commission on Transnational Corporations (UNCTC). Talks came to an end altogether in 1992, when the UNCTC was closed down by Secretary General Boutros-Ghali.

- 1992 -Earth Summit, Rio de Janeiro (Agenda 21): At the 1992 Earth Summit in Rio de Janeiro, a small group of pioneer executives instituted the first business participation in an official UN event. As an out-turn of these conferences, the UN established various offices to support civil society engagement. The effort later would stall, however, for political reasons. Despite such global outreach efforts, the UN failed to engage the private sector on a substantive, ongoing basis. This failure was due an agglutination of an embedded stifling bureaucracies within the UN and the already long held negative perception the private sector had of the Organization.

- 1997 -Rio+5, special session of UN General Assembly (Programme for further Implementation) With the appointment of Kofi Annan as UN Secretary-General in 1997 came a new wave of dynamism within the UN. The relationship between the UN and the Private Sector was resuscitated which would eventually become a forerunner to an unprecedented spate of UN-Private partnerships in the future.

- 1998 -In an unprecedented gesture, Ted Turner, American billionaire and business tycoon, in 1998 donated US\$ 1 billion to support the UN's causes and activities as well as creation of the United Nations Foundation. This action would inadvertently sow a seed of restored trust in the private sector by the UN.

- 1999/2000 – The UN Global Compact was formed: The 1999 Global Compact speech laid the foundation for a thriving initiative while simultaneously enabling other UN entities to explore cooperation with the private sector. It gave strong impulse to the political articulation of the role of business in the work of the Organization. At the launch of the UN Global Compact Initiative, the First Guidelines on Cooperation between the UN and the Business Sector were laid. The creation of the UN Global Compact and the unanimous endorsement of the UN Guiding principles on Business and Human Rights by the UN Human Rights

Council in 2011, have been crucial milestones in the evolving engagement between the UN and businesses.

- 2000 – The Millennium Declaration: The Millennium Declaration of 2000 recognized and articulated the key role of the private sector to the achievement of the Organization's goals in the statement: "To give greater opportunities to the private sector, non-governmental organizations and civil society, in general, to contribute to the realization of the Organization's goals and programmes". The Millennium Declaration, from which the Millennium Development Goals are derived, contained proposals on cooperation with business and called for "greater opportunities for the private sector, non-governmental organizations and civil society in general to contribute to the realization of the Organization's goals and programmes".

- 2001- Item "Towards global partnerships" was placed on the agenda of the 56th UN General Assembly to be considered every two years thereafter. This item formulated a constructive basis for the UN-private sector relationship. Succeeding resolutions elaborated on the relationship and provided critical political support.

- 2002- In 2002, The Monterrey Consensus on Financing for Development also articulated at the level of Heads of State that the private sector has a significant role to play. The Consensus brought together finance ministers with Heads of State and foreign ministers and was the first ever high-level UN gathering to involve an exchange of views between governments, civil society and the business community.

- 2004- On 24 June 2004, Secretary-General Kofi Annan convened the 1st Global Compact Leaders Summit at United Nations Headquarters in New York. Nearly 500 leaders attended the Summit - including Chief Executive Officers, government officials, and the heads of various labour groups, Civil Society Organizations and UN agencies — to discuss and debate the Global Compact and the topic of global corporate citizenship, and to produce strategic recommendations and action imperatives related to the future evolution of the initiative.

- 2005 – The 1st UN System Private Sector Focal Points Meeting convening staff from across the UN and a few business and civil society representatives was held. The Private Sector Focal Points Meeting was co-organized by the Global Compact and the ILO. Additionally, The Global Compact continued to come up with innovative ways of engaging institutional investors by launching the "Principles for Responsible Investment" (PRI) at the New York Stock Exchange in 2005.

- 2006 - Launch of quarterly "UN-Business Focal Point" electronic newsletter to foster information exchange and learning on partnerships across the entire UN system.

- 2007 - 2nd Global Compact Leaders Summit held where it was established that working with business in a principled and pragmatic approach is one effective means for the United Nations to achieve its goals of global security, development and realization of human rights.

- 2008 – The 1st United Nations Private Sector Forum on the Millennium Development Goals and food sustainability was held.

- 2009 – In 2009, the Revised Guidelines on Cooperation between the UN and the Business Sector were published. Also, the 2nd UN Private Sector Forum on Climate Change.

- 2010 – The year 2010 marked the 3rd Global Compact Leaders Summit and launch of the Global Compact Leadership Blueprint. Another significant milestone that year was the launch of business.un.org, the first UN-business partnership gateway for matching private sector resources with UN needs.

- 2011- In 2011, after a decade of experimentation, at the Fourth United Nations Conference on the Least Developed Countries (LDC-IV), taking place in Istanbul, Turkey, in 2011, a parallel Private Sector Track was organized to explore ways to overcome barriers to investment in LDCs and to form risk-mitigating collaborations.

- 2012 - In Rio De Janeiro in June 2012, the largest ever private sector gathering held in parallel to a UN conference, the Corporate Sustainability Forum, which attracted over 3,000 corporate and civil society participants. Emerging from workshops and meetings were numerous new initiatives and a new global narrative on the corporate sustainability agenda. The Corporate Sustainability Forum influenced the official Rio+20 outcome document, inspired over 200 commitments from business, and helped to launch new initiatives and scale-up existing ones. It showed for the first time that business was willing to move ahead on sustainability irrespective of progress logged at inter-governmental negotiations.

- 2015- Adoption of the 2030 Agenda: On September 25, 2015, the United Nations General Assembly adopted the 2030 Agenda for Sustainable Development with the 17 Sustainable Development Goals and 169 targets. The SDGs were adopted to build on the Millennium Development Goals and complete what they did not achieve by aiming to end poverty, fight inequality and injustice and tackle climate change by 2030. This resolution clearly reaffirmed the United Nations strong commitment to the full implementation of this new Agenda. It was clearly stated that the ambitious Goals and targets will only be achieved by revitalizing Global Partnership with the private sector, Governments, civil society, the United Nations system and other actors. It was agreed that the role of the diverse private sector, ranging from micro-enterprises to cooperatives to multinationals and philanthropic organizations in the implementation of the new Agenda cannot be underestimated in the attainment of the global goals.

III. THE CHANGING ROLE OF THE PRIVATE SECTOR-A REDEFINED PARTNERSHIP

The 2030 Agenda cannot be achieved without meaningful engagement by business200, where the private sector has a critical role to play as the driver of innovation and technological development and as the key engine for economic growth and employment. The concept of universality201 under the 2030 Agenda provides the opportunity to involve the private sector in a new innovative way to collaborate towards the achievement of the SDGs. Since the adoption of the goals, there has been a major shift in the way business is done around the world in ensuring that the SDGs are achieved by 2030.

The Sustainable Development Goals have provided significant opportunities for change in social, environmental and economic issues. The goals which were set by the UN and accepted by governments all over the world are aimed at reducing inequalities, improving standards of living, protecting lives and the planet.

The SDGs are being adopted by the private sector at a record pace. The starting point for the private sector was the fact that they were considered as actors and not donors in the new 2030 agenda. In addition, the goals presented clear business opportunities for the companies that understand that sustainable change can be met through innovative products and services. By aligning business strategies with the SDGs, organizations are turning global challenges into business opportunities while at the same time contribute to a better world. Global challenges such as population growth, inequality, scarcity of resources and climate change are being translated into tangible risks and opportunities for businesses to manage. Experts suggest that to achieve the SDGs, the world is dependent on the Private Sector. Due to the enormous role that private sector plays in the social and economic landscape, it would be impossible to achieve the SDGs without them. The private sector represents the most effective way to achieve the SDGs as the reach of multinational cooperation's goes far beyond the boundaries of any government or any nation.

Similarly, at a time when many governments are increasingly failing to provide solutions to issues affecting their populace, the society increasingly is turning to the private sector and asking that companies respond to broader societal challenges. Undeniably, the public expectations of companies have never been greater. Society is demanding that public and private companies serve a social purpose. To remain profitable and sustainable over time, businesses are not only expected to deliver financial performance, but to also show how they make a positive contribution to society.

Companies must be seen to benefit all their stakeholders, including shareholders, employees, customers, and the communities in which they operate.

For this performance to be sustained, companies must also understand the societal impact of their business as well as the ways that broad, structural trends – from gender imbalance to slow wage growth to rising automation to climate change – affect their potential for growth. Nowadays, stakeholders are demanding that businesses demonstrate greater leadership on a wider range of issues. This should be evident in a company's ability to manage environmental, social, and governance matters which demonstrate the leadership and good governance that is so essential to sustainable growth. Many businesses understand the importance of the changes which is why they are increasingly integrating these issues into their business processes.

In leading the incorporation of SDGs into business operations, companies have started to ask themselves certain questions:

- What role are we playing in the community?

- How are we managing the impact of our activities on the environment?

- How are we working to create a diverse workforce?

- In what ways are we adapting to the ever rapidly changing technological space?

- In what ways are we creating the relevant opportunities for our employees and business to adapt to the societal changes?

Today more than ever, the private sector has demonstrated that they are willing to show the leadership and clarity that will drive not only their own investment returns, but also the prosperity and security of their fellow citizens.

IV. A PRACTICAL APPROACH TO PRIVATE SECTOR PARTNERSHIPS- THE SUSTAINABLE DEVELOMENT GOALS FUND

In March 2014, the Sustainable Development Goals Fund was established under UNDP (SDG Fund, www.sdgfund.org). The Fund was created following the success of the Millennium Development Goals Achievement Fund (MDG-F) which was established in 2007 based on an agreement between the Government of Spain and the UNDP on behalf of the United Nations system to actively support MDG achievement and inter-agency cooperation.

With an initial contribution from the Government of Spain and as part of the post-2015 agenda, the SDG Fund was created to serve as a bridge between the experience of the MDGs and the SDGs with the private sector as the key partner in this transformative development mechanism. Since inception, the SDG Fund has worked within the selected regions of Latin America and the Caribbean, Asia, Arab States and Africa to support national actions towards the achievement of the SDGs through the initiation of new Joint

Programmes and a multi-sectoral approach with special emphasis on the participation of the private sector with the 3 cross-cutting issues of gender equality and women's empowerment; public-private partnerships and sustainability.

Because partnerships are a key component of our mandate, the SDG Fund developed global initiatives related to advocacy in addition to the joint programmes on the ground. The SDG Fund recognizes the immense potential and added value that partnering with traditional and non-traditional development actors can have on delivering sustainable development on the ground, hence we have constantly worked to bridge the efforts of different development partners such as UN agencies, businesses, civil society, and academia. Partnerships within the SDG Fund have been organized in four categories:

1. Partnerships with the private sector- The SDG Fund recognized the immense potential and added value that partnering with responsible companies can have in delivering sustainable development on the ground.

2. Global partnerships with the UN system- The SDG Fund has collaborated with UN Agencies, funds, programmes and other entities in the system through global partnerships to advance the 2030 Agenda for Sustainable Development.

3. Partnerships with Academia- Academia has also been a priority for the advocacy work in the SDG Fund in order to make better use of academic expertise and mobilize researchers and university students in the achievement of the SDGs.

4. Partnerships with Creative Industries- For the SDG Fund, working with world renowned artists, chefs, musicians and architects led the way to finding new approaches to move the SDGs forward.

V.   THE SDG FUND AND THE PRIVATE SECTOR

Since 2015, the SDG Fund has worked with the private sector to adopt the SDGs by managing risks, adding value and enhancing opportunities for the businesses and their stakeholders. For the SDG Fund, an increased involvement of the private sector not only enhances the sustainability of business by forming a sound business climate open to investment, enhanced productivity and entrepreneurship through attending to issues of resource scarcity, poverty and market integration; it is also a demand of civil society and other actors who request private sector practice of Corporate Social Responsibility (CSR). As an entity of the United Nations, the SDG Fund became particularly interested in working with businesses that share common values based on the United Nations Guiding Principles on Business and Human Rights. In line with this, the SDG Fund has supported private sector initiatives aimed at overcoming the common challenges of contemporary sustainable development by pooling the expertise, technology, resources and capacities of both actors towards fulfilling the globally shared responsibility of improving the livelihoods of all.

From the onset, the SDG Fund proposed a modality where private sector is treated as a partner and not only a donor. The SDG Fund firmly believes that each company, regardless their sizes, geographical location, or sectors, can making critical contributions towards shared economic, social, and environmental progress. This is being achieved through core business operations and value chains, social investments, and advocacy efforts.

Though some of the goals are specific to certain industries, others can be supported by every company regardless of its industry. Issues such as gender equality and reduced inequality are critical to every business and companies were quick to realize that a more diversified work force creates new markets and fosters innovation. As a leader in the implementation of the SDG's, the SDG Fund carried out workshops with private sector organizations in different continents of the world to promote the awareness and understanding of the SDGs.

Feedback from these sessions revealed that the private sector welcomed the idea of making profits while also generating measurable beneficial social or environmental impacts through the adoption of the SDGs. For several years, businesses have carried out philanthropic/Corporate Social Responsibility activities in their various areas of operation without much support from governments. Most of these activities were not carried out for financial gains and had become an integral part of these businesses. As these activities continued to grow in scale, businesses started to look for more sustainable ways to carry them out. Based on this, the private sector has become a major player working with the SDGs to make businesses investments that are good for the society and for their businesses.

Under this context, the SDG Fund addressed the challenge of how businesses can become more involved in joint development initiatives with governments, civil society, and UN Agencies. This process can be viewed as challenge, the bigger issue and this purpose, is the broad reaching scope and complexity of the SDGs, that no one should be left behind, that different partners have different comparative advantages and that coordination and concerted efforts are needed to achieve them. More specifically, the SDG Fund acted as a key convener in collaborating with the private sector and a bridge between the private sector, the public sector and the UN system. These joint programmes offer a scalable, innovative model of public – private partnership that could be replicated in other countries and regions, adapting to the local context.

The SDG Fund provided businesses with a one-stop shop to engage with the United Nations and served as a UN platform that allowed partners to work with several specialized UN Agencies simultaneously, aiming to facilitate global projects while leveraging UN Agencies' complementary expertise, knowledge and networks. In a multi-agency mechanism, all SDG Fund programmes could leverage additional funding from different partners to increase impact. This increased sustainability, impact, national ownership and the potential to scale up by working with local and national partners that allow business actors to actively participate and engage in the design, selection and monitoring of the programmes.

What the SDG Fund offered businesses

1. Provision of technical expertise: leveraging the SDG Fund's deep understanding and proven experience of development challenges in the local context to address issues businesses encounter along their value chains in developing countries.

2. Access to extensive network: By engaging the SDG Fund, Business were able to take advantage of our vast network of stakeholders (local and national governments, NGOs, other public and private sector actors) to strengthen sectoral policies and thereby facilitate the ease of doing business particularly in developing countries.

3. Pooled funding: Combining financial resources from the SDG Fund, the private sector and other partners were able to maximize investments and achieve greater impact.

4. Knowledge-Sharing: Our public-private dialogues provided businesses with guidance on how to conduct their operations in a sustainable manner using the SDGs as a framework.

What Businesses gained from the partnership:

Improved stakeholder relations: the SDG Fund provided support to government and private sector relations by promoting robust legal frameworks that ensured an enabling environment for businesses to thrive.

Accountability: by providing sustainable practices and solutions, the SDG Fund addressed the increasing demands of consumers and investors for identified private sector companies.

Greater brand value and equity: the SDG Fund facilitated the implementation of sustainable practices with a potential to create new markets and opportunities in which businesses could reap positive rewards. This ultimately had positive impacts on their bottom line.

Increased global reputation: through their partnership with the SDG Fund, the businesses developed partnerships that were capable of building investor confidence and attract responsible investments.

Experiences of the SDG Fund working with the private sector demonstrate how the UN system, public sector actors and businesses could effectively work together to implement the SDGs. It also demonstrates how the private sector can play a critical role in accelerating the achievement of the SDGs by promoting public-private partnerships, social investments and aligning the 2030 Agenda with corporate social responsibility. Through positive development results on improved infrastructure, greater gender equality and stable social conditions, economic growth can be generated to lead to the creation of new markets, boost innovations and minimize risks.

VI.   STRATEGIES FOR PRIVATE SECTOR ENGAGEMENT

VI.1 Private Sector Advisory Group (PSAG)

The SDG Fund has been championing the role of the private sector in sustainable development projects through its "co-design, co-financing, co-implementation" approach, striving to make the private sector an active partner in its work. By establishing in 2015 a Private Sector Advisory Group (PSAG), formed by business leaders of different industries and from all regions of the world. The PSAG provided the SDG Fund valuable knowledge and assets to jointly work towards the achievement of the SDGs and engaged in a multi-dimensional way - by offering industry-specific training for SDG Fund joint programmes, engaging in dialogues with public and private stakeholders to provide alternative viewpoints and engagement opportunities, actively participating in research and knowledge sharing, providing financial, human and/or natural resources as well as infrastructure support and a lot more. As a result, the SDG Fund accumulated solid experience and understanding on how the private sector works and how it can be involved in public-private partnerships. Under the SDG Fund, the PSAG has presented a powerful platform for business leaders to leverage comparative advantages, ensure change across the global private sector, exchange lessons learned, and resource development activities. As such, its member companies are afforded an unparalleled opportunity to contribute to extraordinary social impacts, elevate their discreet and collective brands, and cultivate partnerships of tremendous transformative capacity.

Since joining the PSAG and attending the private sector workshops, most members have started to integrate the SDG framework into their corporate reporting. Most notable, Nutresa has done a complete mapping of their sustainability strategies using the SDGs as a guide. Sahara Group has reevaluated some of their ESG policies to ensure that they are meeting the SDG targets. In their 2016 sustainability report, BBVAMF measured their impact using the SDGs.

Inspire

Actions to motivate and mobilise business, UN staff and Member States around specific strategic SDG engagement opportunities, especially at the country level.

Connect

Actions to simplify and facilitate the process of business engagement with UN agencies and other delivery partners, especially at the country level.

Equip

Actions to build and share knowledge and skills for business engagement, including partnering and measuring impact, and to explore co-investment models.

VI.2 Creating the PSAG in Nigeria- A case of Local Ownership

In a bid to expand the PSAG activities in Africa, the SDG Fund tasked Sahara Group to coordinate the efforts of the organized private sector in Nigeria and across the continent. Sahara Group is a leading international energy and infrastructure conglomerate headquartered in Lagos Nigeria but with operations in 38 countries across Africa, Middle east, Europe and Asia. Leveraging on its conveying power within the private sector, the company engaged other businesses as well as the Nigerian Presidency to support the formation of the Nigerian sector of the PSAG.

On the 28th of February 2017, the Nigerian chapter of the PSAG was inaugurated by the Vice President of the country. The inauguration of the PSAG was done in line with the efforts of the Federal Government of Nigeria through the Office of the Senior Special Assistant to the President on Sustainable Development Goals to work with the organized private sector towards achieving the SDGs through sustainable partnerships.

Since then, the PSAG has supported the Office of the Senior Special Assistant to the President of Nigeria on Sustainable Development Goals (OSSAP- SDGs) as well as other key stakeholders to build a roadmap for how public-private alliances can provide large-scale solutions towards achieving the SDGs. This has been carried out in many ways, some of which include the following:

A. Reporting tool: through one of its members (PWC), the PSAG has recently developed a SDG Reporting Tool which is the localized reporting instrument designed to help companies report their progress and work in contributing towards the achievement of the SDGs. This tool is unique as it helps organizations create their sustainability report as well as their SDGs contributions at the same time. Developing the reporting tool became imperative because there is no central unit for private sector to report their SDG related activities to the government. There was also the need to develop a tool that allow businesses carry out their reporting themselves and to showcase to the public and other stakeholders what they are about. The success or otherwise of the PSAG clusters largely depends on how well cluster members report their work.

B. Promoting collaboration: the PSAG has encouraged companies that are already carrying out SDG related projects as part of their CSR and have them collaborate in clusters for stronger impact and have them report their work so that Nigeria's SDGs can be met. Cluster Leads regularly encourage competing companies within their clusters to meet and have conversations about how they can combine resources to achieve their common sustainability goals.

C. Ensuring Africa Wide SDG achievement: The aim of the PSAG is beyond just contributing to the achievement of the goals, it is about helping Africa attain them. This will be achieved by setting the tone for the private sector in other Africa countries to fully participate for the goals to be reached. Over the last few months, the Nigerian PSAG has received invitations from 9 African countries interested in learning and adopting the PSAG Nigeria Model.

D. Ensuring Government Representation and Involvement: The PSAG is working to ensure that at government level, there is an SDGs informed vision that is beyond tenure-based development plans of countries for them to move forward and progress to be made in development. By developing pilot initiatives that can bring global best practice into view, the PSAG plans to create critical models for development that can be replicated.

Based on the momentum that the PSAG has generated within the country, plans are underway to replicate same in other African countries thereby scaling impact across the African continent.

VI.3 Private Sector Advisory Group Reports

Following the creation of the PSAG, it was agreed upon that one of the PSAG's main contribution would be to prepare an annual report about the role of the private sector in development focusing on specific issues. The first report, entitled, Business and the United Nations: Working together towards the Sustainable Development Goals: A

Framework for Action, was released in 2015 in conjunction with Harvard's Kennedy School and Business Fights Poverty, and outlines the business and development case for increased UN business engagement as well as recommendations on the ways that the UN can work more effectively on this shared imperative.

This report offers fresh perspectives on a variety of topics including improving the climate for partnership design, co-creation, combining complementary skills, and developing solutions to harness the full potential of what business can bring to the development table. This publication focuses on insight and best practices culled from interviews with business leaders which are designed to help both the private sector, the UN, and other practitioners learn from each other.

Following the positive reception of the first report, the PSAG published the second report, Universality and the SDGs: A Business Perspective in 2016. This report, written in collaboration with Global Compact, highlights varied perspectives from both large and small companies working to understand the commonality of the new development agenda. This report is based on interviews and input from private sector leaders through workshops in Africa, Latin America, Europe and the United States, with more than 100 firms representing various regions and industry sectors. Each workshop was moderated by a Global Compact representative and a questionnaire was developed to facilitate the discussions. The year-long series of workshops and interactive discussions provided valuable insight in to how companies were working to address the new set of goals. It also suggests many firms are working in the areas of SDGs, yet their work is not always linked to the goals or articulated as such.

The report and workshop relied on the Global Compact's SDG Compass. The Compass guides companies on how they can align their strategies as well as measure and manage their contribution to the realization of the SDGs. The SDG Compass presents five steps that assist companies in maximizing their contribution to the SDGs: understanding the SDGs, defining priorities, goal setting, integrating sustainability and reporting.

In 2017, The SDG Fund, in collaboration with, Pennsylvania University Law School and with the legal specialized support from the law firm McDermott Will & Emery examined how Sustainable Development Goal 16 (peace, justice and strong institutions) is relevant to the private sector and offers perspectives on the link between peace and the development agenda. The report, Business and SDG 16: Contributing to peaceful, just and inclusive societies, serves as a practical guide for sharing best practices on how the private sector can incorporate SDG 16 - which focuses on building peaceful, just and inclusive societies - into business planning. It shows how an effective legal framework can help the private sector build trust with the public and civil society and details the role of business in creating conditions that would improve areas such as corporate social responsibility, governance, transparency and accountability. Companies from the PSAG are also working to prevent corruption by instituting a zero-tolerance policy and implementing a reporting system for potential compliance violations. For example, a number of leading companies in Colombia are collaborating to integrate thousands of small farmers in high-conflict areas into their supply chain in order to help create jobs as well as support reconciliation efforts.

Furthermore, McDermott Will & Emery LLP supported the University of Pennsylvania Law School by conducting research in six countries on their efforts to advance the rule of law and suppress corruption (Cambodia, India, Lebanon, the United Kingdom, Uzbekistan and Zimbabwe). Practices and trends in these countries were evaluated, including legislative and regulatory changes.

At a glance: PSAG Reports by the numbers

- All three reports were launched at the United Nations Headquarters (November 2015, 2016, and 2017) to an audience of over 800 participants combined.

- Additionally, the 2016 report was presented in December 2016 at Telefonica Foundation Headquarters to an audience of around 200.

- The 2017 report was presented in December 2017 in Madrid to an audience of around 40.

- Up-to-date, The SDG Fund has disseminated more than 900 copies to UN Member States, UN agencies, private sector and academia.

- SDG Fund website analytics show that both Report websites have received over 20,000 clicks from users around the world.

Apart from disseminating these reports among various stakeholders such as the UN, private sector, NGOs and academia, the SDG Fund was invited to many events to discuss the contents of these reports. The SDG Fund participated in Global Compact, The Economist, Oekom Summit, and Concordia Summit events around the world, just to name a few examples. The PSAG model and the expertise captured in each report elevated the visibility of the SDG Fund. As mentioned, for many in the United Nations, working with the Private Sector as a key implementing partner is a novel approach, therefore, many entities within the UN system sought out the experience of the SDG Fund to enhance and develop their private sector strategies. The reports served as guiding tools and reference points for many as well. The reports offer the voice of the private sector. Moreover, companies themselves also rely on the reports as tools to frame their sustainability strategies and to understand how they can collaborate with the United Nations.

VI.4. Other forms of Engagement

Apart from the ongoing partnership with the PSAG, the SDG Fund had a unique position to collaborate with the private sector, where each private sector actor is encouraged to identify together with the Fund the partnership modality that goes best with its company's core business, values and interests. While being flexible and open for various partnership modalities, private sector actors collaborated with the SDG Fund through three main ways: a) joining force with the SDG Fund on-the-ground for joint programmes; b) supporting of ongoing private sector initiatives, such as the PSAG, sustainability campaign or initiatives on creative industries202; c) pilot initiatives and independent partnerships under the co-design, co-create and co-invest modality, where this new modality was strongly encouraged and focused in current and future work of the SDG Fund.

The co-design, co-create, and co-implement modality originated from the main conclusions of the Business and UN report prepared with the PSAG in 2015. The premise is that companies are eager and prepared to work alongside the United Nations and Governments to co-design, co-create and co-implement programmes. Typically, in the past, the private sector has been a donor but today, more companies want to co-implement programmes with the UN to unite and leverage their strengths and expertise. Rather than involve the private sector at the end of the process, the SDG Fund created a framework of engagement to ensure that they were included from the outset in the design of the programme (see Framework below). This proved quite challenging for both the UN agencies and the Private sector that aren't typically used to working together. What was most arduous was understanding each other's languages, agreement documents, and timeline considerations. For the most part, companies tend to launch programmes faster than the UN but with smaller budgets. Additionally, each agency has their own policies so reconciling those with that of private sectors can be extremely challenging.

The modalities for partnerships included working with the private sector to jointly support the development of integrated value chains in market sectors that offer the prospects of sustainable growth and transition to better remunerated forms of employment. In some cases, these alliances could be commercially viable from the outset, in others they require various forms of seed or venture financing, or hybrid approaches that include ongoing public, donor or philanthropic support. The SDG Fund used diverse types of resource-mobilization support and utilized a range of resources from the private sector including cash as well as core competencies. This meant contributing with different types of non-commercial financial support, from traditional philanthropy to social venture funds and hybrid or "blended-value" financing mechanisms, corporate volunteers, pro-bono goods and services, technical expertise and support and other in-kind contributions. Finally, advocacy, institutional framework and policy dialogue is essential part of working the private sector. The SDG Fund promoted a multi-stakeholder dialogue on issues related to the purposes and activities of the UN.

VII.   FRAMEWORK OF ENGAGEMENT WITH PRIVATE SECTOR

The SDG Fund created a step-by-step management processes for developing and managing partnerships between the private sector and the SDG Fund. This process has been streamlined for a quick turnaround time:

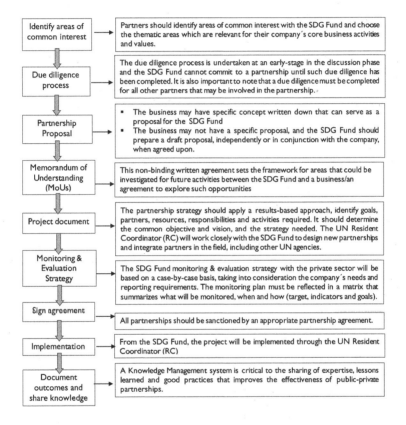

VIII.   CASE STUDIES

VIII.1 Co-Design and Co-Implementation Case Study: Food Africa

Food Africa Project is an innovate public-private partnership between Sahara Group, the United Nations' Sustainable Development Goals Fund, United Nation System in Nigeria, the Roca Brothers and the Kaduna State Government, directed at improving food security and nutrition and alleviating poverty through strengthening of the agro-food value chains, improving agricultural productivity and yields, creation of a food processing facilities and promotion of access to markets in Nigeria.

Following the creation of the PSAG in 2015 and the 'co-design and co-implement' methodology derived from the 2015 PSAG report, Sahara Group approached the SDG Fund with the idea of partnering to tackle the food security issues faced in Nigeria. Sahara Group and the SDG Fund, met with all the relevant UN agencies in the field and together began drafting the necessary documents to execute this programme. Each partner brought their expertise and funds to the table. Throughout the co-design process, the Roca Brothers as Goodwill Ambassadors and the Government of Kaduna were included in the programme.

The aim of this programme is introduce more sustainable practices in the value chain, reduce crop waste, and improve smallholder farmers' profitability. Recognizing the link between the gaps in skills and structural unemployment in the region, the project promotes income generating opportunities and offer technical support to promote trade of local goods and services.

Still at the construction stage, the program will feature an agro processing facility and serve as a Center of Excellence to increase farmers' income and efforts to reduce food loss. The center will provide training in the food industry on issues linked to food safety, business planning and product diversification. Designed as a hybrid public-private facility, the program will eventually be sustained and managed by the community's local farmers.

Sahara Group, a leading African energy conglomerate and member of the SDG Fund Private Sector Advisory Group and major co-financer of the project will bring its business perspective to the program to ensure the viability of the facility's operations.

It is expected that 5,000 women and men of Kaduna will be directly impacted with new job prospects, increased income and additional skills to compete in the thriving food industry. In addition, an estimated 500,000 residents will indirectly benefit from the Food Africa Project which is designed to be scaled-up in the region and eventually replicated in other parts of Sub-Saharan Africa.

Food Africa Partners and Roles:

The SDG Fund and Sahara Group are responsible for project design and will together provide the bulk of the co-financing, mobilize matching fund contributions and oversee the preparation and implementation of the work plan in agreement with all partners. They will identify best practice and seek to replicate lessons learnt in Sub-Saharan Africa and beyond.

UN Nations System in Nigeria – the Resident Coordinators Office will play a role in the coordination of the specialized UN agencies, FAO, ILO and ITC will leverage their areas of expertise to provide technical assistance in implementing those activities agreed upon in the work plan, including the feasibility, baseline and market studies, training of farmers, cooperatives and farmer-based organizations, occupational and safety and health. They will assume responsibility for monitoring, including routine reporting on their respective activities. They would bring the latest know-how, including tools to track and effectively reduce post-harvest losses and full-cost accounting in line with international best practice.

The Roca Brothers – will together with project partners, mentor a select group of farmers in cultivation, processing and bringing to market, specialized horticultural products. They will play a key role in establishing the Centre of Excellence, through Training-of-Trainers modality to build the capacity of a team of local trainers. They will provide their technical expertise, including the sharing of best practices in resource efficiency, recycling and recovering of waste as secondary resources to help optimize the operations of the processing facilities. The Rocas' team will also contribute to the communications and advocacy campaign.

Kaduna State Government provided as an in-kind contribution to the project, the land upon which the facility will be constructed and other arable land within the identified Local Government Areas in addition to access to utilities and all-year round armed security for the facility. The state government will collaborate with other state-level stakeholders to improve local infrastructure and including rural roads to allow access to the facility and farmland and will share relevant policy information, databases, etc. at its disposal. They would also play a vital role in assisting in the identification of potential farmers that would take part in the out-grower's scheme.

VIII.2. Private Sector engagement in Colombia Joint Programme Case Study: Ferrovial

Ferrovial, a member of the Private Sector Advisory Group, joined forces with the SDG Fund on-the-ground to enrich the joint programme, Productive and food secure territories for a peaceful and resilient in Cauca, Colombia. Ferrovial, in partnership with Save the Children, provided reliable, affordable and sustainable access to water and sanitation services for the community as part of the efforts to reduce deforestation and the deterioration of water sources in the region. Their main activities included technical review of the community water source, taking measures to prevent and control overflow of the community water storage, installing water storage tanks in nearby schools, and protecting water sources from pollution. This is an example of how a private sector partner worked with the SDG Fund and the Colombia country team to provide technical support to enhance and ongoing joint programme.

IX. MITIGATING REPUTATIONAL RISKS

To ensure the success of any initiative or mechanism with the private sector, the SDG Fund always completed a rigorous due diligence process of each potential private sector partner following UNDP's Policy on due Diligence and Partnerships with the Private Sector. Part of this process included clearly articulating the underlying concepts and ideas behind the initiative and establishing good guidance tools for staff to ensure consistent implementation of the approach, processes and procedures for key elements. Prior to the creation of the PSAG, the SDG Fund carried out a due diligence process for over 100 companies. Many of which didn't meet the criteria set forth by the policy.

While observing all "exclusionary criteria" and those specifically identified "high-risk sectors" in addition to the principle of non-exclusivity, the SDG Fund recognized the need for a "principles-based approach" to private sector engagement,203 with partnerships based on mutual accountability, a co-design and co-decision process which is inclusive of all other relevant partners (not just private sector) and fully reflects national priorities/ownership.204

When identifying partners, the SDG Fund assessed companies based on ESG policies, corporate governance, past controversies and took any allegations and violations extremely seriously but also weighed the potential benefits of the intended partnership. If a company faced controversial allegations, it was also important to take into in consideration their response and responsibility to remedy the situation and strengthen their monitoring systems. Where the SDG Fund partnered with companies in high risk sectors where controversy was very common, all companies proved that they took each allegation very seriously and were committed to improving the operating environment and avoiding recurrences. The SDG Fund recognized the implications and the reputational risks involved however, The SDG Fund also saw a unique opportunity to make an impact in the industry with one of the sector's key leaders. The SDG Fund believed that these partnerships offered a tremendous opportunity to not only harness the expertise and technical support of the company, but also to advise and inspire companies to transform and expand their sustainability strategies and impact.

The SDG Fund developed a robust Crisis Communication Plan to monitor and address any risks that might be associated with a partnership. Part of the strategy included monthly monitoring of international and local media outlets and NGO watchdogs to see if there are any potential controversies.

The 2030 Agenda requires a greater involvement among governments, civil society, private sector and international organizations. It provides opportunities to work beyond silos and communities of practice and the involvement of the private sector is no longer optional. By building increased stability, improved economic prospects and better social and economic conditions in the community, the private sector also demonstrates its contribution for a peaceful and inclusive societies, which in turn provide businesses with more economic opportunities and growth. By engaging businesses through innovative public-private partnerships, the SDG Fund sought to promote a new development model towards achieving the SDGs.

X.   REFERENCES

1945: THE SAN FRANCISCO CONFERENCE. (n.d.). Retrieved from http://www.un.org/en/sections/history-united-nations-charter/1945-san-francisco-conference/index.html

ABOUT THE ILO. (n.d.). Retrieved from https://www.ilo.org/global/about-the-ilo/lang--en/index.htm

FACING REALITIES: Getting Down to Business[Pdf]. (2007). Retrieved from https://www.unglobalcompact.org/docs/news_events/8.1/GC_Summit_Report_07.pdf

HISTORY. (2017, July 15). Retrieved from http://www.sdgfund.org/history

HISTORY OF THE UNITED NATIONS. (n.d.). Retrieved from http://www.un.org/en/sections/history/history-united-nations/

HOXTELL, W., PREYSING, D., & STEETS, J. (2010). Coming of Age: UN-Private Sector Collaboration Since 2000[Pdf]. Retrieved from http://www.gppi.net/fileadmin/user_upload/media/pub/2010/Hoxtell_Preysing_Steets_20102_Coming_of_Age.pdf

INFOTEAM SA. (n.d.). The UPU. Retrieved from http://www.upu.int/en/the-upu/the-upu.html

PHILIP D. REED. (2018, October 01). Retrieved from https://en.wikipedia.org/wiki/Philip_D._Reed

RESOLUTION ADOPTED BY THE GENERAL ASSEMBLY ON 25 SEPTEMBER 2015[Pdf]. (2015). Retrieved from http://www.un.org/en/development/desa/population/migration/generalassembly/docs/globalcompact/A_RES_70_1_E.pdf

RESOLUTION ADOPTED BY THE GENERAL ASSEMBLY ON 20 DECEMBER 2013. (2014). Retrieved from http://www.un.org/en/ga/search/view_doc.asp?symbol=A/RES/68/234

SDG FUND PRIVATE SECTOR ADVISORY GROUP. (2018, February 02). Retrieved from http://www.sdgfund.org/sdg-fund-private-sector-advisory-group

TESSNER, S (2000). The United Nations and Business: A Partnership Recovered, St. Martin's Press, New York, p. xix.

THE GLOBAL COMPACT LEADERS SUMMIT [Pdf]. (n.d.). Retrieved from https://www.unglobalcompact.org/docs/news_events/8.1/summit_rep_fin.pdf

THE UN-PRIVATE SECTOR RELATIONSHIP: A PARTNERSHIP RECOVERED[Pdf]. (2015). Retrieved from http://www.unprme.org/resource-docs/UNPrivateSectorRelationshipArticleGKApril2015.pdf

UNITED NATIONS. Department of Economic and Social Affairs. (1973) Multinational Corporations in World Development. New York: United Nations.

UNITED NATIONS. Department of Economic and Social Affairs. (1974). The Impact of Multinational Corporations on Development and on International Relations. New York: United Nations, p.5.

WHO CARES WINS: Connecting Financial Markets to a Changing World [Pdf]. (2004). Retrieved from https://www.unglobalcompact.org/docs/issues_doc/Financial_markets/who_cares_who_wins.pdf

Chapter 8

PUBLIC DIPLOMACY AND SDGs

SDGs AS A GOAL AND AS A MEANS OF PUBLIC DIPLOMACY

RAUL DE MORA JIMENEZ

Communications Specialist, UN Sustainable Development Goals Fund.

SUMMARY: I. INTRODUCTION. PUBLIC DIPLOMACY IN THE CONTEXT OF THE 2030 AGENDA II. THE CONCEPT AND PRACTICE OF PUBLIC DIPLOMACY, SOME NOTES. III. THE SDG FUND'S PUBLIC DIPLOMACY INITIATIVE. IV. PUBLIC DIPLOMACY AND SDGS: HOW CAN PUBLIC DIPLOMACY SUPPORT SDG IMPLEMENTATION?. V. PUBLIC DIPLOMACY ACTORS FOR SDGS. VI. CONCLUSION: THE SDGS AS A TOOL FOR PUBLIC DIPLOMACY.

* * *

I.   INTRODUCTION: PUBLIC DIPLOMACY IN THE CONTEXT OF THE 2030 AGENDA

Public diplomacy as an academic discipline lingers on the confluence of communication theory and international relations. By bringing together elements of these two disciplines, a public diplomacy framework allows us to analyze and provide strategic advice to international relations actors on how they can use strategic communications to advance their objectives, in particular to reach audiences and the public abroad. In this regard, public diplomacy can provide a new vantage point to understand the Sustainable Development Goals (SDGs) and the 2030 Agenda for Sustainable Development and, most importantly, to guide communications on and around the SDGs. This article uses the experience of the SDG Fund, particularly insights from its Public Diplomacy Initiative, which ran from 2016-2018, in order to share lessons learned. It tries to address two questions: how can public diplomacy advance implementation of the SDGs and how can different actors use the SDGs as a tool in their public diplomacy efforts.

The argument underpinning this chapter is that the SDGs can be both an "objective" and a means of "public diplomacy." This applies to state actors (the traditional diplomatic actors) as well as non-traditional diplomacy and development actors (sub-national government actors, international organizations, private sector, and civil society). This has a practical consequence: the implementation of SDGs at the global, national and local level can benefit from the public diplomacy toolset; at the same time, the SDGs as a framework and lens can be powerful for those in public diplomacy. In terms of professional practice, this also means that the SDGs should be part of the toolset of diplomats and public diplomacy should be part of the toolset of development actors.

But how can what have traditionally been two very separate worlds (diplomacy and international development) come together when using similar tools? As Pamment (2016) described, "the common trajectory" of aid and public diplomacy "is unmistakable, and is the result of very clear trends in both fields." While the Millennium Development Goals and aid effectiveness debates of the past 20 years pushed international development actors to think in terms of "partnerships" and "participation," public diplomacy has shifted its debates toward "dialogue," "engagement," and "collaboration." As such, "the act of giving aid" can be "in itself considered a form of public diplomacy." It is important, however, to understand that the SDGs framework goes beyond a traditional "aid giving" vision of development as it is envisaged as a universal and global shared responsibility to be adapted to local contexts. Thus, the relationship between public diplomacy and development needs to be reconsidered. But let's start with the concept and origins of public diplomacy.

II.   THE CONCEPT AND PRACTICE OF PUBLIC DIPLOMACY, SOME NOTES

Public diplomacy is usually understood as strategic communication actions by an international player in order to advance its objectives and policies in the global arena. As explained by Laporte and Pamment (unpublished, 2016) as part of their seminal work for the SDG Fund (described in the next section), it is 'public' in the sense that the content of the messages is accessible and open to be discussed with any interested interlocutor. That means that traditional international actors use public media and communications actions to achieve specific purposes, develop a policy or present a particular understanding of global affairs. The purpose of public diplomacy is to bring the public component to the profession of diplomacy, which is characterized by its reliance on personal relationships among diplomats, closed meetings and undisclosed memorandums and notes.

The current concept of public diplomacy originated in 1965, at the height of the Cold War, by Edmund Gullion, a former U.S. diplomat and academic (Hunt, 2015) and the concept has substantially evolved in the last few decades. In fact, many transformations in the concept and practice of public diplomacy justify its relevance in the context of the 2030 Agenda and the SDGs.

Public diplomacy as a concept and as a practice originated with a purpose to influence external audiences and the public, mostly from state actors (most typically, the State Department, the Ministry of Foreign Affairs or their equivalent). It was unidirectional, following an approach to communications that had many elements of a "propaganda" model and conductivist behavioral theories of psychology. This means using communications as a means of influencing "minds" and "hearts" to generate changes in behavior beneficial for the interest of the foreign actor. This approach in the international arena followed the experience of governments, which had already created their departments of public information for their national constituencies to influence foreign policy. This was the model that the United States followed under the presidency of Woodrow Wilson. The Committee for Public Information (also known as the Creel Committee) was established as an independent agency to convince U.S. citizens to support government efforts during World War I (Creel, 1920). Several decades later, international organizations followed suit. For example, the United Nations established its Public Information Department in 1946; the department is still named "public information."

Public information and communications substantially changed in the following decades. In 2005 - even before many transformations in the communications landscape that generated almost global penetration of the Internet, widespread use of mobile networks and the expansion of the social media networks - Jan Melissen (2005) argued for the emergence of what he called a "New Public Diplomacy." With this term he referred to how public diplomacy is particularly suitable to adapt in this context so, with a greater focus on Joseph Nye's definition of "soft power", to engage non-traditional actors. Public diplomacy became an "indispensable ingredient for such a collaborative model of diplomacy."

This "New Public Diplomacy" is particularly suitable for the 2030 Agenda era. On one hand, a substantial change is about actors; public diplomacy is now not only practiced by state actors and foreign services, but also other actors who are increasingly using strategies characteristic of public diplomacy. The 2030 Agenda is an all-actors agenda, as governments alone cannot fulfill the commitments included in the 17 goals (Duran, Barrado, Liesa and Blanco, 2016). On the other hand, as described by Laporte and Pamment (2016), the emergence of non-state political players in the sphere of international politics, the complexity of communications networks that connect citizens and communities, and new forms of exercising power have forced traditional political actors to redefine their diplomacy strategies (Kerr and Wiseman, 2013). Since the SDGs are not legally binding from an international law's point of view, their relevance resides precisely in their normative and soft power nature.

In this new communications and development context, it is important to understand the objectives of public diplomacy, which undoubtedly vary among the many actors that use it. Public diplomacy usually performs one of these three roles and objectives (Löffelholz, Auer, and Srugies, 2015): to influence the attitudes and decisions of the foreign public and governments and manage perceptions (role of the persuader); to generate understanding for political programs, ideas, ideals and values (role of the generator of understanding); and to establish and maintain relationships and partnerships (role of the facilitator). Influencing policy makers, raising awareness and building partnerships are at the core of achieving the SDGs.

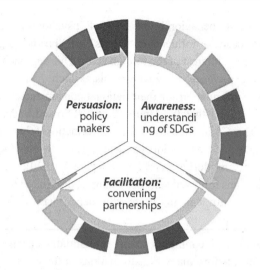

Graph 1. How public diplomacy can impact SDG achievement

It is clear that public diplomacy can have an important role in advancing the 2030 Agenda by contributing to any of these three objectives. With this, public diplomacy becomes an instrument to promote the SDGs, not only to raise awareness on sustainable development, but to influence policy makers and convene partnerships. As any framework of global engagement, the value of the SDGs resides considerably on the extent of how much people are aware of them. This is important, no doubt, but the real potential of public diplomacy regarding the SDGs can only be achieved if the other two potential objectives of public diplomacy (influencing policymakers and convening partnerships) are also taken into account. This requires us to look at public diplomacy beyond its role of simply promoting the SDGs.

III.   THE SDG FUND'S PUBLIC DIPLOMACY INITIATIVE

To better understand the relationship between public diplomacy and the SDGs, the SDG Fund gathered a group of experts to bring a public diplomacy perspective to the 2030 Agenda. The SDG Fund was a development mechanism established by the UN Development Programme, on behalf of the UN System, thanks to the initial contribution of the government of Spain. From 2014 to 2018, the SDG Fund served as a bridge between the MDGs and the SDGs. With programmes in more than 20 countries that benefitted 5.4 million people, the SDG Fund brought together governments, UN agencies, civil society and the private sector. One of its objectives was to test and try new approaches to communications and advocacy. As part of these efforts, the initiative took advantage of the SDG Fund's on-the-ground work as a basis to discuss public diplomacy for the SDGs in action.

The premise of the SDG Fund's Public Development Initiative was that the effectiveness of the 2030 Agenda depends on how this ambitious global Agenda is communicated and how stakeholders take ownership. For this reason, the growing academic field of public diplomacy could provide relevant tools and advocacy strategies to benefit the SDG Fund. They aimed to produce, research and analyze how to make use of public diplomacy tools and prepare an action plan.

The SDG Fund's Public Diplomacy Initiative was led by professors Teresa LaPorte of the University of Navarra in Spain and James Pamment of Lund University in Sweden. It also included these recognized academics, researchers and thought leaders in the area of public diplomacy: Nicholas Cull, professor of public diplomacy at the USC Annenberg School for Communication and Journalism and director of the USC Master's program in Public Diplomacy, University of Southern California; Sieglinde Gstöhl, Director of EU International Relations and Diplomacy Department, College of Europe; Antoinette Kankindi, senior lecturer at Strathmore University, Kenya; Jan Melissen, senior research fellow at the Netherlands Institute of International Relations 'Clingendael' and professor of diplomacy in the Department of Political Sciences at Antwerp University; Shaun Riordan, principal consultant at Aurora Partners and senior visiting fellow of the Clingendael Institute; Karen Sanders, head of the School of Arts and Humanities, St Mary's University in Twickenham, London and Karin Wilkins, professor of media studies, University of Texas.

By convening this group of leading public diplomacy experts to share their experiences and insights, the SDG Fund was able "to identify some areas of common interest and promote the sustainability of global public goods with the primary objective of establishing effective communication, dialogue, participation and engagement strategies with key partners," as established in the initiative's terms of reference. The group met annually and these public diplomacy workshops also supported and fed the SDG Fund's Communications and Advocacy Strategy and framework of action with the private sector. It also facilitated a dialogue between key stakeholders (member states, the private sector, media, think tanks, other development organizations and civil society) and the SDG Fund in order to find areas for collaboration and synergies, both at the conceptual and at the programme level.

Topics discussed included: SDG Fund as a mechanism to promote the SDGs; trends in public perceptions of development aid and how the SDG Fund can position itself in this new context; and a public diplomacy initiative proposal with the European Union, developed by professors and Pamment (2016). Moreover, the group discussed what the role of public diplomacy could be in the context of the UN Development System's repositioning. Another key element of discussion was how the role of the UN Resident Coordinator could be recast as an actor of public diplomacy, taking into account the similarities and differences with the role of country ambassadors. The group raised the question of the universality of the 2030 Agenda and what it means, from a public diplomacy perspective, to have a development agenda that applies to developed and developing countries alike. This text is highly inspired by these discussions and reflections.

IV.   PUBLIC DIPLOMACY AND SDGS: HOW CAN PUBLIC DIPLOMACY SUPPORT SDG IMPLEMENTATION?

One of the starting points of the SDG Fund's Public Diplomacy Initiative was that public diplomacy has been closely linked to cooperation for development since its inception. As explained by Laporte and Pamment (2016), in this context, development aid as an instrument of diplomatic action has developed in four directions: 1) from the countries providing aid, especially when it was a matter of introducing social change (North-South flow); 2) from the receiving countries to the donating countries, in order to ask for closer collaboration or denounce harmful practices (South-North flow); 3) between developing countries, to establish common practices or orchestrate their demands (South-South flow), and 4) between countries providing aid to lead and coordinate specific actions (North-North flow).

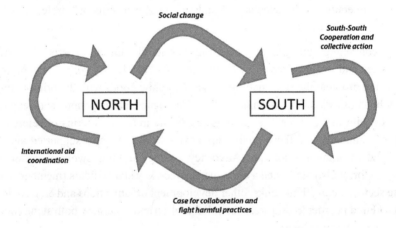

Graph 2. Flows of public diplomacy between traditional State development actors

These four flows continue to be a useful model to analyze public diplomacy as a means of achieving the SDGs, but the universality of the 2030 Agenda requires us to rethink how to apply public diplomacy in this new understanding of international cooperation. This is explained in the SDG Fund's 2016 report "Universality and the SDGs: A Business Perspective:"

"Universal means that the subject belongs or extends to all countries and their people. The SDG Agenda is no longer about developed and developing countries, the rich and the poor; it now extends worldwide. The agenda commits all countries to contribute towards a comprehensive effort for global sustainability in all its dimensions – social, economic and environmental – while ensuring equity, peace and security. These goals show that our society, from each individual to every collective organization, has an agenda to achieve and that sustainable development has become a must for all if the world is to survive and progress is to be shared".

As a consequence, the distinction between South and North might not be completely relevant within the 2030 Agenda paradigm (Mawdsley, 2017). It is not only about countries that were traditionally considered the South, as is the case of China or India, which have become part of the North by becoming development aid donors. With aid grants becoming just a small portion of the total overseas development assistance (ODA), albeit with a catalyzing role, the transfers of aid from the North to the South may not reflect the character and nature of the 2030 Agenda. While the Millennium Declaration (and its MDGs) was in some extent an initiative from developed countries to the developing countries, the 2030 Agenda is a roadmap for all countries. In this context, "development aid" responded to a normative framework with the overall aim of transforming developing countries into developed countries.

By contrast, the 2030 Agenda provides a roadmap for all countries and societies to become sustainable. With a stronger environmental component (SDGs 11, 12, 13, 14 and 15) and the embedment of global governance-related matters (such as illicit trade or the participation of developing countries in global governance structures, as stated in SDG 16) challenges become not only country-dependent, but interdependent. There are no model countries to follow as all countries have to change if the SDGs are going to be achieved. Even a very developed country like Sweden requires some work in more than 75 percent of the 'non-development cooperation' SDG targets (Kamphof and Melissen, 2018). While the MDGs looked into building model societies that some believe existed or could be taken as a reference, the SDGs aimed to achieve a model of society that doesn't exist as such and therefore can be considered as a pathway to uncharted territories.

With this, the three objectives of public diplomacy described in Graph 1 (persuasion, awareness and facilitating) become even more important, and transboundary action is required. This is what makes public diplomacy a particularly relevant tool of strategic communications for state, as well as non-state actors. While traditional diplomatic practice is associated with actors involved in largely closed processes of international relations, public diplomacy is about diplomatic engagement with people (Welsh and Fearn, 2008). A universal and ambitious framework of action can only be achieved if everyone is on board.

Moreover, it is important to also understand the relationship between communications and development. Laporte and Pamment (2016) advocate for the need to differentiate between "communication *about* development" (improving the quality and efficiency of the politics of cooperation) and the "communication *of* development" (actions of marketing with the end goal of promoting projects among potential donors and collaborators). A third dimension, "communication *for* development," takes place when communications is part of development. If we replace development for sustainable development, we could see how public diplomacy can advance the SDGs in at least three fronts:

- **Communications *about* sustainable development**. The first strategic use of communications in the context of the SDGs is to explain to wider audiences what is sustainable development and why it is important. Regarding persuasion of policy makers, public diplomacy can move the SDGs beyond the purview of international aid and development line ministries and ensure that sustainable development is the responsibility of all the line ministries. In particular, Finance and Economy ministries become key agents in the success of the 2030 Agenda as they decide how investments are allocated for the SDGs. Public diplomacy can also help raise awareness about sustainable development, which in many societies it is still linked to environment protection. Public diplomacy can also showcase the relationships between the three dimensions of sustainable development (environmental, social and economic) and how they interact. Communications strategies can present sustainable development in the most compelling and simplified manner, so it can be digested by population groups ranging from students to policy makers. Public diplomacy can also facilitate partnerships; for example, a partnership between the private and public sector can communicate what sustainable development is and why sustainable development of other societies and communities is important as a common and global endeavor. The ultimate goal of communications about sustainable development follows Pamment and La Porte's model to improve the quality and efficiency of sustainable development policies and actions.

- **Communications *of* sustainable development.** The second type of contribution of public diplomacy to the SDGs is about communicating what is being done to achieve the SDGs. This includes efforts to persuade policy makers to invest in particular SDG projects and initiatives. In this case, marketing and corporate communications tools are particularly relevant. But communication of sustainable development is not only about communicating with donors and funding partners. It is about communicating with all stakeholders of a concrete development initiative and about how communications can contribute to national ownership so that relevant partners - in particular governmental partners - take full ownership of a particular project of initiative. In addition, communicating about sustainable development can raise awareness among the general public about what is being done with public, private or mixed resources. In this case, the objective is to provide examples of what sustainable development means in practice and why investment in particular SDGs is important. A public diplomacy dimension helps address one of the risks of a universal agenda: that societies that have been traditionally donors have to act for sustainable development both within and outside their own territory, ensuring that greater internal sustainable development action doesn't go in detriment of international development cooperation. Lastly, communications about sustainable development facilitates partnerships. As almost no sustainable development action can be a single-actor or a one-entity endeavor, by communicating together partners of a sustainable development initiative deepen and strengthen their relationship and involve also other partners, such as the media.

- **Communications** *for* **sustainable development**. Third, strategic communications can advance the SDGs by becoming part of sustainable development themselves. For example, in order to persuade relevant policy makers, development projects frequently include advocacy actions for changing laws, plans and policies to make them more aligned with the SDGs. Communications is a powerful way to promote social change among participants and communities, following the traditional communication for development (C4D) approaches, including changing behavior through entertainment and education (Singhal and Rogers, 2012). As the SDGs are more numerous and ambitious in comparison to MDGs, the areas for social change have expanded and now incorporate aspects such as responsible consumption, which were not a part of the MDGs. Finally, communications for sustainable development can facilitate partnerships as part of SDG-related projects. For example, partnerships with media companies can fight gender-based violence, and partnerships with telecommunications providers and social media companies can address social problems like hate speech.

By combining the three roles and objectives of public diplomacy with the three types of relationships between communications and sustainable development, we can build a framework for public diplomacy in regards to the SDGs. In the next section, we will discuss how different actors are already using public diplomacy in the context of the 2030 Agenda.

V.   PUBLIC DIPLOMACY ACTORS FOR SDGS

Public diplomacy, as described at the beginning of this chapter, was created as a new discipline and tool for diplomats to advance foreign policies of state actors. More actors, as a result of the changing geopolitical, economic and communications landscape, have been conducting activities that could be described as public diplomacy. As Wiseman

(2010) says, the 21st century had resulted in a third dimension in the conduct of international relations, which he defines as "polylateralism." Melissen (2011), building on this concept, argues that polylateral diplomacy, or non-state diplomacy, "is equivalent to governments' cooperation with transnational civil-society actors." In conclusion, his view is that public diplomacy thrives in a polylateral world of multiple actors in which governments remain highly relevant in increasingly diverse national networks.

The 2030 Agenda requires collective action, where public actors at different levels of government play a crucial role, but action is also required by international organizations, civil society, the private sector and individuals. This section presents some examples of how all these actors are indeed using public diplomacy strategies and actions to promote the SDGs. For analysis purposes, each actor is presented separately, even though many of them are working together in some of these examples of public diplomacy.

- *International organizations: much more than the custodian of the SDGs.* The 2030 Agenda and its 17 SDGs were approved in September 2015 during the annual meeting of heads of states of the United Nations General Assembly. This took place after a process that started in Rio+20[1] and lasted several years. The association between the UN and the SDGs is so strong that these are often referred to as the UN's Sustainable Development Goals. Indeed, several UN entities are developing different actions and campaigns around the SDGs that could be defined as public diplomacy.

For example, the UN launched "MyWorld" (http://vote.myworld2015.org/) during the consultation process in order to involve citizens around the world in defining and deciding what goals should be included in the final list. It consisted of an online survey to gather citizens' opinions and relied on creative use of citizen mobilization and awareness raising initiatives, both online and offline. The campaign gathered more than 9.5 million votes from all over the world[2]. As stated on the campaign's website, the *"United Nations wanted to know what matters most to you."*

The UN leadership has been very clear in making sure the SDGs were not just the UN's goals, but everyone's goals. The UN Secretary General said in his report on repositioning the UN Development System in the context of the 2030 Agenda: *"building on existing partnership efforts, the United Nations is uniquely placed to offer the platforms needed for all actors to come together, build trust and mobilize their respective assets to achieve the Sustainable Development Goals"* (United Nations, 2017). The UN's entities are facilitating new partnerships between public and private sectors in what could be understood as a form of public diplomacy. Some examples from the SDG Fund can be found in this volume, in the article on the transition from the MDGs to the SDGs and private sector engagement.

---

[1] For an exhaustive description with relevant information from the inside of the debates and negotiations that led to the approval of the 2030 Agenda, Dodds, Donoghue and Roesch (2016) provide a good in-detail overview of the process.
[2] The results and analytics of the campaign are available online at: http://data.myworld2015.org/ (last retrieved 15 October 2018).

The UN, however, is a clear example of a traditional diplomacy instrument, established as an intergovernmental organization by member states, and is therefore an evident product of diplomacy. UN conferences and summits can be considered in many regards as conventional diplomacy tools. But the UN is trying to make them more than just a traditional event organized by and for diplomats. In relation to the SDGs, good examples can be found on how communications is being used not only as a public information tool, but as a platform to engage with people worldwide, well beyond the limited number of participants in these type of events. For example, the UN now convenes "Global Goals Week" during the UN General Assembly in order to raise awareness and political engagement with the SDGs. The UN has put into place communications strategies to turn "diplomatic events" into "people's events." For example, during the UN General Assembly, the "SDG Media Zone" allows bloggers and social media influencers to connect what is happening at the UN headquarters with people around the world. Through a strategic use of communications, the High Level Political Forum on Sustainable Development, which takes place every July to review progress towards the SDGs, has become an opportunity for communications and online discussion on the SDGs beyond the UN's walls in New York.

Other international organizations are also using public diplomacy around the SDGs. The European Union, through the European Development Days, has actively promoted the SDGs. The African Union has launched "Agenda 2063-SDGs," linking the SDGs with the African Agenda 2063, a framework for guiding Africa's development over the next five decades. Similarly, the Secretary General for Iberoamerica (SEGIB) made the SDGs the central theme of its 2018 summit, launching several communications campaigns around it.

- *Governments: facilitating and enabling collective action*. The 2030 Agenda was agreed upon by all UN member states and is therefore first and foremost an agenda of national governments, with responsibility both within and outside their countries. As such, communications around the SDGs by national governments have components of public communications and public diplomacy. Governments of donor countries from the North and the South use public diplomacy to communicate about, of and for sustainable development.

Strictly speaking, only those engagement activities with foreign audiences are public diplomacy. However, if internal/national audiences are not aware of the SDGs and of their country's actions for sustainable development, it is unlikely that their governments will invest heavily in SDG public diplomacy abroad. Knowledge of the SDGs is still low, even though it is higher than it was for the MDGs at any point. For example, while more than 4 in 10 Europeans are aware of the SDGs, just over 1 in 10 know what the SDGs are, according to the 2017 Eurobarometer. A review of surveys on the SDGs in different countries shows that even if they are familiar, they are usually not well known (OECD, 2017).

When communicating about the SDGs, government actors need to make several strategic decisions. Should the agenda be communicated as a whole? Or should communications focus on particular SDGs? Can a government invest heavily in public diplomacy abroad for the SDGs when its own citizens do not know about the SDGs? Beyond the traditional role of public diplomacy to raise awareness in third countries, governments are using other forms of public diplomacy, too.

A good example is convening the SDG public-private partnerships. For instance, the Danish Cooperation is behind the "Partnering for Green Growth and Global Goals 2030 (P4G)" initiative, whose objective is to convene partnerships around food and agriculture, water, energy, cities and the circular economy. However, public-private partnerships around the SDGs, as argued by Kamphof and Melissen (2018), are not always easy; they pose a test for ministries of foreign affairs as SDG partnerships differ from early 21st-century public–private partnerships. They identify three main challenges: time-consuming consultations on government structures do not work well for the private sector; multi-stakeholder partnerships operate in horizontal networks rather than in the hierarchical structures of government; and long-term sustainability objectives should be aligned with short-term business priorities.

Some countries have decided to focus their public diplomacy on initiatives around certain SDGs in order to position themselves as leaders in sustainability in a particular field. This is the case for Sweden and Fiji, who took a prominent role in promoting SDG 14 (Life below water) worldwide and protecting oceans as part of the Ocean Conference of 2017. Similarly, Germany has made jobs creation a key priority; in October 2018, Chancellor Angela Merkel pledged a €1 billion development fund to tackle unemployment in Africa as part of the G20 Compact with Africa, which started under the German G20 presidency to promote private investment in Africa (https://www.compactwithafrica.org/).

• *Civil society: watchdogs and advocates*. Civil society organizations (CSOs) played an important advocacy role in shaping the 2030 Agenda. Many CSOs contributed directly to discussions on the SDGs through the so-called UN Major Groups (Women, Children and Youth, Indigenous Peoples, Non-Governmental Organizations, Local Authorities, Workers and Trade Unions, Business and Industry, Scientific and Technological Community, Farmers, and Persons with disabilities). These groups, created at the Earth Summit of 1992, are part of a mechanism of participation at the UN that brings the voices of a broad part of society[3]. Without this broad participation of civil society, it is unlikely that some of the goals and targets would have made it into the final list. For example, major groups played a significant role in ensuring that the particular rights of some groups of vulnerable populations were incorporated during the negotiations within the Open Working Group on Sustainable Development Goals, rights that in its most part had not been taken into consideration as such when the MDGs were approved. A good example is the inclusion of the rights of people with disabilities across

---

[3] For more information on the UN Major Groups it is recommended to visit the website created by UN DESA to this end: https://sustainabledevelopment.un.org/majorgroups/about.

different goals and targets, even if some authors have said additional efforts were still needed (Tardi and Njelesani, 2015).

From a public diplomacy perspective, civil society organizations also had an important role in promoting the SDGs, acting both as advocates and watchdogs for their implementation. After analyzing different actions of NGOs around the SDGs, Demailly and Hege (2018) identified four roles they can play in SDG implementation at the national level: holding governments to account, communicating the SDGs to a broad audience, implementing projects, and holding the private sector to account.

These efforts by CSOs have been accompanied by international collaboration, with several international and cross-sectoral alliances of civil society groups launching communications initiatives around the SDGs, sometimes in collaboration with governments, the UN and the private sector. A notorious example is Civicus - with more than 4,000 members in more than 175 countries, and a headquarters in Johannesburg[4] - which was instrumental in launching the "Beyond 2015" campaign with other partners.

- *Private sector: beyond corporate social responsibility.* One of the most significant changes in landscape between the Millennium Declaration and the 2030 Agenda has been the incremental role the private sector has acquired. Several of the SDG Fund's reports referenced in this book are a good reminder of the quick uptake of SDGs by the private sector, across industries and countries. Perhaps one of the most significant changes is about seeing the role of the private sector beyond the traditional donor perspective. This requires moving beyond the most common approach to SDGs from private sector companies who frequently address through corporate social responsibility and philanthropy initiatives, than as crucial to core business operations. This coincides with the rise of corporate public diplomacy as cited by Ordeix-Rigo and Duarte (2009) to advance business interests abroad. In contrast with civil society organizations, some of the actions that could be defined as public diplomacy tend to be efforts by a particular company trying to position itself as playing a role in achieving the SDGs. The Global Compact has had a particularly relevant role in articulating the advocacy actions of the private sector, especially through its local networks.

- *Citizens: individuals as public diplomats of the SDGs.* Perhaps as a result of the different campaigns and initiatives launched by other actors, citizens around the world are acting as public diplomats for the SDGs. Using visual elements from the SDGs, citizens across countries and continents are launching communications micro-initiatives and participating in international mobilization efforts. Social media and new technologies of communications allow people in different parts of the world to interact and connect, and the SDGs have proven to be a good connecting narrative thread. A good example is "Global Citizen," whose own name reflects the possibilities of citizens to engage with the SDGs across borders and frontiers. It is a good model of citizen activism around the SDGs, with its primary focus on ending poverty by 2030. Interestingly, its impact is

---

[4] More information can be found in the institutional website of the organization at http://www.civicus.org/.

measured in terms of citizens mobilized (its goal, as described on its website, is to mobilize "100M action-taking Global Citizens").

As a result, awareness and mobilization around the SDGs are increasing, even if they are still far from the levels required for a global agenda. For example, in September 2018, Ipsos surveyed people in 15 countries on the SDGs, finding that adults and youth agreed that the SDGs are important (67%), while only 17% indicated not having heard of them. Awareness is lowest in Great Britain, the United States, Australia and Nigeria, while it is the highest in Indonesia, China, Mexico and Brazil[5]. Globescan, in a survey for the OECD, found that citizens in non-OECD countries were more likely than OECD citizens to see themselves as "global citizens."

VI.   CONCLUSION: THE SDGS AS A TOOL FOR PUBLIC DIPLOMACY

In this brief overview of public diplomacy and the SDGs, this chapter tried to make the argument for SDG advocates to look into public diplomacy as a discipline that can greatly help them advance the SDGs. Indeed, as shown in these pages, there are already many initiatives around the SDGs that have components and characteristics of public diplomacy. This is the view of public diplomacy as a tool for the SDGs: it does not doubt its value to create awareness, persuade policy makers and convene partnerships around the SDGs.

The reverse can also apply, and the SDGs should be equally understood as a tool for public diplomacy. First of all, the SDGs, with their iconography, visual identity and global endorsement, allow a different angle and lens for looking into complicated matters. This facilitates engagement with external audiences as the SDGs are a common narrative that unites countries, societies and cultures. For example, in post-conflict contexts, wounds can be difficult to cure with traditional communications strategies focused on the conflict itself. But the SDGs can provide a different framework and narrative to tackle and talk about the conflict's root causes from a different angle.

Moreover, the SDGs allow for a new generation of partnerships that was uncommon before. The SDG Fund's partnerships with creative industries, for example, showed the value of the SDGs as generators of partnerships between the government, the private sector, civil society and even celebrity chefs. This was the case with the Food Africa project, described in this book's chapter on the private sector. In this same vein, one of the recommendations of the SDG Fund's Public Diplomacy Initiative was to look into public-private partnerships for the SDGs. The 2030 Agenda allows a variety of modalities of engagement that need to be explored and adapted with different public diplomacy strategic purposes.

---

[5] Information extracted from Goalkeepers Global Youth Outlook Poll (September 2018): https://www.ipsos.com/sites/default/files/ct/news/documents/2018-09/gates_ipsos_topline_report_09_24_2018.pdf (last retrieved 27 Oct 2018).

As a global and universal agenda, the SDGs can perhaps help reconfigure the practice of public diplomacy itself. The origins of contemporary public diplomacy are clearly dominated by the U.S. experience. By bringing perspectives from different actors and geographical areas and thematic areas, not only ministries of foreign affairs, the SDGs can contribute to more global and inclusive public diplomacy. Public diplomacy is not only about communications, as coherence between action and discourse is required. The SDGs cannot just be seen as a communications instrument to advance other interests. The 2030 Agenda requires us to rethink how we act and interact with external constituencies to achieve the SDGs, which are both global and local goals. The clock is ticking if we collectively aim to have a more prosperous, sustainable and fair planet by 2030.

VII. REFERENCES

CREEL, G. (1920). How we advertised America: The first telling of the amazing story of the committee on public information that carried the gospel of Americanism to every corner of the globe. Harper & brothers.

DODDS, F., DONOGHUE, A. D., & ROESCH, J. L. (2016). *Negotiating the Sustainable Development Goals: A transformational agenda for an insecure world.* Taylor & Francis.

DURAN Y LALAGUNA AND ADESIDA, 2018

DURAN Y LALAGUNA, P., BARRADO, C. M. D., LIESA, C. R. F., & BLANCO, S. M. (Eds.). (2016). *International Society and Sustainable Development Goals.* Thomson Reuters Aranzadi.

HEGE, E., & DEMAILLY, D. (2018). NGO mobilisation around the SDGs.

HUNT, A *(2015) Public diplomacy. What it is and how to do it, Geneva,* UNITAR, 2015.

JAN MELISSEN (2011) beyond the new diplomacy

KAMPHOF, RIES, AND JAN MELISSEN. "SDG s, Foreign Ministries and the Art of Partnering with the Private Sector." *Global Policy* 9.3 (2018): 327-335.

KERR, P., & WISEMAN, G. (Eds.). (2013). *Diplomacy in a globalizing world: Theories and practices* (p. 123). New York: Oxford university press.

LAPORTE, M.T. AND PAMMENT, J. (2016, unpublished) "Sharing Innovation: Potential Contribution of the SDGF to the European Cooperation for Development. Proposal for a Public Diplomacy Strategy".

LÖFFELHOLZ, M., AUER, C., & SRUGIES, A. *(2015). Strategic Dimensions of Public Diplomacy. In D. Holtzhausen, & A. Zerfass (Eds.), The Routledge Handbook of Strategic Communication (pp. 439-458).*

MAWDSLEY, E. (2017). Development geography 1: Cooperation, competition and convergence between 'North'and 'South'. *Progress in Human Geography, 41*(1), 108-117.

MELISSEN, J. (2005). The new public diplomacy: Between theory and practice. In *The new public diplomacy* (pp. 3-27). Palgrave Macmillan, London.

MELISSEN, J. (2011). Beyond the new public diplomacy. Netherlands Institute of International Relations' Clingendael'.

OECD (2017) "What People Know and Think About the Sustainable Development Goals: Selected Findings from Public Opinion Surveys", Policy Note. Compiled by the OECD Development Communication Network (DevCom).

ORDEIX-RIGO, E. AND DUARTE, J. (2009) "From public diplomacy to corporate diplomacy: Increasing corporation's legitimacy and influence." *American Behavioral Scientist*

PAMMENT, J. (2016). Intersections between public diplomacy & international development: Case studies in converging fields. *CPD Perspectives.*

SDG FUND (2016). Universality and the SDGs: A business perspective. *Sustainable Development Goals Fund.*

SINGHAL, A., AND ROGERS, E. (2012). *Entertainment-education: A communication strategy for social change.* Routledge.

TARDI, RACHELE, AND JANET NJELESANI. "Disability and the post-2015 development agenda." Disability and rehabilitation 37.16 (2015): 1496-1500.

UNITED NATIONS (2017). *"Repositioning the United Nations development system to deliver on the 2030 Agenda: our promise for dignity, prosperity and peace on a healthy planet"*, Secretary General Report

WELSH, J., & FEARN, D. (2008). Engagement: Public diplomacy in a globalized world. *London: Foreign and Commonwealth Office.*

WISEMAN, G. (2010). Polylateralism: Diplomacy's third dimension. *Public Diplomacy Magazine, 4*(1), 24-39.

ANNEX

General Assembly	Distr.: General 21 October 2015

Seventieth session
Agenda items 15 and 116

Resolution adopted by the General Assembly on 25 September 2015

[without reference to a Main Committee (*A/70/L.1*)]

70/1.   Transforming our world: the 2030 Agenda for Sustainable Development

The General Assembly

Adopts the following outcome document of the United Nations summit for the adoption of the post-2015 development agenda:

Transforming our world: the 2030 Agenda for Sustainable Development

Preamble

This Agenda is a plan of action for people, planet and prosperity. It also seeks to strengthen universal peace in larger freedom. We recognize that eradicating poverty in all its forms and dimensions, including extreme poverty, is the greatest global challenge and an indispensable requirement for sustainable development.

All countries and all stakeholders, acting in collaborative partnership, will implement this plan. We are resolved to free the human race from the tyranny of poverty and want and to heal and secure our planet. We are determined to take the bold and transformative steps which are urgently needed to shift the world on to a sustainable and resilient path. As we embark on this collective journey, we pledge that no one will be left behind.

The 17 Sustainable Development Goals and 169 targets which we are announcing today demonstrate the scale and ambition of this new universal Agenda. They seek to build on the Millennium Development Goals and complete what they did not achieve. They seek to realize the human rights of all and to achieve gender equality and the empowerment of all women and girls. They are integrated and indivisible and balance the three dimensions of sustainable development: the economic, social and environmental.

The Goals and targets will stimulate action over the next 15 years in areas of critical importance for humanity and the planet.

15-16301 (E)
1516301

Please recycle ♻

People

We are determined to end poverty and hunger, in all their forms and dimensions, and to ensure that all human beings can fulfil their potential in dignity and equality and in a healthy environment.

Planet

We are determined to protect the planet from degradation, including through sustainable consumption and production, sustainably managing its natural resources and taking urgent action on climate change, so that it can support the needs of the present and future generations.

Prosperity

We are determined to ensure that all human beings can enjoy prosperous and fulfilling lives and that economic, social and technological progress occurs in harmony with nature.

Peace

We are determined to foster peaceful, just and inclusive societies which are free from fear and violence. There can be no sustainable development without peace and no peace without sustainable development.

Partnership

We are determined to mobilize the means required to implement this Agenda through a revitalized Global Partnership for Sustainable Development, based on a spirit of strengthened global solidarity, focused in particular on the needs of the poorest and most vulnerable and with the participation of all countries, all stakeholders and all people.

The interlinkages and integrated nature of the Sustainable Development Goals are of crucial importance in ensuring that the purpose of the new Agenda is realized. If we realize our ambitions across the full extent of the Agenda, the lives of all will be profoundly improved and our world will be transformed for the better.

Declaration

Introduction

1. We, the Heads of State and Government and High Representatives, meeting at United Nations Headquarters in New York from 25 to 27 September 2015 as the Organization celebrates its seventieth anniversary, have decided today on new global Sustainable Development Goals.

2. On behalf of the peoples we serve, we have adopted a historic decision on a comprehensive, far-reaching and people-centred set of universal and transformative Goals and targets. We commit ourselves to working tirelessly for the full implementation of this Agenda by 2030. We recognize that eradicating poverty in all its forms and dimensions, including extreme poverty, is the greatest global challenge and an indispensable requirement for sustainable development. We are committed to achieving sustainable development in its three dimensions – economic, social and environmental – in a balanced and integrated manner. We will also build upon the achievements of the Millennium Development Goals and seek to address their unfinished business.

3. We resolve, between now and 2030, to end poverty and hunger everywhere; to combat inequalities within and among countries; to build peaceful, just and inclusive societies; to protect human rights and promote gender equality and the empowerment of women and girls; and to ensure the lasting protection of the planet and its natural resources. We resolve also to create conditions for sustainable, inclusive and sustained economic growth, shared prosperity and decent work for all, taking into account different levels of national development and capacities.

4. As we embark on this great collective journey, we pledge that no one will be left behind. Recognizing that the dignity of the human person is fundamental, we wish to see the Goals and targets met for all nations and peoples and for all segments of society. And we will endeavour to reach the furthest behind first.

5. This is an Agenda of unprecedented scope and significance. It is accepted by all countries and is applicable to all, taking into account different national realities, capacities and levels of development and respecting national policies and priorities. These are universal goals and targets which involve the entire world, developed and developing countries alike. They are integrated and indivisible and balance the three dimensions of sustainable development.

6. The Goals and targets are the result of over two years of intensive public consultation and engagement with civil society and other stakeholders around the world, which paid particular attention to the voices of the poorest and most vulnerable. This consultation included valuable work done by the Open Working Group of the General Assembly on Sustainable Development Goals and by the United Nations, whose Secretary-General provided a synthesis report in December 2014.

Our vision

7. In these Goals and targets, we are setting out a supremely ambitious and transformational vision. We envisage a world free of

poverty, hunger, disease and want, where all life can thrive. We envisage a world free of fear and violence. A world with universal literacy. A world with equitable and universal access to quality education at all levels, to health care and social protection, where physical, mental and social well-being are assured. A world where we reaffirm our commitments regarding the human right to safe drinking water and sanitation and where there is improved hygiene; and where food is sufficient, safe, affordable and nutritious. A world where human habitats are safe, resilient and sustainable and where there is universal access to affordable, reliable and sustainable energy.

8.   We envisage a world of universal respect for human rights and human dignity, the rule of law, justice, equality and non-discrimination; of respect for race, ethnicity and cultural diversity; and of equal opportunity permitting the full realization of human potential and contributing to shared prosperity. A world which invests in its children and in which every child grows up free from violence and exploitation. A world in which every woman and girl enjoys full gender equality and all legal, social and economic barriers to their empowerment have been removed. A just, equitable, tolerant, open and socially inclusive world in which the needs of the most vulnerable are met.

9.   We envisage a world in which every country enjoys sustained, inclusive and sustainable economic growth and decent work for all. A world in which consumption and production patterns and use of all natural resources – from air to land, from rivers, lakes and aquifers to oceans and seas – are sustainable. One in which democracy, good governance and the rule of law, as well as an enabling environment at the national and international levels, are essential for sustainable development, including sustained and inclusive economic growth, social development, environmental protection and the eradication of poverty and hunger. One in which development and the application of technology are climate-sensitive, respect biodiversity and are resilient. One in which humanity lives in harmony with nature and in which wildlife and other living species are protected.

Our shared principles and commitments

10.   The new Agenda is guided by the purposes and principles of the Charter of the United Nations, including full respect for international law. It is grounded in the Universal Declaration of Human Rights,[1] international human rights treaties, the Millennium Declaration[2] and the 2005 World Summit Outcome.[3] It is informed by other instruments such as the Declaration on the Right to Development.[4]

11.   We reaffirm the outcomes of all major United Nations conferences and summits which have laid a solid foundation for sustainable development and have helped to shape the new Agenda. These include the Rio Declaration on Environment and Development,[5] the World Summit on Sustainable Development, the

---

[1] Resolution 217 A (III).

[2] Resolution 55/2.

[3] Resolution 60/1.

[4] Resolution 41/128, annex.

[5] *Report of the United Nations Conference on Environment and Development, Rio de Janeiro, 3–14 June 1992*, vol. I, *Resolutions Adopted by the Conference* (United Nations publication, Sales No. E.93.I.8 and corrigendum), resolution 1, annex I.

World Summit for Social Development, the Programme of Action of the International Conference on Population and Development,[6] the Beijing Platform for Action[7] and the United Nations Conference on Sustainable Development. We also reaffirm the follow-up to these conferences, including the outcomes of the Fourth United Nations Conference on the Least Developed Countries, the third International Conference on Small Island Developing States, the second United Nations Conference on Landlocked Developing Countries and the Third United Nations World Conference on Disaster Risk Reduction.

12.   We reaffirm all the principles of the Rio Declaration on Environment and Development, including, inter alia, the principle of common but differentiated responsibilities, as set out in principle 7 thereof.

13.   The challenges and commitments identified at these major conferences and summits are interrelated and call for integrated solutions. To address them effectively, a new approach is needed. Sustainable development recognizes that eradicating poverty in all its forms and dimensions, combating inequality within and among countries, preserving the planet, creating sustained, inclusive and sustainable economic growth and fostering social inclusion are linked to each other and are interdependent.

Our world today

14.   We are meeting at a time of immense challenges to sustainable development. Billions of our citizens continue to live in poverty and are denied a life of dignity. There are rising inequalities within and among countries. There are enormous disparities of opportunity, wealth and power. Gender inequality remains a key challenge. Unemployment, particularly youth unemployment, is a major concern. Global health threats, more frequent and intense natural disasters, spiralling conflict, violent extremism, terrorism and related humanitarian crises and forced displacement of people threaten to reverse much of the development progress made in recent decades. Natural resource depletion and adverse impacts of environmental degradation, including desertification, drought, land degradation, freshwater scarcity and loss of biodiversity, add to and exacerbate the list of challenges which humanity faces. Climate change is one of the greatest challenges of our time and its adverse impacts undermine the ability of all countries to achieve sustainable development. Increases in global temperature, sea level rise, ocean acidification and other climate change impacts are seriously affecting coastal areas and low-lying coastal countries, including many least developed countries and small island developing States. The survival of many societies, and of the biological support systems of the planet, is at risk.

15.   It is also, however, a time of immense opportunity. Significant progress has been made in meeting many development challenges. Within the past generation, hundreds of millions of people have emerged from extreme poverty. Access to education has greatly increased for both boys and girls. The spread of information and communications technology and global interconnectedness has great

---

[6] *Report of the International Conference on Population and Development, Cairo, 5– 13 September 1994* (United Nations publication, Sales No. E.95.XIII.18), chap. I, resolution 1, annex.

[7] *Report of the Fourth World Conference on Women, Beijing, 4–15 September 1995* (United Nations publication, Sales No. E.96.IV.13), chap. I, resolution 1, annex II.

potential to accelerate human progress, to bridge the digital divide and to develop knowledge societies, as does scientific and technological innovation across areas as diverse as medicine and energy.

16. Almost 15 years ago, the Millennium Development Goals were agreed. These provided an important framework for development and significant progress has been made in a number of areas. But the progress has been uneven, particularly in Africa, least developed countries, landlocked developing countries and small island developing States, and some of the Millennium Development Goals remain off-track, in particular those related to maternal, newborn and child health and to reproductive health. We recommit ourselves to the full realization of all the Millennium Development Goals, including the off-track Millennium Development Goals, in particular by providing focused and scaled-up assistance to least developed countries and other countries in special situations, in line with relevant support programmes. The new Agenda builds on the Millennium Development Goals and seeks to complete what they did not achieve, particularly in reaching the most vulnerable.

17. In its scope, however, the framework we are announcing today goes far beyond the Millennium Development Goals. Alongside continuing development priorities such as poverty eradication, health, education and food security and nutrition, it sets out a wide range of economic, social and environmental objectives. It also promises more peaceful and inclusive societies. It also, crucially, defines means of implementation. Reflecting the integrated approach that we have decided on, there are deep interconnections and many cross-cutting elements across the new Goals and targets.

The new Agenda

18. We are announcing today 17 Sustainable Development Goals with 169 associated targets which are integrated and indivisible. Never before have world leaders pledged common action and endeavour across such a broad and universal policy agenda. We are setting out together on the path towards sustainable development, devoting ourselves collectively to the pursuit of global development and of "win-win" cooperation which can bring huge gains to all countries and all parts of the world. We reaffirm that every State has, and shall freely exercise, full permanent sovereignty over all its wealth, natural resources and economic activity. We will implement the Agenda for the full benefit of all, for today's generation and for future generations. In doing so, we reaffirm our commitment to international law and emphasize that the Agenda is to be implemented in a manner that is consistent with the rights and obligations of States under international law.

19. We reaffirm the importance of the Universal Declaration of Human Rights, as well as other international instruments relating to human rights and international law. We emphasize the responsibilities of all States, in conformity with the Charter of the United Nations, to respect, protect and promote human rights and fundamental freedoms for all, without distinction of any kind as to race, colour, sex, language, religion, political or other opinion, national or social origin, property, birth, disability or other status.

20. Realizing gender equality and the empowerment of women and girls will make a crucial contribution to progress across all the Goals and targets. The achievement of full human potential and of

sustainable development is not possible if one half of humanity continues to be denied its full human rights and opportunities. Women and girls must enjoy equal access to quality education, economic resources and political participation as well as equal opportunities with men and boys for employment, leadership and decision-making at all levels. We will work for a significant increase in investments to close the gender gap and strengthen support for institutions in relation to gender equality and the empowerment of women at the global, regional and national levels. All forms of discrimination and violence against women and girls will be eliminated, including through the engagement of men and boys. The systematic mainstreaming of a gender perspective in the implementation of the Agenda is crucial.

21.   The new Goals and targets will come into effect on 1 January 2016 and will guide the decisions we take over the next 15 years. All of us will work to implement the Agenda within our own countries and at the regional and global levels, taking into account different national realities, capacities and levels of development and respecting national policies and priorities. We will respect national policy space for sustained, inclusive and sustainable economic growth, in particular for developing States, while remaining consistent with relevant international rules and commitments. We acknowledge also the importance of the regional and subregional dimensions, regional economic integration and interconnectivity in sustainable development. Regional and subregional frameworks can facilitate the effective translation of sustainable development policies into concrete action at the national level.

22.   Each country faces specific challenges in its pursuit of sustainable development. The most vulnerable countries and, in particular, African countries, least developed countries, landlocked developing countries and small island developing States, deserve special attention, as do countries in situations of conflict and post-conflict countries. There are also serious challenges within many middle-income countries.

23.   People who are vulnerable must be empowered. Those whose needs are reflected in the Agenda include all children, youth, persons with disabilities (of whom more than 80 per cent live in poverty), people living with HIV/AIDS, older persons, indigenous peoples, refugees and internally displaced persons and migrants. We resolve to take further effective measures and actions, in conformity with international law, to remove obstacles and constraints, strengthen support and meet the special needs of people living in areas affected by complex humanitarian emergencies and in areas affected by terrorism.

24.   We are committed to ending poverty in all its forms and dimensions, including by eradicating extreme poverty by 2030. All people must enjoy a basic standard of living, including through social protection systems. We are also determined to end hunger and to achieve food security as a matter of priority and to end all forms of malnutrition. In this regard, we reaffirm the important role and inclusive nature of the Committee on World Food Security and welcome the Rome Declaration on Nutrition and the Framework for Action.[8] We will devote resources to developing rural areas and sustainable agriculture and fisheries, supporting smallholder farmers,

---

[8] World Health Organization, document EB 136/8, annexes I and II.

especially women farmers, herders and fishers in developing countries, particularly least developed countries.

25. We commit to providing inclusive and equitable quality education at all levels – early childhood, primary, secondary, tertiary, technical and vocational training. All people, irrespective of sex, age, race or ethnicity, and persons with disabilities, migrants, indigenous peoples, children and youth, especially those in vulnerable situations, should have access to life-long learning opportunities that help them to acquire the knowledge and skills needed to exploit opportunities and to participate fully in society. We will strive to provide children and youth with a nurturing environment for the full realization of their rights and capabilities, helping our countries to reap the demographic dividend, including through safe schools and cohesive communities and families.

26. To promote physical and mental health and well-being, and to extend life expectancy for all, we must achieve universal health coverage and access to quality health care. No one must be left behind. We commit to accelerating the progress made to date in reducing newborn, child and maternal mortality by ending all such preventable deaths before 2030. We are committed to ensuring universal access to sexual and reproductive health-care services, including for family planning, information and education. We will equally accelerate the pace of progress made in fighting malaria, HIV/AIDS, tuberculosis, hepatitis, Ebola and other communicable diseases and epidemics, including by addressing growing anti-microbial resistance and the problem of unattended diseases affecting developing countries. We are committed to the prevention and treatment of non-communicable diseases, including behavioural, developmental and neurological disorders, which constitute a major challenge for sustainable development.

27. We will seek to build strong economic foundations for all our countries. Sustained, inclusive and sustainable economic growth is essential for prosperity. This will only be possible if wealth is shared and income inequality is addressed. We will work to build dynamic, sustainable, innovative and people-centred economies, promoting youth employment and women's economic empowerment, in particular, and decent work for all. We will eradicate forced labour and human trafficking and end child labour in all its forms. All countries stand to benefit from having a healthy and well-educated workforce with the knowledge and skills needed for productive and fulfilling work and full participation in society. We will strengthen the productive capacities of least developed countries in all sectors, including through structural transformation. We will adopt policies which increase productive capacities, productivity and productive employment; financial inclusion; sustainable agriculture, pastoralist and fisheries development; sustainable industrial development; universal access to affordable, reliable, sustainable and modern energy services; sustainable transport systems; and quality and resilient infrastructure.

28. We commit to making fundamental changes in the way that our societies produce and consume goods and services. Governments, international organizations, the business sector and other non-State actors and individuals must contribute to changing unsustainable consumption and production patterns, including through the mobilization, from all sources, of financial and technical assistance to strengthen developing countries' scientific, technological and innovative capacities to move towards more sustainable patterns of

166

consumption and production. We encourage the implementation of the 10-Year Framework of Programmes on Sustainable Consumption and Production Patterns. All countries take action, with developed countries taking the lead, taking into account the development and capabilities of developing countries.

29.   We recognize the positive contribution of migrants for inclusive growth and sustainable development. We also recognize that international migration is a multidimensional reality of major relevance for the development of countries of origin, transit and destination, which requires coherent and comprehensive responses. We will cooperate internationally to ensure safe, orderly and regular migration involving full respect for human rights and the humane treatment of migrants regardless of migration status, of refugees and of displaced persons. Such cooperation should also strengthen the resilience of communities hosting refugees, particularly in developing countries. We underline the right of migrants to return to their country of citizenship, and recall that States must ensure that their returning nationals are duly received.

30.   States are strongly urged to refrain from promulgating and applying any unilateral economic, financial or trade measures not in accordance with international law and the Charter of the United Nations that impede the full achievement of economic and social development, particularly in developing countries.

31.   We acknowledge that the United Nations Framework Convention on Climate Change[9] is the primary international, intergovernmental forum for negotiating the global response to climate change. We are determined to address decisively the threat posed by climate change and environmental degradation. The global nature of climate change calls for the widest possible international cooperation aimed at accelerating the reduction of global greenhouse gas emissions and addressing adaptation to the adverse impacts of climate change. We note with grave concern the significant gap between the aggregate effect of parties' mitigation pledges in terms of global annual emissions of greenhouse gases by 2020 and aggregate emission pathways consistent with having a likely chance of holding the increase in global average temperature below 2 degrees Celsius, or 1.5 degrees Celsius above pre-industrial levels.

32.   Looking ahead to the twenty-first session of the Conference of the Parties in Paris, we underscore the commitment of all States to work for an ambitious and universal climate agreement. We reaffirm that the protocol, another legal instrument or agreed outcome with legal force under the Convention applicable to all parties shall address in a balanced manner, inter alia, mitigation, adaptation, finance, technology development and transfer and capacity-building; and transparency of action and support.

33.   We recognize that social and economic development depends on the sustainable management of our planet's natural resources. We are therefore determined to conserve and sustainably use oceans and seas, freshwater resources, as well as forests, mountains and drylands and to protect biodiversity, ecosystems and wildlife. We are also determined to promote sustainable tourism, to tackle water scarcity and water pollution, to strengthen cooperation on desertification, dust storms, land degradation and drought and to promote resilience and disaster risk reduction. In this regard, we look forward to the thirteenth

---

[9] United Nations, *Treaty Series*, vol. 1771, No. 30822.

meeting of the Conference of the Parties to the Convention on Biological Diversity to be held in Mexico.

34. We recognize that sustainable urban development and management are crucial to the quality of life of our people. We will work with local authorities and communities to renew and plan our cities and human settlements so as to foster community cohesion and personal security and to stimulate innovation and employment. We will reduce the negative impacts of urban activities and of chemicals which are hazardous for human health and the environment, including through the environmentally sound management and safe use of chemicals, the reduction and recycling of waste and the more efficient use of water and energy. And we will work to minimize the impact of cities on the global climate system. We will also take account of population trends and projections in our national rural and urban development strategies and policies. We look forward to the upcoming United Nations Conference on Housing and Sustainable Urban Development to be held in Quito.

35. Sustainable development cannot be realized without peace and security; and peace and security will be at risk without sustainable development. The new Agenda recognizes the need to build peaceful, just and inclusive societies that provide equal access to justice and that are based on respect for human rights (including the right to development), on effective rule of law and good governance at all levels and on transparent, effective and accountable institutions. Factors which give rise to violence, insecurity and injustice, such as inequality, corruption, poor governance and illicit financial and arms flows, are addressed in the Agenda. We must redouble our efforts to resolve or prevent conflict and to support post-conflict countries, including through ensuring that women have a role in peacebuilding and State-building. We call for further effective measures and actions to be taken, in conformity with international law, to remove the obstacles to the full realization of the right of self-determination of peoples living under colonial and foreign occupation, which continue to adversely affect their economic and social development as well as their environment.

36. We pledge to foster intercultural understanding, tolerance, mutual respect and an ethic of global citizenship and shared responsibility. We acknowledge the natural and cultural diversity of the world and recognize that all cultures and civilizations can contribute to, and are crucial enablers of, sustainable development.

37. Sport is also an important enabler of sustainable development. We recognize the growing contribution of sport to the realization of development and peace in its promotion of tolerance and respect and the contributions it makes to the empowerment of women and of young people, individuals and communities as well as to health, education and social inclusion objectives.

38. We reaffirm, in accordance with the Charter of the United Nations, the need to respect the territorial integrity and political independence of States.

Means of implementation

39. The scale and ambition of the new Agenda requires a revitalized Global Partnership to ensure its implementation. We fully commit to this. This Partnership will work in a spirit of global solidarity, in particular solidarity with the poorest and with people in vulnerable situations. It will facilitate an intensive global engagement in support

of implementation of all the Goals and targets, bringing together Governments, the private sector, civil society, the United Nations system and other actors and mobilizing all available resources.

40. The means of implementation targets under Goal 17 and under each Sustainable Development Goal are key to realizing our Agenda and are of equal importance with the other Goals and targets. The Agenda, including the Sustainable Development Goals, can be met within the framework of a revitalized Global Partnership for Sustainable Development, supported by the concrete policies and actions as outlined in the outcome document of the third International Conference on Financing for Development, held in Addis Ababa from 13 to 16 July 2015. We welcome the endorsement by the General Assembly of the Addis Ababa Action Agenda,[10] which is an integral part of the 2030 Agenda for Sustainable Development. We recognize that the full implementation of the Addis Ababa Action Agenda is critical for the realization of the Sustainable Development Goals and targets.

41. We recognize that each country has primary responsibility for its own economic and social development. The new Agenda deals with the means required for implementation of the Goals and targets. We recognize that these will include the mobilization of financial resources as well as capacity-building and the transfer of environmentally sound technologies to developing countries on favourable terms, including on concessional and preferential terms, as mutually agreed. Public finance, both domestic and international, will play a vital role in providing essential services and public goods and in catalysing other sources of finance. We acknowledge the role of the diverse private sector, ranging from micro-enterprises to cooperatives to multinationals, and that of civil society organizations and philanthropic organizations in the implementation of the new Agenda.

42. We support the implementation of relevant strategies and programmes of action, including the Istanbul Declaration and Programme of Action,[11] the SIDS Accelerated Modalities of Action (SAMOA) Pathway[12] and the Vienna Programme of Action for Landlocked Developing Countries for the Decade 2014–2024,[13] and reaffirm the importance of supporting the African Union's Agenda 2063 and the programme of the New Partnership for Africa's Development,[14] all of which are integral to the new Agenda. We recognize the major challenge to the achievement of durable peace and sustainable development in countries in conflict and post-conflict situations.

43. We emphasize that international public finance plays an important role in complementing the efforts of countries to mobilize public resources domestically, especially in the poorest and most vulnerable countries with limited domestic resources. An important use of international public finance, including official development assistance (ODA), is to catalyse additional resource mobilization from other sources, public and private. ODA providers reaffirm their

---

[10] The Addis Ababa Action Agenda of the Third International Conference on Financing for Development (Addis Ababa Action Agenda), adopted by the General Assembly on 27 July 2015 (resolution 69/313, annex).

[11] *Report of the Fourth United Nations Conference on the Least Developed Countries, Istanbul,* *Turkey,* *9–13 May 2011* (A/CONF.219/7), chaps. I and II.

[12] Resolution 69/15, annex.

[13] Resolution 69/137, annex II.

[14] A/57/304, annex.

respective commitments, including the commitment by many developed countries to achieve the target of 0.7 per cent of gross national income for official development assistance (ODA/GNI) to developing countries and 0.15 per cent to 0.2 per cent of ODA/GNI to least developed countries.

44. We acknowledge the importance for international financial institutions to support, in line with their mandates, the policy space of each country, in particular developing countries. We recommit to broadening and strengthening the voice and participation of developing countries – including African countries, least developed countries, landlocked developing countries, small island developing States and middle-income countries – in international economic decision-making, norm-setting and global economic governance.

45. We acknowledge also the essential role of national parliaments through their enactment of legislation and adoption of budgets and their role in ensuring accountability for the effective implementation of our commitments. Governments and public institutions will also work closely on implementation with regional and local authorities, subregional institutions, international institutions, academia, philanthropic organizations, volunteer groups and others.

46. We underline the important role and comparative advantage of an adequately resourced, relevant, coherent, efficient and effective United Nations system in supporting the achievement of the Sustainable Development Goals and sustainable development. While stressing the importance of strengthened national ownership and leadership at the country level, we express our support for the ongoing dialogue in the Economic and Social Council on the longer-term positioning of the United Nations development system in the context of this Agenda.

Follow-up and review

47. Our Governments have the primary responsibility for follow-up and review, at the national, regional and global levels, in relation to the progress made in implementing the Goals and targets over the coming 15 years. To support accountability to our citizens, we will provide for systematic follow-up and review at the various levels, as set out in this Agenda and the Addis Ababa Action Agenda. The high-level political forum under the auspices of the General Assembly and the Economic and Social Council will have the central role in overseeing follow-up and review at the global level.

48. Indicators are being developed to assist this work. Quality, accessible, timely and reliable disaggregated data will be needed to help with the measurement of progress and to ensure that no one is left behind. Such data is key to decision-making. Data and information from existing reporting mechanisms should be used where possible. We agree to intensify our efforts to strengthen statistical capacities in developing countries, particularly African countries, least developed countries, landlocked developing countries, small island developing States and middle-income countries. We are committed to developing broader measures of progress to complement gross domestic product.

A call for action to change our world

49. Seventy years ago, an earlier generation of world leaders came together to create the United Nations. From the ashes of war and division they fashioned this Organization and the values of peace, dialogue and

international cooperation which underpin it. The supreme embodiment of those values is the Charter of the United Nations.

50. Today we are also taking a decision of great historic significance. We resolve to build a better future for all people, including the millions who have been denied the chance to lead decent, dignified and rewarding lives and to achieve their full human potential. We can be the first generation to succeed in ending poverty; just as we may be the last to have a chance of saving the planet. The world will be a better place in 2030 if we succeed in our objectives.

51. What we are announcing today – an Agenda for global action for the next 15 years – is a charter for people and planet in the twenty-first century. Children and young women and men are critical agents of change and will find in the new Goals a platform to channel their infinite capacities for activism into the creation of a better world.

52. "We the peoples" are the celebrated opening words of the Charter of the United Nations. It is "we the peoples" who are embarking today on the road to 2030. Our journey will involve Governments as well as parliaments, the United Nations system and other international institutions, local authorities, indigenous peoples, civil society, business and the private sector, the scientific and academic community – and all people. Millions have already engaged with, and will own, this Agenda. It is an Agenda of the people, by the people and for the people – and this, we believe, will ensure its success.

53. The future of humanity and of our planet lies in our hands. It lies also in the hands of today's younger generation who will pass the torch to future generations. We have mapped the road to sustainable development; it will be for all of us to ensure that the journey is successful and its gains irreversible.

Sustainable Development Goals and targets

54. Following an inclusive process of intergovernmental negotiations, and based on the proposal of the Open Working Group on Sustainable Development Goals,[15] which includes a chapeau contextualizing the latter, set out below are the Goals and targets which we have agreed.

55. The Sustainable Development Goals and targets are integrated and indivisible, global in nature and universally applicable, taking into account different national realities, capacities and levels of development and respecting national policies and priorities. Targets are defined as aspirational and global, with each Government setting its own national targets guided by the global level of ambition but taking into account national circumstances. Each Government will also decide how these aspirational and global targets should be incorporated into national planning processes, policies and strategies. It is important to recognize the link between sustainable development and other relevant ongoing processes in the economic, social and environmental fields.

56. In deciding upon these Goals and targets, we recognize that each country faces specific challenges to achieve sustainable development, and we underscore the special challenges facing the most vulnerable countries and, in particular, African countries, least developed countries, landlocked developing countries and small island developing States, as well as the specific challenges facing the middle-income countries. Countries in situations of conflict also need special attention.

57. We recognize that baseline data for several of the targets remains unavailable, and we call for increased support for strengthening data collection and capacity-building in Member States, to develop national and global baselines where they do not yet exist. We commit to addressing this gap in data collection so as to better inform the measurement of progress, in particular for those targets below which do not have clear numerical targets.

58. We encourage ongoing efforts by States in other forums to address key issues which pose potential challenges to the implementation of our Agenda, and we respect the independent mandates of those processes. We intend that the Agenda and its implementation would support, and be without prejudice to, those other processes and the decisions taken therein.

59. We recognize that there are different approaches, visions, models and tools available to each country, in accordance with its national circumstances and priorities, to achieve sustainable development; and we reaffirm that planet Earth and its ecosystems are our common home and that "Mother Earth" is a common expression in a number of countries and regions.

---

[15] Contained in the report of the Open Working Group of the General Assembly on Sustainable Development Goals (A/68/970 and Corr.1; see also A/68/970/Add.1–3).

Sustainable Development Goals

Goal 1. End poverty in all its forms everywhere

Goal 2. End hunger, achieve food security and improved nutrition and promote sustainable agriculture

Goal 3. Ensure healthy lives and promote well-being for all at all ages

Goal 4. Ensure inclusive and equitable quality education and promote lifelong learning opportunities for all

Goal 5. Achieve gender equality and empower all women and girls

Goal 6. Ensure availability and sustainable management of water and sanitation for all

Goal 7 Ensure access to affordable, reliable, sustainable and modern energy for all

Goal 8. Promote sustained, inclusive and sustainable economic growth, full and productive employment and decent work for all

Goal 9. Build resilient infrastructure, promote inclusive and sustainable industrialization and foster innovation

Goal 10. Reduce inequality within and among countries

Goal 11. Make cities and human settlements inclusive, safe, resilient and sustainable

Goal 12. Ensure sustainable consumption and production patterns

Goal 13. Take urgent action to combat climate change and its impacts[*]

Goal 14. Conserve and sustainably use the oceans, seas and marine resources for sustainable development

Goal 15. Protect, restore and promote sustainable use of terrestrial ecosystems, sustainably manage forests, combat desertification, and halt and reverse land degradation and halt biodiversity loss

Goal 16. Promote peaceful and inclusive societies for sustainable development, provide access to justice for all and build effective, accountable and inclusive institutions at all levels

Goal 17.   Strengthen the means of implementation and revitalize the Global Partnership for Sustainable Development

---

Goal 1.   End poverty in all its forms everywhere

1.1   By 2030, eradicate extreme poverty for all people everywhere, currently measured as people living on less than $1.25 a day

1.2   By 2030, reduce at least by half the proportion of men, women and children of all ages living in poverty in all its dimensions according to national definitions

1.3   Implement nationally appropriate social protection systems and measures for all, including floors, and by 2030 achieve substantial coverage of the poor and the vulnerable

1.4   By 2030, ensure that all men and women, in particular the poor and the vulnerable, have equal rights to economic resources, as well as access to basic services, ownership and control over land and other forms of property, inheritance, natural resources, appropriate new technology and financial services, including microfinance

1.5   By 2030, build the resilience of the poor and those in vulnerable situations and reduce their exposure and vulnerability to climate-related extreme events and other economic, social and environmental shocks and disasters

1.a   Ensure significant mobilization of resources from a variety of sources, including through enhanced development cooperation, in order to provide adequate and predictable means for developing countries, in particular least developed countries, to implement programmes and policies to end poverty in all its dimensions

1.b   Create sound policy frameworks at the national, regional and international levels, based on pro-poor and gender-sensitive development strategies, to support accelerated investment in poverty eradication actions

Goal 2.   End hunger, achieve food security and improved nutrition and promote sustainable agriculture

2.1   By 2030, end hunger and ensure access by all people, in particular the poor and people in vulnerable situations, including infants, to safe, nutritious and sufficient food all year round

2.2   By 2030, end all forms of malnutrition, including achieving, by 2025, the internationally agreed targets on stunting and wasting in children under 5 years of age, and address the nutritional needs of adolescent girls, pregnant and lactating women and older persons

2.3   By 2030, double the agricultural productivity and incomes of small-scale food producers, in particular women, indigenous peoples, family farmers, pastoralists and fishers, including through secure and equal access to land, other productive resources and inputs, knowledge, financial services, markets and opportunities for value addition and non-farm employment

2.4 By 2030, ensure sustainable food production systems and implement resilient agricultural practices that increase productivity and production, that help maintain ecosystems, that strengthen capacity for adaptation to climate change, extreme weather, drought, flooding and other disasters and that progressively improve land and soil quality

2.5 By 2020, maintain the genetic diversity of seeds, cultivated plants and farmed and domesticated animals and their related wild species, including through soundly managed and diversified seed and plant banks at the national, regional and international levels, and promote access to and fair and equitable sharing of benefits arising from the utilization of genetic resources and associated traditional knowledge, as internationally agreed

2.a Increase investment, including through enhanced international cooperation, in rural infrastructure, agricultural research and extension services, technology development and plant and livestock gene banks in order to enhance agricultural productive capacity in developing countries, in particular least developed countries

2.b Correct and prevent trade restrictions and distortions in world agricultural markets, including through the parallel elimination of all forms of agricultural export subsidies and all export measures with equivalent effect, in accordance with the mandate of the Doha Development Round

2.c Adopt measures to ensure the proper functioning of food commodity markets and their derivatives and facilitate timely access to market information, including on food reserves, in order to help limit extreme food price volatility

Goal 3. Ensure healthy lives and promote well-being for all at all ages

3.1 By 2030, reduce the global maternal mortality ratio to less than 70 per 100,000 live births

3.2 By 2030, end preventable deaths of newborns and children under 5 years of age, with all countries aiming to reduce neonatal mortality to at least as low as 12 per 1,000 live births and under-5 mortality to at least as low as 25 per 1,000 live births

3.3 By 2030, end the epidemics of AIDS, tuberculosis, malaria and neglected tropical diseases and combat hepatitis, water-borne diseases and other communicable diseases

3.4 By 2030, reduce by one third premature mortality from non-communicable diseases through prevention and treatment and promote mental health and well-being

3.5 Strengthen the prevention and treatment of substance abuse, including narcotic drug abuse and harmful use of alcohol

3.6 By 2020, halve the number of global deaths and injuries from road traffic accidents

3.7 By 2030, ensure universal access to sexual and reproductive health-care services, including for family planning, information and education, and the integration of reproductive health into national strategies and programmes

3.8 Achieve universal health coverage, including financial risk protection, access to quality essential health-care services and access to safe, effective, quality and affordable essential medicines and vaccines for all

3.9 By 2030, substantially reduce the number of deaths and illnesses from hazardous chemicals and air, water and soil pollution and contamination

3.a Strengthen the implementation of the World Health Organization Framework Convention on Tobacco Control in all countries, as appropriate

3.b Support the research and development of vaccines and medicines for the communicable and non-communicable diseases that primarily affect developing countries, provide access to affordable essential medicines and vaccines, in accordance with the Doha Declaration on the TRIPS Agreement and Public Health, which affirms the right of developing countries to use to the full the provisions in the Agreement on Trade-Related Aspects of Intellectual Property Rights regarding flexibilities to protect public health, and, in particular, provide access to medicines for all

3.c Substantially increase health financing and the recruitment, development, training and retention of the health workforce in developing countries, especially in least developed countries and small island developing States

3.d Strengthen the capacity of all countries, in particular developing countries, for early warning, risk reduction and management of national and global health risks

Goal 4. Ensure inclusive and equitable quality education and promote lifelong learning opportunities for all

4.1 By 2030, ensure that all girls and boys complete free, equitable and quality primary and secondary education leading to relevant and effective learning outcomes

4.2 By 2030, ensure that all girls and boys have access to quality early childhood development, care and pre-primary education so that they are ready for primary education

4.3 By 2030, ensure equal access for all women and men to affordable and quality technical, vocational and tertiary education, including university

4.4 By 2030, substantially increase the number of youth and adults who have relevant skills, including technical and vocational skills, for employment, decent jobs and entrepreneurship

4.5 By 2030, eliminate gender disparities in education and ensure equal access to all levels of education and vocational training for the vulnerable, including persons with disabilities, indigenous peoples and children in vulnerable situations

4.6 By 2030, ensure that all youth and a substantial proportion of adults, both men and women, achieve literacy and numeracy

4.7 By 2030, ensure that all learners acquire the knowledge and skills needed to promote sustainable development, including, among others, through education for sustainable development and sustainable lifestyles, human rights, gender equality, promotion of a culture of peace and non-violence, global citizenship and appreciation of cultural diversity and of culture's contribution to sustainable development

4.a Build and upgrade education facilities that are child, disability and gender sensitive and provide safe, non-violent, inclusive and effective learning environments for all

4.b By 2020, substantially expand globally the number of scholarships available to developing countries, in particular least developed countries, small island developing States and African countries, for enrolment in higher education, including vocational training and information and communications technology, technical, engineering and scientific programmes, in developed countries and other developing countries

4.c By 2030, substantially increase the supply of qualified teachers, including through international cooperation for teacher training in developing countries, especially least developed countries and small island developing States

Goal 5. Achieve gender equality and empower all women and girls

5.1 End all forms of discrimination against all women and girls everywhere

5.2 Eliminate all forms of violence against all women and girls in the public and private spheres, including trafficking and sexual and other types of exploitation

5.3 Eliminate all harmful practices, such as child, early and forced marriage and female genital mutilation

5.4 Recognize and value unpaid care and domestic work through the provision of public services, infrastructure and social protection policies and the promotion of shared responsibility within the household and the family as nationally appropriate

5.5 Ensure women's full and effective participation and equal opportunities for leadership at all levels of decision-making in political, economic and public life

5.6 Ensure universal access to sexual and reproductive health and reproductive rights as agreed in accordance with the Programme of Action of the International Conference on Population and Development and the Beijing Platform for Action and the outcome documents of their review conferences

5.a Undertake reforms to give women equal rights to economic resources, as well as access to ownership and control over land and other forms of property, financial services, inheritance and natural resources, in accordance with national laws

5.b Enhance the use of enabling technology, in particular information and communications technology, to promote the empowerment of women

5.c   Adopt and strengthen sound policies and enforceable legislation for the promotion of gender equality and the empowerment of all women and girls at all levels

Goal 6.   Ensure availability and sustainable management of water and sanitation for all

6.1   By 2030, achieve universal and equitable access to safe and affordable drinking water for all

6.2   By 2030, achieve access to adequate and equitable sanitation and hygiene for all and end open defecation, paying special attention to the needs of women and girls and those in vulnerable situations

6.3   By 2030, improve water quality by reducing pollution, eliminating dumping and minimizing release of hazardous chemicals and materials, halving the proportion of untreated wastewater and substantially increasing recycling and safe reuse globally

6.4   By 2030, substantially increase water-use efficiency across all sectors and ensure sustainable withdrawals and supply of freshwater to address water scarcity and substantially reduce the number of people suffering from water scarcity

6.5   By 2030, implement integrated water resources management at all levels, including through transboundary cooperation as appropriate

6.6   By 2020, protect and restore water-related ecosystems, including mountains, forests, wetlands, rivers, aquifers and lakes

6.a   By 2030, expand international cooperation and capacity-building support to developing countries in water- and sanitation-related activities and programmes, including water harvesting, desalination, water efficiency, wastewater treatment, recycling and reuse technologies

6.b   Support and strengthen the participation of local communities in improving water and sanitation management

Goal 7.   Ensure access to affordable, reliable, sustainable and modern energy for all

7.1   By 2030, ensure universal access to affordable, reliable and modern energy services

7.2   By 2030, increase substantially the share of renewable energy in the global energy mix

7.3   By 2030, double the global rate of improvement in energy efficiency

7.a   By 2030, enhance international cooperation to facilitate access to clean energy research and technology, including renewable energy, energy efficiency and advanced and cleaner fossil-fuel technology, and promote investment in energy infrastructure and clean energy technology

7.b   By 2030, expand infrastructure and upgrade technology for supplying modern and sustainable energy services for all in developing countries, in particular least developed countries, small island developing States and landlocked developing countries, in accordance with their respective programmes of support

Goal 8. Promote sustained, inclusive and sustainable economic growth, full and productive employment and decent work for all

8.1 Sustain per capita economic growth in accordance with national circumstances and, in particular, at least 7 per cent gross domestic product growth per annum in the least developed countries

8.2 Achieve higher levels of economic productivity through diversification, technological upgrading and innovation, including through a focus on high-value added and labour-intensive sectors

8.3 Promote development-oriented policies that support productive activities, decent job creation, entrepreneurship, creativity and innovation, and encourage the formalization and growth of micro-, small- and medium-sized enterprises, including through access to financial services

8.4 Improve progressively, through 2030, global resource efficiency in consumption and production and endeavour to decouple economic growth from environmental degradation, in accordance with the 10-Year Framework of Programmes on Sustainable Consumption and Production, with developed countries taking the lead

8.5 By 2030, achieve full and productive employment and decent work for all women and men, including for young people and persons with disabilities, and equal pay for work of equal value

8.6 By 2020, substantially reduce the proportion of youth not in employment, education or training

8.7 Take immediate and effective measures to eradicate forced labour, end modern slavery and human trafficking and secure the prohibition and elimination of the worst forms of child labour, including recruitment and use of child soldiers, and by 2025 end child labour in all its forms

8.8 Protect labour rights and promote safe and secure working environments for all workers, including migrant workers, in particular women migrants, and those in precarious employment

8.9 By 2030, devise and implement policies to promote sustainable tourism that creates jobs and promotes local culture and products

8.10 Strengthen the capacity of domestic financial institutions to encourage and expand access to banking, insurance and financial services for all

8.a Increase Aid for Trade support for developing countries, in particular least developed countries, including through the Enhanced Integrated Framework for Trade-related Technical Assistance to Least Developed Countries

8.b By 2020, develop and operationalize a global strategy for youth employment and implement the Global Jobs Pact of the International Labour Organization

Goal 9. Build resilient infrastructure, promote inclusive and sustainable industrialization and foster innovation

9.1 Develop quality, reliable, sustainable and resilient infrastructure, including regional and transborder infrastructure, to support economic development and human well-being, with a focus on affordable and equitable access for all

9.2 Promote inclusive and sustainable industrialization and, by 2030, significantly raise industry's share of employment and gross domestic product, in line with national circumstances, and double its share in least developed countries

9.3 Increase the access of small-scale industrial and other enterprises, in particular in developing countries, to financial services, including affordable credit, and their integration into value chains and markets

9.4 By 2030, upgrade infrastructure and retrofit industries to make them sustainable, with increased resource-use efficiency and greater adoption of clean and environmentally sound technologies and industrial processes, with all countries taking action in accordance with their respective capabilities

9.5 Enhance scientific research, upgrade the technological capabilities of industrial sectors in all countries, in particular developing countries, including, by 2030, encouraging innovation and substantially increasing the number of research and development workers per 1 million people and public and private research and development spending

9.a Facilitate sustainable and resilient infrastructure development in developing countries through enhanced financial, technological and technical support to African countries, least developed countries, landlocked developing countries and small island developing States

9.b Support domestic technology development, research and innovation in developing countries, including by ensuring a conducive policy environment for, inter alia, industrial diversification and value addition to commodities

9.c Significantly increase access to information and communications technology and strive to provide universal and affordable access to the Internet in least developed countries by 2020

Goal 10. Reduce inequality within and among countries

10.1 By 2030, progressively achieve and sustain income growth of the bottom 40 per cent of the population at a rate higher than the national average

10.2 By 2030, empower and promote the social, economic and political inclusion of all, irrespective of age, sex, disability, race, ethnicity, origin, religion or economic or other status

10.3 Ensure equal opportunity and reduce inequalities of outcome, including by eliminating discriminatory laws, policies and practices and promoting appropriate legislation, policies and action in this regard

10.4 Adopt policies, especially fiscal, wage and social protection policies, and progressively achieve greater equality

10.5 Improve the regulation and monitoring of global financial markets and institutions and strengthen the implementation of such regulations

10.6 Ensure enhanced representation and voice for developing countries in decision-making in global international economic and financial institutions in order to deliver more effective, credible, accountable and legitimate institutions

10.7 Facilitate orderly, safe, regular and responsible migration and mobility of people, including through the implementation of planned and well-managed migration policies

10.a Implement the principle of special and differential treatment for developing countries, in particular least developed countries, in accordance with World Trade Organization agreements

10.b Encourage official development assistance and financial flows, including foreign direct investment, to States where the need is greatest, in particular least developed countries, African countries, small island developing States and landlocked developing countries, in accordance with their national plans and programmes

10.c By 2030, reduce to less than 3 per cent the transaction costs of migrant remittances and eliminate remittance corridors with costs higher than 5 per cent

Goal 11. Make cities and human settlements inclusive, safe, resilient and sustainable

11.1 By 2030, ensure access for all to adequate, safe and affordable housing and basic services and upgrade slums

11.2 By 2030, provide access to safe, affordable, accessible and sustainable transport systems for all, improving road safety, notably by expanding public transport, with special attention to the needs of those in vulnerable situations, women, children, persons with disabilities and older persons

11.3 By 2030, enhance inclusive and sustainable urbanization and capacity for participatory, integrated and sustainable human settlement planning and management in all countries

11.4 Strengthen efforts to protect and safeguard the world's cultural and natural heritage

11.5 By 2030, significantly reduce the number of deaths and the number of people affected and substantially decrease the direct economic losses relative to global gross domestic product caused by disasters, including water-related disasters, with a focus on protecting the poor and people in vulnerable situations

11.6 By 2030, reduce the adverse per capita environmental impact of cities, including by paying special attention to air quality and municipal and other waste management

11.7 By 2030, provide universal access to safe, inclusive and accessible, green and public spaces, in particular for women and children, older persons and persons with disabilities

11.a Support positive economic, social and environmental links between urban, peri-urban and rural areas by strengthening national and regional development planning

11.b By 2020, substantially increase the number of cities and human settlements adopting and implementing integrated policies and plans towards inclusion, resource efficiency, mitigation and adaptation to climate change, resilience to disasters, and develop and implement, in line with the Sendai Framework for Disaster Risk Reduction 2015–2030, holistic disaster risk management at all levels

11.c Support least developed countries, including through financial and technical assistance, in building sustainable and resilient buildings utilizing local materials

Goal 12. Ensure sustainable consumption and production patterns

12.1 Implement the 10-Year Framework of Programmes on Sustainable Consumption and Production Patterns, all countries taking action, with developed countries taking the lead, taking into account the development and capabilities of developing countries

12.2 By 2030, achieve the sustainable management and efficient use of natural resources

12.3 By 2030, halve per capita global food waste at the retail and consumer levels and reduce food losses along production and supply chains, including post-harvest losses

12.4 By 2020, achieve the environmentally sound management of chemicals and all wastes throughout their life cycle, in accordance with agreed international frameworks, and significantly reduce their release to air, water and soil in order to minimize their adverse impacts on human health and the environment

12.5 By 2030, substantially reduce waste generation through prevention, reduction, recycling and reuse

12.6 Encourage companies, especially large and transnational companies, to adopt sustainable practices and to integrate sustainability information into their reporting cycle

12.7 Promote public procurement practices that are sustainable, in accordance with national policies and priorities

12.8 By 2030, ensure that people everywhere have the relevant information and awareness for sustainable development and lifestyles in harmony with nature

12.a Support developing countries to strengthen their scientific and technological capacity to move towards more sustainable patterns of consumption and production

12.b Develop and implement tools to monitor sustainable development impacts for sustainable tourism that creates jobs and promotes local culture and products

12.c Rationalize inefficient fossil-fuel subsidies that encourage wasteful consumption by removing market distortions, in accordance with national circumstances, including by restructuring taxation and phasing out those harmful subsidies, where they exist, to reflect their environmental impacts, taking fully into account the specific needs and conditions of developing countries and minimizing the possible adverse impacts on their development in a manner that protects the poor and the affected communities

Goal 13. Take urgent action to combat climate change and its impacts[*]

13.1 Strengthen resilience and adaptive capacity to climate-related hazards and natural disasters in all countries

13.2 Integrate climate change measures into national policies, strategies and planning

13.3 Improve education, awareness-raising and human and institutional capacity on climate change mitigation, adaptation, impact reduction and early warning

13.a Implement the commitment undertaken by developed-country parties to the United Nations Framework Convention on Climate Change to a goal of mobilizing jointly $100 billion annually by 2020 from all sources to address the needs of developing countries in the context of meaningful mitigation actions and transparency on implementation and fully operationalize the Green Climate Fund through its capitalization as soon as possible

13.b Promote mechanisms for raising capacity for effective climate change-related planning and management in least developed countries and small island developing States, including focusing on women, youth and local and marginalized communities

Goal 14. Conserve and sustainably use the oceans, seas and marine resources for sustainable development

14.1 By 2025, prevent and significantly reduce marine pollution of all kinds, in particular from land-based activities, including marine debris and nutrient pollution

14.2 By 2020, sustainably manage and protect marine and coastal ecosystems to avoid significant adverse impacts, including by strengthening their resilience, and take action for their restoration in order to achieve healthy and productive oceans

14.3 Minimize and address the impacts of ocean acidification, including through enhanced scientific cooperation at all levels

14.4 By 2020, effectively regulate harvesting and end overfishing, illegal, unreported and unregulated fishing and destructive fishing practices and implement science-based management plans, in order to restore fish stocks in the shortest time feasible, at least to levels that can produce maximum sustainable yield as determined by their biological characteristics

14.5 By 2020, conserve at least 10 per cent of coastal and marine areas, consistent with national and international law and based on the best available scientific information

14.6 By 2020, prohibit certain forms of fisheries subsidies which contribute to overcapacity and overfishing, eliminate subsidies that

---

[*] Acknowledging that the United Nations Framework Convention on Climate Change is the primary international, intergovernmental forum for negotiating the global response to climate change.

contribute to illegal, unreported and unregulated fishing and refrain from introducing new such subsidies, recognizing that appropriate and effective special and differential treatment for developing and least developed countries should be an integral part of the World Trade Organization fisheries subsidies negotiation[16]

14.7 By 2030, increase the economic benefits to small island developing States and least developed countries from the sustainable use of marine resources, including through sustainable management of fisheries, aquaculture and tourism

14.a Increase scientific knowledge, develop research capacity and transfer marine technology, taking into account the Intergovernmental Oceanographic Commission Criteria and Guidelines on the Transfer of Marine Technology, in order to improve ocean health and to enhance the contribution of marine biodiversity to the development of developing countries, in particular small island developing States and least developed countries

14.b Provide access for small-scale artisanal fishers to marine resources and markets

14.c Enhance the conservation and sustainable use of oceans and their resources by implementing international law as reflected in the United Nations Convention on the Law of the Sea, which provides the legal framework for the conservation and sustainable use of oceans and their resources, as recalled in paragraph 158 of "The future we want"

Goal 15. Protect, restore and promote sustainable use of terrestrial ecosystems, sustainably manage forests, combat desertification, and halt and reverse land degradation and halt biodiversity loss

15.1 By 2020, ensure the conservation, restoration and sustainable use of terrestrial and inland freshwater ecosystems and their services, in particular forests, wetlands, mountains and drylands, in line with obligations under international agreements

15.2 By 2020, promote the implementation of sustainable management of all types of forests, halt deforestation, restore degraded forests and substantially increase afforestation and reforestation globally

15.3 By 2030, combat desertification, restore degraded land and soil, including land affected by desertification, drought and floods, and strive to achieve a land degradation-neutral world

15.4 By 2030, ensure the conservation of mountain ecosystems, including their biodiversity, in order to enhance their capacity to provide benefits that are essential for sustainable development

15.5 Take urgent and significant action to reduce the degradation of natural habitats, halt the loss of biodiversity and, by 2020, protect and prevent the extinction of threatened species

15.6 Promote fair and equitable sharing of the benefits arising from the utilization of genetic resources and promote appropriate access to such resources, as internationally agreed

---

[16] Taking into account ongoing World Trade Organization negotiations, the Doha Development Agenda and the Hong Kong ministerial mandate.

15.7 Take urgent action to end poaching and trafficking of protected species of flora and fauna and address both demand and supply of illegal wildlife products

15.8 By 2020, introduce measures to prevent the introduction and significantly reduce the impact of invasive alien species on land and water ecosystems and control or eradicate the priority species

15.9 By 2020, integrate ecosystem and biodiversity values into national and local planning, development processes, poverty reduction strategies and accounts

15.a Mobilize and significantly increase financial resources from all sources to conserve and sustainably use biodiversity and ecosystems

15.b Mobilize significant resources from all sources and at all levels to finance sustainable forest management and provide adequate incentives to developing countries to advance such management, including for conservation and reforestation

15.c Enhance global support for efforts to combat poaching and trafficking of protected species, including by increasing the capacity of local communities to pursue sustainable livelihood opportunities

Goal 16. Promote peaceful and inclusive societies for sustainable development, provide access to justice for all and build effective, accountable and inclusive institutions at all levels

16.1 Significantly reduce all forms of violence and related death rates everywhere

16.2 End abuse, exploitation, trafficking and all forms of violence against and torture of children

16.3 Promote the rule of law at the national and international levels and ensure equal access to justice for all

16.4 By 2030, significantly reduce illicit financial and arms flows, strengthen the recovery and return of stolen assets and combat all forms of organized crime

16.5 Substantially reduce corruption and bribery in all their forms

16.6 Develop effective, accountable and transparent institutions at all levels

16.7 Ensure responsive, inclusive, participatory and representative decision-making at all levels

16.8 Broaden and strengthen the participation of developing countries in the institutions of global governance

16.9 By 2030, provide legal identity for all, including birth registration

16.10 Ensure public access to information and protect fundamental freedoms, in accordance with national legislation and international agreements

16.a Strengthen relevant national institutions, including through international cooperation, for building capacity at all levels, in particular in developing countries, to prevent violence and combat terrorism and crime

16.b Promote and enforce non-discriminatory laws and policies for sustainable development

Goal 17. Strengthen the means of implementation and revitalize the Global Partnership for Sustainable Development

Finance

17.1 Strengthen domestic resource mobilization, including through international support to developing countries, to improve domestic capacity for tax and other revenue collection

17.2 Developed countries to implement fully their official development assistance commitments, including the commitment by many developed countries to achieve the target of 0.7 per cent of gross national income for official development assistance (ODA/GNI) to developing countries and 0.15 to 0.20 per cent of ODA/GNI to least developed countries; ODA providers are encouraged to consider setting a target to provide at least 0.20 per cent of ODA/GNI to least developed countries

17.3 Mobilize additional financial resources for developing countries from multiple sources

17.4 Assist developing countries in attaining long-term debt sustainability through coordinated policies aimed at fostering debt financing, debt relief and debt restructuring, as appropriate, and address the external debt of highly indebted poor countries to reduce debt distress

17.5 Adopt and implement investment promotion regimes for least developed countries

Technology

17.6 Enhance North-South, South-South and triangular regional and international cooperation on and access to science, technology and innovation and enhance knowledge sharing on mutually agreed terms, including through improved coordination among existing mechanisms, in particular at the United Nations level, and through a global technology facilitation mechanism

17.7 Promote the development, transfer, dissemination and diffusion of environmentally sound technologies to developing countries on favourable terms, including on concessional and preferential terms, as mutually agreed

17.8 Fully operationalize the technology bank and science, technology and innovation capacity-building mechanism for least developed countries by 2017 and enhance the use of enabling technology, in particular information and communications technology

Capacity-building

17.9 Enhance international support for implementing effective and targeted capacity-building in developing countries to support national plans to implement all the Sustainable Development Goals, including through North-South, South-South and triangular cooperation

Trade

17.10 Promote a universal, rules-based, open, non-discriminatory and equitable multilateral trading system under the World Trade Organization, including through the conclusion of negotiations under its Doha Development Agenda

17.11 Significantly increase the exports of developing countries, in particular with a view to doubling the least developed countries' share of global exports by 2020

17.12 Realize timely implementation of duty-free and quota-free market access on a lasting basis for all least developed countries, consistent with World Trade Organization decisions, including by ensuring that preferential rules of origin applicable to imports from least developed countries are transparent and simple, and contribute to facilitating market access

Systemic issues

Policy and institutional coherence

17.13 Enhance global macroeconomic stability, including through policy coordination and policy coherence

17.14 Enhance policy coherence for sustainable development

17.15 Respect each country's policy space and leadership to establish and implement policies for poverty eradication and sustainable development

Multi-stakeholder partnerships

17.16 Enhance the Global Partnership for Sustainable Development, complemented by multi-stakeholder partnerships that mobilize and share knowledge, expertise, technology and financial resources, to support the achievement of the Sustainable Development Goals in all countries, in particular developing countries

17.17 Encourage and promote effective public, public-private and civil society partnerships, building on the experience and resourcing strategies of partnerships

Data, monitoring and accountability

17.18 By 2020, enhance capacity-building support to developing countries, including for least developed countries and small island developing States, to increase significantly the availability of high-quality, timely and reliable data disaggregated by income, gender, age, race, ethnicity, migratory status, disability, geographic location and other characteristics relevant in national contexts

17.19 By 2030, build on existing initiatives to develop measurements of progress on sustainable development that complement gross domestic product, and support statistical capacity-building in developing countries

Means of implementation and the Global Partnership

60. We reaffirm our strong commitment to the full implementation of this new Agenda. We recognize that we will not be able to achieve our ambitious Goals and targets without a revitalized and enhanced Global Partnership and comparably ambitious means of

implementation. The revitalized Global Partnership will facilitate an intensive global engagement in support of implementation of all the Goals and targets, bringing together Governments, civil society, the private sector, the United Nations system and other actors and mobilizing all available resources.

61. The Agenda's Goals and targets deal with the means required to realize our collective ambitions. The means of implementation targets under each Sustainable Development Goal and Goal 17, which are referred to above, are key to realizing our Agenda and are of equal importance with the other Goals and targets. We shall accord them equal priority in our implementation efforts and in the global indicator framework for monitoring our progress.

62. This Agenda, including the Sustainable Development Goals, can be met within the framework of a revitalized Global Partnership for Sustainable Development, supported by the concrete policies and actions outlined in the Addis Ababa Action Agenda, which is an integral part of the 2030 Agenda for Sustainable Development. The Addis Ababa Action Agenda supports, complements and helps to contextualize the 2030 Agenda's means of implementation targets. It relates to domestic public resources, domestic and international private business and finance, international development cooperation, international trade as an engine for development, debt and debt sustainability, addressing systemic issues and science, technology, innovation and capacity-building, and data, monitoring and follow-up.

63. Cohesive nationally owned sustainable development strategies, supported by integrated national financing frameworks, will be at the heart of our efforts. We reiterate that each country has primary responsibility for its own economic and social development and that the role of national policies and development strategies cannot be overemphasized. We will respect each country's policy space and leadership to implement policies for poverty eradication and sustainable development, while remaining consistent with relevant international rules and commitments. At the same time, national development efforts need to be supported by an enabling international economic environment, including coherent and mutually supporting world trade, monetary and financial systems, and strengthened and enhanced global economic governance. Processes to develop and facilitate the availability of appropriate knowledge and technologies globally, as well as capacity-building, are also critical. We commit to pursuing policy coherence and an enabling environment for sustainable development at all levels and by all actors, and to reinvigorating the Global Partnership for Sustainable Development.

64. We support the implementation of relevant strategies and programmes of action, including the Istanbul Declaration and Programme of Action, the SIDS Accelerated Modalities of Action (SAMOA) Pathway and the Vienna Programme of Action for Landlocked Developing Countries for the Decade 2014–2024, and reaffirm the importance of supporting the African Union's Agenda 2063 and the programme of the New Partnership for Africa's Development, all of which are integral to the new Agenda. We recognize the major challenge to the achievement of durable peace and sustainable development in countries in conflict and post-conflict situations.

65.   We recognize that middle-income countries still face significant challenges to achieve sustainable development. In order to ensure that achievements made to date are sustained, efforts to address ongoing challenges should be strengthened through the exchange of experiences, improved coordination, and better and focused support of the United Nations development system, the international financial institutions, regional organizations and other stakeholders.

66.   We underscore that, for all countries, public policies and the mobilization and effective use of domestic resources, underscored by the principle of national ownership, are central to our common pursuit of sustainable development, including achieving the Sustainable Development Goals. We recognize that domestic resources are first and foremost generated by economic growth, supported by an enabling environment at all levels.

67.   Private business activity, investment and innovation are major drivers of productivity, inclusive economic growth and job creation. We acknowledge the diversity of the private sector, ranging from micro-enterprises to cooperatives to multinationals. We call upon all businesses to apply their creativity and innovation to solving sustainable development challenges. We will foster a dynamic and well-functioning business sector, while protecting labour rights and environmental and health standards in accordance with relevant international standards and agreements and other ongoing initiatives in this regard, such as the Guiding Principles on Business and Human Rights[17] and the labour standards of the International Labour Organization, the Convention on the Rights of the Child[18] and key multilateral environmental agreements, for parties to those agreements.

68.   International trade is an engine for inclusive economic growth and poverty reduction, and contributes to the promotion of sustainable development. We will continue to promote a universal, rules-based, open, transparent, predictable, inclusive, non-discriminatory and equitable multilateral trading system under the World Trade Organization, as well as meaningful trade liberalization. We call upon all members of the World Trade Organization to redouble their efforts to promptly conclude the negotiations on the Doha Development Agenda.[19] We attach great importance to providing trade-related capacity-building for developing countries, including African countries, least developed countries, landlocked developing countries, small island developing States and middle-income countries, including for the promotion of regional economic integration and interconnectivity.

69.   We recognize the need to assist developing countries in attaining long-term debt sustainability through coordinated policies aimed at fostering debt financing, debt relief, debt restructuring and sound debt management, as appropriate. Many countries remain vulnerable to debt crises and some are in the midst of crises, including a number of least developed countries, small island developing States and some developed countries. We reiterate that debtors and creditors must work together to prevent and resolve unsustainable debt situations. Maintaining sustainable debt levels is the responsibility of the

---

[17] A/HRC/17/31, annex.

[18] United Nations, *Treaty Series*, vol. 1577, No. 27531.

[19] A/C.2/56/7, annex.

borrowing countries; however we acknowledge that lenders also have a responsibility to lend in a way that does not undermine a country's debt sustainability. We will support the maintenance of debt sustainability of those countries that have received debt relief and achieved sustainable debt levels.

70.   We hereby launch a Technology Facilitation Mechanism which was established by the Addis Ababa Action Agenda in order to support the Sustainable Development Goals. The Technology Facilitation Mechanism will be based on a multi-stakeholder collaboration between Member States, civil society, the private sector, the scientific community, United Nations entities and other stakeholders and will be composed of a United Nations inter-agency task team on science, technology and innovation for the Sustainable Development Goals, a collaborative multi-stakeholder forum on science, technology and innovation for the Sustainable Development Goals and an online platform.

•The United Nations inter-agency task team on science, technology and innovation for the Sustainable Development Goals will promote coordination, coherence and cooperation within the United Nations system on science, technology and innovation-related matters, enhancing synergy and efficiency, in particular to enhance capacity-building initiatives. The task team will draw on existing resources and will work with 10 representatives from civil society, the private sector and the scientific community to prepare the meetings of the multi-stakeholder forum on science, technology and innovation for the Sustainable Development Goals, as well as in the development and operationalization of the online platform, including preparing proposals for the modalities for the forum and the online platform. The 10 representatives will be appointed by the Secretary-General, for periods of two years. The task team will be open to the participation of all United Nations agencies, funds and programmes and the functional commissions of the Economic and Social Council and it will initially be composed of the entities that currently integrate the informal working group on technology facilitation, namely, the Department of Economic and Social Affairs of the Secretariat, the United Nations Environment Programme, the United Nations Industrial Development Organization, the United Nations Educational, Scientific and Cultural Organization, the United Nations Conference on Trade and Development, the International Telecommunication Union, the World Intellectual Property Organization and the World Bank.

•The online platform will be used to establish a comprehensive mapping of, and serve as a gateway for, information on existing science, technology and innovation initiatives, mechanisms and programmes, within and beyond the United Nations. The online platform will facilitate access to information, knowledge and experience, as well as best practices and lessons learned, on science, technology and innovation facilitation initiatives and policies. The online platform will also facilitate the dissemination of relevant open access scientific publications generated worldwide. The online platform will be developed on the basis of an independent technical assessment which will take into account best practices and lessons learned from other initiatives, within and beyond the United Nations, in order to ensure that it will complement, facilitate access to and provide adequate information on existing science, technology and innovation platforms, avoiding duplications and enhancing synergies.

• The multi-stakeholder forum on science, technology and innovation for the Sustainable Development Goals will be convened once a year, for a period of two days, to discuss science, technology and innovation cooperation around thematic areas for the implementation of the Sustainable Development Goals, congregating all relevant stakeholders to actively contribute in their area of expertise. The forum will provide a venue for facilitating interaction, matchmaking and the establishment of networks between relevant stakeholders and multi-stakeholder partnerships in order to identify and examine technology needs and gaps, including on scientific cooperation, innovation and capacity-building, and also in order to help to facilitate development, transfer and dissemination of relevant technologies for the Sustainable Development Goals. The meetings of the forum will be convened by the President of the Economic and Social Council before the meeting of the high-level political forum under the auspices of the Council or, alternatively, in conjunction with other forums or conferences, as appropriate, taking into account the theme to be considered and on the basis of a collaboration with the organizers of the other forums or conferences. The meetings of the forum will be co-chaired by two Member States and will result in a summary of discussions elaborated by the two co-Chairs, as an input to the meetings of the high-level political forum, in the context of the follow-up and review of the implementation of the post-2015 development agenda.

• The meetings of the high-level political forum will be informed by the summary of the multi-stakeholder forum. The themes for the subsequent multi-stakeholder forum on science, technology and innovation for the Sustainable Development Goals will be considered by the high-level political forum on sustainable development, taking into account expert inputs from the task team.

71.   We reiterate that this Agenda and the Sustainable Development Goals and targets, including the means of implementation, are universal, indivisible and interlinked.

Follow-up and review

72.   We commit to engaging in systematic follow-up and review of the implementation of this Agenda over the next 15 years. A robust, voluntary, effective, participatory, transparent and integrated follow-up and review framework will make a vital contribution to implementation and will help countries to maximize and track progress in implementing this Agenda in order to ensure that no one is left behind.

73.   Operating at the national, regional and global levels, it will promote accountability to our citizens, support effective international cooperation in achieving this Agenda and foster exchanges of best practices and mutual learning. It will mobilize support to overcome shared challenges and identify new and emerging issues. As this is a

universal Agenda, mutual trust and understanding among all nations will be important.

74.   Follow-up and review processes at all levels will be guided by the following principles:

(*a*)   They will be voluntary and country-led, will take into account different national realities, capacities and levels of development and will respect policy space and priorities. As national ownership is key to achieving sustainable development, the outcome from national-level processes will be the foundation for reviews at the regional and global levels, given that the global review will be primarily based on national official data sources.

(*b*)   They will track progress in implementing the universal Goals and targets, including the means of implementation, in all countries in a manner which respects their universal, integrated and interrelated nature and the three dimensions of sustainable development.

(*c*)   They will maintain a longer-term orientation, identify achievements, challenges, gaps and critical success factors and support countries in making informed policy choices. They will help to mobilize the necessary means of implementation and partnerships, support the identification of solutions and best practices and promote the coordination and effectiveness of the international development system.

(*d*)   They will be open, inclusive, participatory and transparent for all people and will support reporting by all relevant stakeholders.

(*e*)   They will be people-centred, gender-sensitive, respect human rights and have a particular focus on the poorest, most vulnerable and those furthest behind.

(*f*)   They will build on existing platforms and processes, where these exist, avoid duplication and respond to national circumstances, capacities, needs and priorities. They will evolve over time, taking into account emerging issues and the development of new methodologies, and will minimize the reporting burden on national administrations.

(*g*)   They will be rigorous and based on evidence, informed by country-led evaluations and data which is high-quality, accessible, timely, reliable and disaggregated by income, sex, age, race, ethnicity, migration status, disability and geographic location and other characteristics relevant in national contexts.

(*h*)   They will require enhanced capacity-building support for developing countries, including the strengthening of national data systems and evaluation programmes, particularly in African countries, least developed countries, small island developing States, landlocked developing countries and middle-income countries.

(*i*)   They will benefit from the active support of the United Nations system and other multilateral institutions.

75.   The Goals and targets will be followed up and reviewed using a set of global indicators. These will be complemented by indicators at the regional and national levels which will be developed by Member States, in addition to the outcomes of work undertaken for the development of the baselines for those targets where national and global baseline data does not yet exist. The global indicator

framework, to be developed by the Inter-Agency and Expert Group on Sustainable Development Goal Indicators, will be agreed by the Statistical Commission by March 2016 and adopted thereafter by the Economic and Social Council and the General Assembly, in line with existing mandates. This framework will be simple yet robust, address all Sustainable Development Goals and targets, including for means of implementation, and preserve the political balance, integration and ambition contained therein.

76. We will support developing countries, particularly African countries, least developed countries, small island developing States and landlocked developing countries, in strengthening the capacity of national statistical offices and data systems to ensure access to high-quality, timely, reliable and disaggregated data. We will promote transparent and accountable scaling-up of appropriate public-private cooperation to exploit the contribution to be made by a wide range of data, including earth observation and geospatial information, while ensuring national ownership in supporting and tracking progress.

77. We commit to fully engage in conducting regular and inclusive reviews of progress at the subnational, national, regional and global levels. We will draw as far as possible on the existing network of follow-up and review institutions and mechanisms. National reports will allow assessments of progress and identify challenges at the regional and global level. Along with regional dialogues and global reviews, they will inform recommendations for follow-up at various levels.

National level

78. We encourage all Member States to develop as soon as practicable ambitious national responses to the overall implementation of this Agenda. These can support the transition to the Sustainable Development Goals and build on existing planning instruments, such as national development and sustainable development strategies, as appropriate.

79. We also encourage Member States to conduct regular and inclusive reviews of progress at the national and subnational levels which are country-led and country-driven. Such reviews should draw on contributions from indigenous peoples, civil society, the private sector and other stakeholders, in line with national circumstances, policies and priorities. National parliaments as well as other institutions can also support these processes.

Regional level

80. Follow-up and review at the regional and subregional levels can, as appropriate, provide useful opportunities for peer learning, including through voluntary reviews, sharing of best practices and discussion on shared targets. We welcome in this respect the cooperation of regional and subregional commissions and organizations. Inclusive regional processes will draw on national-level reviews and contribute to follow-up and review at the global level, including at the high-level political forum on sustainable development.

81. Recognizing the importance of building on existing follow-up and review mechanisms at the regional level and allowing adequate policy space, we encourage all Member States to identify the most suitable regional forum in which to engage. United Nations regional

commissions are encouraged to continue supporting Member States in this regard.

Global level

82. The high-level political forum will have a central role in overseeing a network of follow-up and review processes at the global level, working coherently with the General Assembly, the Economic and Social Council and other relevant organs and forums, in accordance with existing mandates. It will facilitate sharing of experiences, including successes, challenges and lessons learned, and provide political leadership, guidance and recommendations for follow-up. It will promote system-wide coherence and coordination of sustainable development policies. It should ensure that the Agenda remains relevant and ambitious and should focus on the assessment of progress, achievements and challenges faced by developed and developing countries as well as new and emerging issues. Effective linkages will be made with the follow-up and review arrangements of all relevant United Nations conferences and processes, including on least developed countries, small island developing States and landlocked developing countries.

83. Follow-up and review at the high-level political forum will be informed by an annual progress report on the Sustainable Development Goals to be prepared by the Secretary-General in cooperation with the United Nations system, based on the global indicator framework and data produced by national statistical systems and information collected at the regional level. The high-level political forum will also be informed by the *Global Sustainable Development Report*, which shall strengthen the science-policy interface and could provide a strong evidence-based instrument to support policymakers in promoting poverty eradication and sustainable development. We invite the President of the Economic and Social Council to conduct a process of consultations on the scope, methodology and frequency of the global report as well as its relation to the progress report, the outcome of which should be reflected in the ministerial declaration of the session of the high-level political forum in 2016.

84. The high-level political forum, under the auspices of the Economic and Social Council, shall carry out regular reviews, in line with General Assembly resolution 67/290 of 9 July 2013. Reviews will be voluntary, while encouraging reporting, and include developed and developing countries as well as relevant United Nations entities and other stakeholders, including civil society and the private sector. They shall be State-led, involving ministerial and other relevant high-level participants. They shall provide a platform for partnerships, including through the participation of major groups and other relevant stakeholders.

85. Thematic reviews of progress on the Sustainable Development Goals, including cross-cutting issues, will also take place at the high-level political forum. These will be supported by reviews by the functional commissions of the Economic and Social Council and other intergovernmental bodies and forums which should reflect the integrated nature of the Goals as well as the interlinkages between them. They will engage all relevant stakeholders and, where possible, feed into, and be aligned with, the cycle of the high-level political forum.

86. We welcome, as outlined in the Addis Ababa Action Agenda, the dedicated follow-up and review for the financing for development

outcomes as well as all the means of implementation of the Sustainable Development Goals which is integrated with the follow-up and review framework of this Agenda. The intergovernmentally agreed conclusions and recommendations of the annual Economic and Social Council forum on financing for development will be fed into the overall follow-up and review of the implementation of this Agenda in the high-level political forum.

87. Meeting every four years under the auspices of the General Assembly, the high-level political forum will provide high-level political guidance on the Agenda and its implementation, identify progress and emerging challenges and mobilize further actions to accelerate implementation. The next high-level political forum under the auspices of the General Assembly will be held in 2019, with the cycle of meetings thus reset, in order to maximize coherence with the quadrennial comprehensive policy review process.

88. We also stress the importance of system-wide strategic planning, implementation and reporting in order to ensure coherent and integrated support to the implementation of the new Agenda by the United Nations development system. The relevant governing bodies should take action to review such support to implementation and to report on progress and obstacles. We welcome the ongoing dialogue in the Economic and Social Council on the longer-term positioning of the United Nations development system and look forward to taking action on these issues, as appropriate.

89. The high-level political forum will support participation in follow-up and review processes by the major groups and other relevant stakeholders in line with resolution 67/290. We call upon those actors to report on their contribution to the implementation of the Agenda.

90. We request the Secretary-General, in consultation with Member States, to prepare a report, for consideration at the seventieth session of the General Assembly in preparation for the 2016 meeting of the high-level political forum, which outlines critical milestones towards coherent, efficient and inclusive follow-up and review at the global level. The report should include a proposal on the organizational arrangements for State-led reviews at the high-level political forum under the auspices of the Economic and Social Council, including recommendations on voluntary common reporting guidelines. It should clarify institutional responsibilities and provide guidance on annual themes, on a sequence of thematic reviews, and on options for periodic reviews for the high-level political forum.

91. We reaffirm our unwavering commitment to achieving this Agenda and utilizing it to the full to transform our world for the better by 2030.

4th plenary meeting
25 September 2015

Instruments mentioned in the section entitled
"Sustainable Development Goals and targets"

World Health Organization Framework Convention on Tobacco Control (United Nations, *Treaty Series*, vol. 2302, No. 41032)

Sendai Framework for Disaster Risk Reduction 2015–2030 (resolution 69/283, annex II)

United Nations Convention on the Law of the Sea (United Nations, *Treaty Series*, vol. 1833, No. 31363)

"The future we want" (resolution 66/288, annex)